THE NEW WHITEHALL SERIES
NO. 16

The Department of
Education and Science

THE NEW WHITEHALL SERIES
NO. 16

The Department of Education and Science

SIR WILLIAM PILE

GCB, MBE

Permanent Under-Secretary of State 1970-1976
Department of Education and Science

London
GEORGE ALLEN & UNWIN
Boston   Sydney

First published in 1979

GEORGE ALLEN & UNWIN LTD
40 Museum Street, London WC1A 1LU

© George Allen & Unwin (Publishers) Ltd, 1979

British Library Cataloguing in Publication Data

Pile, *Sir* William Dennis
    The Department of Education and Science.
    – (The new Whitehall series; no. 16).
    1. Great Britain. Department of Education and
    Science
    I. Title   II. Series
    379'.06'141   JN453.E/   78–41018

    ISBN 0–04–351054–X

Typeset in 10 on 11 point Times by Bedford Typesetters Ltd.
and printed in Great Britain
by Biddles Ltd., Guildford, Surrey

PREFACE

This is not intended to be a definitive history of the Department of Education and Science (DES) in the years since the Second World War. Its primary aim, like that of other volumes in the New Whitehall Series, is to provide a contemporary account of the Department at work, to explain what it tries to do and how it takes its place in the machinery of government, central and local, and to say something about the people who work in it.

This account may well contain more history of the times than is usual in the New Whitehall Series. There are two main reasons for this. First, an education department of state like the DES has both to try to influence the historic development of the education service and to respond sensitively to external events. It works to shape the environment in which it discharges its task and the environment shapes the policies, procedures and personalities of those in the Department. The history of that developing environment is therefore inextricably a part of the life and character of the Department. Secondly, the postwar years have been a very formative period in every sense. The DES is very different today from the old Board of Education. It is now over fifty years since one of its senior officials* gave an account of the work of the Board as it was then. For both these reasons, therefore, something wider and longer than a plain description of the DES as a government department and as it stands at one moment in time may be thought justified.

The difficulty of deciding where to begin and where to end, however, has been sharpened precisely because, however delimited, the essential characterisation of the period has been that of profound and continuous change. The Education Act 1944 is the most obvious starting point. Deciding where to end has been far more difficult.

I have concluded that it would be both impracticable and undesirable to attempt a stop-press finale to this story. Arbitrary though it may appear, it has seemed sensible to concentrate on developments in the Department's work over the three decades following the enactment of the Education Act 1944, during which it acquired its present shape and range of functions; and this is what the following chapters try to do.

There may be disappointment, even criticism, that the most recent events are not reported in detail. There have certainly been significant

---

*Sir Amherst Selby-Bigge (Permanent Secretary 1911–25), *The Board of Education*, Whitehall Series (London and New York, Putnam, 1927). (The Department's responsibilities did not at that time include the universities, civil science, arts or libraries.)

developments since 1974. The resource background has changed dramatically. The birth rate has continued to decline. The fact of unemployed teachers is a new and painful one. Attention is focused much more than in the past on the content of the curriculum, on the educational process as well as the educational system and structure, and on the relationship of this process to that of preparation for the world of work, particularly the world of industry and technology. All this, I hope, is fully recognised, although inevitably in summary, in the last chapter of the book. And the principal developments have been noted in the earlier narrative chapters. To attempt to do more would be impracticable; the physical effort of editing and printing alone imposes its own delays between events and their recording. But it would also in my view be undesirable to attempt in this sort of volume to be 'bang up to date'. Most of the more noticeable recent developments are still unwinding themselves. It is too early to make judgements about their real significance. History may well prove any such judgements profoundly wrong in the longer perspective – and tomorrow's events may make them even out of date in the shorter perspective. If history is to remain history, it has to be a little chary of prophecy.

I am greatly indebted to many former colleagues who have gone to a great deal of trouble in reading and commenting on drafts in the course of preparation of this volume. I must give special thanks to Dennis Routh, a former member of the Department, who has been responsible for assembling the basic material, for coaxing busy colleagues into commenting on successive revisions and for the general editorship of the volume as a whole. The concluding chapter, however, for what it is worth, is my own.

WILLIAM PILE

CONTENTS

PART SIX   ORGANISATION AND PERSONNEL; AND SOME CONCLUSIONS

PART ONE

The Growth and Scope
of the Department

CHAPTER 1

Introduction: From Committee of Council to Department of State

It may seem ironic that throughout the nineteenth century and the first four decades of the twentieth, the country that led the way in the industrial revolution in Europe should have lagged behind other advanced countries in its provision of public education; but it is not difficult to explain. The prevailing *laissez-faire* ideology, religious dissension and the existence of a highly developed private sector of education (the so-called 'public schools') combined to retard the growth of the public service of education in England throughout this period.

One aspect of this retarded development was the absence, right up to the end of the nineteenth century, of any effective central authority to supervise and plan the development of the service. In 1839 a committee of the Privy Council had been established to 'superintend the application' of the moneys voted by Parliament in 1833 in aid of two voluntary church societies which provided schools for the children of the poorer classes, and the first HM Inspectors of Schools were appointed to ensure the necessary scrutiny.

In 1853, in the wake of the Great Exhibition, a Science and Art Department was established, originally under the Board of Trade, to foster instruction in these subjects, and in 1856 this was put, as a largely autonomous unit, under the control of the Education Committee, which was from that time designated the Education Department.

But this Department, although by this time it had its own vice-president responsible for educational matters, was still not 'an ordinary Department created with a Minister at the head of it'.[1] Nor was it, in the latter part of the century, the only central authority concerned with schools in England and Wales. Thus from 1874 the

Charity Commissioners had certain functions in relation to the endowed grammar schools, with powers of inspection.

It was not until 1899 that one of the many attempts to create an effective central authority, this time given a fair wind by the Report of the influential Bryce Commission on Secondary Education, reached the statute book as the Board of Education Act 1899. On 1 April 1900 the Board of Education, in the words of Selby-Bigge[2] 'struggled into existence'. Its ministerial head was in effect, if not in name, a Minister of Education.

This Act was the precursor of the Balfour Act 1902, which brought in the local authorities – the elected municipal and county councils – as the main providers of the public education service throughout England and Wales. The government of the time had recognised that the creation of an effective central education authority was a necessary precondition for the development of a satisfactory local organisation of the service, based on local government bodies. These two enactments of the turn of the century were the beginning of the partnership between central and local government that is the characteristic feature of this country's educational system today.

But it was only a beginning. The new central authority was at this stage – and indeed right up to 1944 – limited to the modest task of 'superintendence of matters relating to education in England and Wales'. The initiative for development rested almost entirely with the local bodies. The central department had no explicit mandate for policy making, and there was nothing like a coherent system of grant aid from central funds for local activity.

The partnership between the central and the local authorities was carried a stage further by the Fisher Act 1918. This recognised that 'the service of public education' was 'in the nature of things expansive', and that it was 'the business of the Central and the Local Education Authorities (LEAs) to provide liberally for its expansion'.[3] It gave a measure of initiative to the centre, empowering the Board to require the LEAs to submit 'schemes' showing how they proposed to carry out their duties and powers under the Education Acts. It also introduced an element of order into the confused system of central grant aid for local expenditure on education, which enabled the central department to exercise control over the activities it was grant aiding. But the effectiveness of the Fisher Act was seriously impaired by the Geddes axe of the early 1920s; a number of its aims were never realised; and up to 1944 the powers of the central Department remained insufficient to enable it to give an effective lead in developing the system. Although the achievements of the interwar years were by no means negligible, that system still, when war broke out in 1939, in many ways trailed well behind the systems of leading powers such as Germany, France and the USA.

THE EDUCATION ACT 1944

The decisive advance towards a coherent national system, giving to the centre sufficient power for policy making and initiative for development, came with the Education Act 1944. This, the first of the great reforming measures of the period of postwar reconstruction, has been described as 'the most comprehensive and complete measure of educational reform in our history',[4] and the description is still apt.

The Board now became a ministry in name as well as fact, its minister charged with the duty to 'promote the education of the people of England and Wales and the progressive development of institutions devoted to that purpose' (Education Act 1944, Section 1). The Minister of Education was no longer to 'superintend'; he was to 'secure the effective execution' by local authorities, 'under his control and direction' of the 'national policy' for providing a varied and comprehensive educational service in every area.

The words 'control and direction' convey an impression of omnipotence which, as later chapters will suggest, has never corresponded with reality. But the fact remains that the 1944 Act resulted, both directly and indirectly, in a very great extension of the powers and responsibilities of the central department.

The Minister himself was given substantial new powers. Thus he was given powers to provide financial assistance to church schools which were to bring about a transformation of the 'dual system'. He was for the first time given effective powers to supervise the standards of privately financed independent schools and to secure the provision by LEAs of sufficient facilities for the training of teachers. He was empowered in various ways to supervise, control and, in the last resort, direct the activities of LEAs, and he was given what was in effect a mandate to initiate national policies.

Indirectly his responsibilities were increased in as much as the Act provided for a great extension of the statutory duties and powers of the LEAs which were to operate under his control and direction. They were to have the duty to secure that there should be available for their area sufficient schools, both primary and secondary, to provide for the different ages, abilities and aptitudes of all pupils in the area – a provision that amongst other things entailed a major reform of secondary education. They were to have the duty to secure the provision of postschool or 'further' education in their area as one of the three statutory stages of education. In a number of other fields the Minister and the LEAs were given new or enlarged duties and powers which were the basis of major developments over the next three decades, notably in the provision of scholarships for students in higher education, in special education for handicapped children, in the provision of meals and milk in school, and in the school health service.

SUBSEQUENT EXTENSIONS OF THE CENTRAL DEPARTMENT'S RESPONSIBILITIES

In 1964, following the Reports of the Robbins Committee on Higher Education,[5] and the Trend Committee on Civil Science,[6] the Department's functions were further enlarged, and it now became a department of state. It was given responsibility for the financing of the universities, which since 1919 had been exercised directly by the Treasury, with the advice of a semi-autonomous University Grants Committee (UGC). The UGC continued in being, but its advice was thenceforward given to the new Secretary of State. As a result of amalgamation with the Office of the Minister for Science, the Department came to have a range of functions in the field of civil science, notably responsibility for the work of the research councils.

In the following year, the Secretary of State was given responsibility for financial assistance for the arts, which is mainly channelled through the Arts Council of Great Britain. A minister was appointed with the special responsibility of supervising this aspect of the Department's work, becoming in effect Minister for the Arts.

In the same year, as a result of the Public Libraries and Museums Act 1964, the Department acquired new powers in relation to the public library service, which in England and Wales has largely developed as a local government service. It has also been closely concerned with the development of the National Central Library, and more recently with the establishment and financing of the British Library, which incorporated this and other national library institutions.

The Department (or its predecessors) has for more than a century also had responsibility for the administration of two major national museums: the Victoria and Albert Museum and its dependencies, and the Science Museum. In assuming its role in civil science it also inherited responsibility for the British Museum (Natural History), and at about the same time it came to have a general concern for provincial museums and galleries. It has also come to have responsibility for the oversight and development of the major trustee museums and art galleries in London.

The Department thus covers a wide range of responsibilities, comprising not only every phase of education from nursery to university, but also civil science and the arts, public libraries and museums. Directly or indirectly it is concerned with the expenditure of very large sums of public money. Total public expenditure on education in Great Britain in 1977–8 accounted for 12 per cent of public expenditure and 7 per cent of gross national product.

Although the Department is now generally reckoned to be one of the dozen or so major departments of central government, it is by current Whitehall standards a small department. Apart from the Treasury it is the smallest of the London-based departments of state. Its entire headquarters staff numbers about 2,500 (excluding museum staff and HM Inspectorate). This is largely because in England and Wales (and the same is true of Scotland) education is a decentralised service. Unlike education ministries in most other countries, the Department has few executive functions. It does not itself run schools, colleges or universities, or employ teachers, or prescribe curricula or operate public libraries. These functions are the responsibility of local authorities or autonomous bodies. Similarly, in the field of civil science the Department does not itself conduct research or maintain research establishments. This is done by research councils and other bodies which are grant aided by the Department. Its assistance to the arts is also mainly channelled through an autonomous body: the Arts Council of Great Britain.

The Department's role in relation to all these bodies is essentially that of a planning, policy-making, resource-providing and supervisory agency, setting national standards, formulating national policies for development and providing funds. To enable it to fulfil this role it has a variety of powers or means of influence, statutory, financial and administrative. Its relationship with the local government bodies which operate the education service on the ground (up to but not including university level) is commonly described as a partnership, and the term is not inapposite to describe its relationship with the universities, with the research councils and with corresponding bodies in the field of library services, the arts and museums.

Since most of the work of the Department is done through these local government and other bodies, much of what follows will be concerned with the work of these bodies, and the Department's relationships with them.

PLAN OF THE BOOK

The plan of the volume is as follows: Part One deals with the historical context within which the Department has developed, and the framework – legal, administrative and financial – within which it now operates. Chapter 1 briefly traces the emergence of the Department itself. Chapter 2 singles out some of the salient features of postwar Britain that have particularly influenced the development of the educational system and therefore of the Department, or have a special bearing on its work. Chapter 3 gives an introductory account of the Department's relationship with the LEAs which are the main providers of statutory education. Chapter 4 looks in greater depth at the 'partnership' that operates the education service, up to but not including university level, to see how it works in practice in the formation of policy. Chapter 5 deals in more detail with the arrangements for the financing of education, which are of key importance for understanding the relationship between the Department and the local authorities and other providing bodies.

Part Two looks at the Department's responsibilities and its role in the development of policies in the main sectors of the statutory system of education: the schools (Chapter 6); the training and supply of teachers (Chapter 7); and further education (Chapter 8).

In Part Three, Chapter 9 deals with the Department's more recently acquired role *vis-à-vis* the universities.

Part Four (Chapter 10) looks at the higher education sector as a whole, and considers some of the problems of growth and cost with which the country has been confronted in this sector in the 1970s.

Part Five deals with the Department's responsibilities in contiguous fields: public library services both local and national (Chapter 11); the arts and museums (Chapter 12); and civil science (Chapter 13).

In Part Six, Chapter 14 describes the headquarters organisation and staff of the Department and HM Inspectorate and says something about the men and women who work in them. Finally, Chapter 15 offers a few conclusions.

A word about the geographical scope of this volume. The geographical areas over which the Department operates vary from one function to another. Its responsibility for schools, for most non-university higher and further education, and for public libraries, extend only to England, though the 1944 and subsequent Education Acts and relevant Local Government Acts apply to both England and Wales; and major issues of policy and priorities in these sectors are handled on the basis of a concerted approach by the Department and the Welsh Office, which has educational functions in these sectors in the Principality. (Scotland has since 1892 had its own Education Department,[7] responsible for all sectors of education in Scotland other than universities, and has its own distinctive law of education.) The Department's responsibilities in relation to the universities, and also to the arts and civil science, extend to Scotland as well as to England and Wales. In what follows it will sometimes be convenient to speak of 'England' or 'English' although properly speaking the reference should be to England and Wales or to Great Britain.

NOTES AND REFERENCES

1 Sir Amherst Selby-Bigge, *The Board of Education*, Whitehall Series (London and New York, Putnam, 1927), preface, p. 7.
2 ibid., preface, p. 14.
3 ibid., p. 20.
4 P. Wilson, *Views and Prospects from Curzon Street* (Oxford, Blackwell, 1961), . p. 15.
5 Committee on Higher Education (Chairman: Lord Robbins), *Higher Education*, Cmnd 2154 (London, HMSO, 1963).
6 *Report of the Committee of Enquiry into the Organisation of Civil Science*, Cmnd 2171 (London, HMSO, 1963).
7 See Sir David Milne, *The Scottish Office*, New Whitehall Series (London, Allen & Unwin, 1957).

CHAPTER 2

Demographic and Social Background

Any attempt to give an account of the work of a department responsible for the educational system of an advanced country in a period of
rapid change needs to be prefaced with some remarks about the
social context in which it operates. This chapter attempts to pick out
a few salient trends and factors in postwar British society – demographic trends, population movements, health of the child population, effects of technological change, and so forth – which have had
major consequences for the Department. The selection of factors
chosen for mention is necessarily arbitrary, although it reflects
experience of what has most affected the Department's work.

DEMOGRAPHIC FACTORS

To start with the tangible and measurable: in Britain, as in most
other Western countries, this has been a period of large changes in
the birth rate, at first upwards and, later, downwards. In 1944
annual births in England and Wales rose from the prewar level of
around 600,000 a year to 751,000 and then, after a brief decline, to
820,000 in 1946 and a peak of 881,000 in 1947. This was the
phenomenon commonly referred to as the 'bulge'. Thereafter they
fell but, contrary to general expectation, they did not revert to the
prewar level; from 1955 onwards they rose again, to a peak of 876,000
in 1964. Only after that did they show a downward trend; but this
has since continued without interruption until 1977.

The postwar rise, as Lord Butler himself has observed[1], was
largely unforeseen at the time that the Education Act 1944 was in
preparation. In the 1920s and early 1930s annual births had been
falling, and the school population was static or declining. During the

war it was widely assumed that this was the normal pattern, and that after a brief upsurge resulting from the ending of the war and demobilisation, births would revert to the prewar level.

The consequent increase in the size of the child population had a major and continuing impact on the educational system throughout the three decades from 1944. This impact was of course most immediately felt in the schools, which have to accommodate children of compulsory age, and also those who stay on voluntarily, as may be seen from Table 2.1.

Table 2.1   *School population of England and Wales in thousands (all schools)*[1]

1947	1950	1955	1960	1965	1970	1975	1977
5,340	6,315	7,199	7,620	7,775	8,628	9,688	9,759

[1] Of these, about 93 per cent at any one time are in schools maintained by LEAs. The 1947 figure, however, excludes a large part of independent sector.

It will be seen that over the thirty-year period from 1947 to 1977 the school population increased by over 4·4 million.

By no means all the growth in school population has been due to increased births. Much of it is attributable to the deliberate policies of successive governments aimed at extending secondary education. Thus in 1947 the period of compulsory schooling was extended to age 15, and in 1972 to 16. These measures added 400,000 to the secondary school rolls by the end of 1948, and by the end of 1973 a further 250,000. Moreover, it has been the policy of all postwar governments to encourage secondary pupils to stay on beyond the statutory leaving age, and there has thus been a continuing 'trend' towards voluntary staying on, which by 1971–2 had added a further half-million to secondary numbers.

Another factor contributing significantly to the increase in numbers in school in this period has been the arrival of a category of pupil that is relatively new to the official statistics. These are the 'immigrant' pupils, who first appear in the Department's statistics in 1966, although they were arriving in the schools in considerable numbers for ten years or more before that. Immigrant pupils are defined for the purposes of the Department's statistics as including both children from outside the British Isles who have come to this country with families of overseas origin and children born in the United Kingdom to parents of overseas origin who had been in the country for less than ten years. By 1972 over 279,000, accounting for 3·3 per cent of all children in maintained schools, were immigrants in this sense, the bulk of them from new Commonwealth countries, mainly the West Indies, India, Pakistan, Kenya and Cyprus.

But the increase in births of children born in Britain to indigenous parents has throughout this period been the major factor in the growth of school population.

It was against this background of large and continuing increases in numbers in the first three decades after the war that the reforms of the 1944 Act had to be carried through. The impact of increasing numbers was of course not felt only by the schools. As the larger birth groups reached the age of further and higher education, and as new policies came into operation designed to extend educational opportunities at these levels, there was also a greatly increased demand for places in colleges of further education and universities, and the continuing increase in school population called for a very large increase in the supply of teachers and therefore in the provision of teacher training.

From the mid-1970s the trend in births changed radically. Instead of the continuing rise which had been one of the Department's main preoccupations, a continuing decline set in. By 1975 the projection of births prepared by the Government Actuary's Department in conjunction with the Office of Population Censuses and Surveys was already registering a figure well below that assumed in the Department's 1972 White Paper *Education: A Framework for Expansion*, and even below that assumed in 1974. This decline, with its implications for future school population, has had major consequences for the education service, particularly as regards the number of teachers needed in the late 1970s and early 1980s, but also in other ways.

POPULATION MOVEMENT

Another characteristic of postwar British society which has had major consequences for the educational system has been the greatly increased mobility of the population. This is of course no new phenomenon in the country that was the first to experience the industrial revolution, but the extent of movement has been growing. In the postwar period mobility has increased still further as a result of technological change, the changing character of British industry and the provision of new housing on a large scale. In the twenty-five years from 1945 to 1970 some 6 million new houses were built in England and Wales, either privately or by local authorities. In this period some 4 million children moved with their families into new housing. Analysis of the 1966 census figures showed that 10 per cent of the population had moved within one year prior to the census and 30 per cent within five years.

Population movements of this order have, in terms of the need for physical provision of schools and other educational facilities, an impact almost as great as the impact of increases in school population.

THE HEALTH OF THE CHILD POPULATION

Now that over 90 per cent of the child population spend upwards of ten years in schools in the public sector, the health of the child population must be of vital concern to the Department.

Early in its life the Board of Education began to interest itself in the health of children in school. An Act of 1907 laid on local education authorities (LEAs) a duty to ensure the medical examination of all children in public elementary schools, and a Medical Branch was set up at the Board. Thus from the early years of the century the Department's medical advisers have been well informed about the state of health of children in school.

Their reports illuminate the transformation that has occurred over this period. The then chief medical officer of the Ministry of Education reported on the fiftieth anniversary of the service's inauguration:

> Contrasted with children of 50 years ago the boys and girls of today are of better physique, are well clad and shod, and are cleaner, and their expectation of life at birth is 20 years longer. Diseases that once killed or disabled thousands of children have been overcome whilst the ravages of others have been restricted. . . . Children everywhere are taller and heavier than their predecessors of 50 years ago; they reach physical maturity earlier . . .[2]

In the period since 1957 the improvement has been maintained. By 1964 and 1965 the Department's chief medical officer was able to report that the proportion of school children found to be in an unsatisfactory physical condition had fallen to 0·38 per cent.[3]

TECHNOLOGICAL CHANGE:
SOME CONSEQUENCES FOR EDUCATION

It is a commonplace of educational debate to say that we live in a period of accelerating technological change, and it would not be difficult to list a score of ways in which this phenomenon has consequences for the educational system. Four may be singled out as particularly relevant to this volume.

Perhaps the most important of all, paradoxical though this may now seem, has been the increase in the country's wealth that it has helped to bring about, and therefore in the resources available for education. Despite the exhaustion of war and the country's diminished role in the world, the last thirty years have been, for most of the time, a period of continuing economic growth in Britain. Although less spectacular than that of other leading European countries and more interrupted by crises, this growth has over the postwar period as a whole been substantial. It has been estimated that the gross national product (GNP) of 1970 was in real terms about three times that of 1938. This has been a crucial factor in making possible the expansion of the educational system which is surveyed in the following chapters. Its importance may be summed up in the proposition that over this period the country has been able to devote to education between two and three times as much of a GNP that has increased threefold.

A further consequence of technological change that is particularly relevant to this volume is the increased demand that it has created for educated and trained manpower. A technologically advanced society requires from the educational system a greatly increased output of qualified scientists and technologists, and of supporting technicians and craftsmen. It also requires many more people with a high level of general education for managerial positions in industry and commerce, the professions, the apparatus of central and local government and the arts, and a higher degree of literacy, numeracy and general adaptability, at all levels, to enable people to cope with what has been described as 'the universal upgrading of jobs'.

The obverse of society's increasing need for qualified people has been a growing realisation amongst all sections of the community of what the Crowther Report called 'the importance of being qualified' and consequently an increasing demand for qualifications of all kinds, which, combined with the universalisation of secondary education, has acted as a powerful stimulus to the development of all forms of further and higher education.

Technological change has also produced a society in which more leisure has led to a large increase in demand for adult education in the widest sense: 'in our changing and evolving society the explicit and latent demands for all kinds of adult education have increased and will continue to increase. Adults in their own right have claims for the provision of a comprehensive service which can satisfy these demands in appropriately adult ways.'[4]

THE PROBLEM OF DEPRIVATION
AND THE DEPRIVED AREAS

While for the great majority of the population economic growth has brought rising living standards, there has remained an underprivileged minority for whom the increased wealth of the community has brought little benefit. In the decaying inner rings of large conurbations, in communities based on declining industries, in urban areas with large immigrant populations and in some depopulated rural areas, poverty and deprivation have persisted; and although statistics appear to show that during this period the gap between rich and poor has narrowed and that the welfare state has mitigated the worst deprivation, there have remained areas where high unemployment, low earnings, poor housing, overcrowding, large families, a high proportion of broken homes and other factors combine to produce multiple deprivation on which the existing social services make limited impact.

During this period, and particularly in the last decade, there has been a wider recognition[5] that such areas constitute a special problem for social policy generally, and for education in particular, and that so long as they persist amid growing prosperity, the educational system must fall short of achieving the greater equality of educational opportunity that has been the broadly agreed aim of all the parties.

THE EXPLOSION OF KNOWLEDGE

A phenomenon closely associated with technological change, and one which has a direct impact not only on the educational work of the Department but also on its work in relation to science and libraries, is the so-called explosion of knowledge.

The most direct impact of the knowledge explosion on the educational system is of course at its upper end, in universities and other advanced institutions doing research and teaching at the frontiers of knowledge. But it also has a continuous impact on all sectors of technical and vocational education, requiring constant revision and extension of curricula, rising standards and the development of new educational systems for new technologies and skills. It has major implications for teacher training. In the schools it has resulted in inflation of the curriculum, overloading of examination syllabuses and pressures for more and earlier specialisation, thus creating an urgent need for curricular reform.

IMPACT OF THE MEDIA

No review of the background against which the education service has operated in the postwar period would be complete without some reference to the development that has taken place in the media of communication. Two aspects of this phenomenon may be singled out as specially relevant to education and to the work of the Department.

First is broadcasting. While radio has commanded a wide audience for more than fifty years, large scale television viewing is almost entirely a postwar development. The television service of the British Broadcasting Corporation (BBC) started in 1936 but at that time reached only a limited audience. It was suspended during the war and resumed only in 1946. Since then the expansion of viewing has been extremely rapid. In 1950 the number of television licences issued was less than 400,000. By 1968 it was 15·5 million. In 1950 it was estimated that 4·3 per cent of the adult population had television receivers in their homes. By 1964 the figure was over 90 per cent. Britain is one of the small number of countries in the world that have aptly been described as 'total television societies'.

From one point of view this development has brought great benefits to all who work in education. The broadcasting authorities have specific responsibilities in relation to education. The charter of the BBC identifies education as one of its three principal purposes, alongside entertainment and information. So, for Independent Television, do the Television Acts 1954 and 1964. The BBC has machinery, in the School Broadcasting Council and in its Further Education Advisory Council, for associating LEAs, other outside bodies and independent individuals with its specifically educational work. The Television Act 1964 requires the Independent Broadcasting Authority to set up an advisory body to give advice on educational policies and programmes. The central source of advice on educational policy for Independent Television as a whole is its Educational Advisory Council. The Council is assisted by a Schools Committee and an Adult Education Committee. There are also educational advisory committees appointed by the programme companies providing school programmes for the network.

It would be widely agreed that the BBC's response to its educational duties has been generous, particularly if education is taken in its broadest sense (as is implicit in the charter) to include the dissemination of what is best in music, literature and the arts as well as documentaries and discussion of public affairs. The educational contribution of the Independent Broadcasting Authority and the programme companies, although more recent, has also been increasingly valued. The establishment of local radio stations has offered further opportunities for collaboration with LEAs. The widespread acceptance of television as a normal means of communication, more effective in many ways than the traditional printed word, has begun to exert a significant influence on methods of teaching and learning.

At the same time there is growing recognition that with the universalisation of television viewing society is confronted with an immensely powerful medium, exerting an influence on the young in particular, beside which, as the Crowther Report pointed out, education has only a strictly limited impact. Few of those concerned with education would maintain that this influence is wholly beneficial or helpful to the aims of education. Many would argue that merely by mirroring society as it is – with its plurality of values, its excessive materialism (as many think) and its increasing preoccupation with violence – television gives currency and encouragement to the more disquieting tendencies in society to an extent that, to say the least, makes the work of the educators more difficult.

A second point about the development of the media deserves mention here because it has had an increasing, and on the whole invigorating, effect on the work of the Department. The remarkable growth in public interest in education that has taken place in the last thirty years has been reflected in a great increase in coverage of educational topics by the media – the daily and periodical press as well as television and sound broadcasting. All the main national dailies and most of the broadcasting networks have their educational correspondents, and there has been a notable growth in the number of educational journals with exceptionally well-informed specialist staffs. All the main issues of national educational policy with which ministers and the Department have to deal are thus the subject of continuous and searching public debate in the press and on the air as well as in Parliament.

THE DEVELOPMENT OF EDUCATIONAL RESEARCH

The period since the war has been the first in which an attempt has been made to apply research systematically to education and to use it in helping to shape national policy. The 1944 Act gave both the new Ministry and the LEAs power to assist educational research, and for a number of years after the war an independent body, the National Foundation for Educational Research, pioneered systematic research on education, with the help of modest grants from the Department and LEAs.

In 1959 the Crowther Report drew attention to the need for educational research on a far larger scale, and thereafter there have been considerable advances. During the 1960s successive central advisory councils for education for England and for Wales – notably the Newsom Report,[6] the Plowden Report and its counterpart for Wales, the Gittins Report[7] – made use of research on an extensive scale in the preparation of their reports. The Report of the Robbins Committee on Higher Education was accompanied by no less than six volumes of appendices containing the results of surveys and research.

In 1961 the Ministry itself set up a Research and Intelligence Branch to keep in touch with educational research throughout the country and to identify areas of promise or need. In recent years the Department has been concentrating its research expenditure on policy-related issues or other work having a practical application to the educational system as a whole.

The Schools Council, since its creation in 1964, has had at its disposal substantial funds for curriculum research and development. The Office of Population Censuses and Surveys has not infrequently been commissioned to undertake surveys related to problems of educational policy. The universities also have paid increasing attention to educational research, and a number of independent trusts, notably the Nuffield Foundation, have financed major projects.

When the Social Science Research Council was created in 1965, one of its early decisions was to set up an educational research board. As a consequence of this and other developments there has been increasing cross-fertilisation between educational researchers and those in disciplines relevant to education, such as sociology, psychology and genetics.

CHANGING IDEAS ABOUT THE NATURE AND AIMS OF EDUCATION

A word about the changes in accepted ideas on the aims of education and the range of the school curriculum: when the state first became involved in the financing of public education, its aim was to promote the instruction of children of 'the labouring classes' in the three Rs. Although successive revisions of the regulations allowed for the widening of the curriculum, this conception of public education survived well beyond the end of the nineteenth century.

It is significant that Lord Butler, in introducing his Bill to the Commons in January 1944, thought it necessary to point out that, instead of elementary instruction in the three Rs, his Bill put upon the parents of every child of compulsory school age the duty to ensure that he or she received efficient full-time education suitable to his age, ability and aptitude.[8] The duties laid upon LEAs are defined in similar terms. Indeed their responsibilities are drawn even more widely, for they are charged with contributing towards the 'spiritual, moral, mental and physical development of the community'; and although some today may dismiss this phrase as rhetoric, it is one that on the whole offers a fair description of the range of the school curriculum as it is today.

One of the fundamental changes in thinking about the aims of education may conveniently be summed up by saying that there has been a more widespread acceptance, particularly at the primary level, of the 'child-centred' approach to education. Such an approach implies an educational system designed to take account of the needs and interests of children, that is, to encourage each child to realise its own potential rather than simply to assimilate knowledge or instruction in skills. This shift of emphasis has had implications over the whole range of educational provision, for example, in the design of school buildings as well as in the development of the curriculum and the training of teachers.

EDUCATION AND EQUALITY

Another area in which there has been a significant shift in traditional thinking about education is that of the relationship between the aims of education and the idea, or rather the ideal, of equality.

From the time of the Benthamites there has been a close association, in the minds of English educational reformers, between education and equality. At the level of practical policies the belief in greater equality of educational opportunity has been a corollary of the modern democratic belief in universal suffrage. It was no coincidence that the Forster Act 1870 came soon after the Reform Act 1867 which extended the franchise to the urban working man.

During the first half of this century it was the generally accepted belief that what the principle of equality required in education was progress towards equality of educational opportunity. This was one of the main principles which underlay the Butler Act – in particular its objective of providing free secondary education for all and wider access to higher education.

In recent years the findings of research in education, sociology and genetics have provided a growing volume of evidence that equality of educational opportunity does not go far enough, that differences in attainment and even in measurable intelligence may be due as much to home background, parental concern (or lack of it) and social environment as to inherited characteristics.

This was the thesis that led the Plowden Council to formulate the idea of 'positive discrimination' for the deprived and underprivileged. Both their diagnosis and the conclusions that they drew for educational policy have been endorsed by subsequent research, notably that of the National Child Development Study[10] and of Dr Halsey and his colleagues,[11] and have come to be widely accepted by educational opinion as a basis of educational policies and resource allocation.

But while this thesis has gained wide support, it would be misleading to suggest that it has been universally accepted. There is room for differences of opinion on the extent to which nature or nurture is the decisive factor in determining the potentialities and achievements of individual children. Equally, where resources are scarce, there is room for argument as to the extent to which resources should be devoted to the underprivileged at the expense of the able, and many would argue that a too exclusive preoccupation with the social aim of education in promoting equality may result in a neglect of other aims such as the pursuit of quality and excellence. There has been a continuing debate in recent years, which by no means follows party lines, between the protagonists of equality and positive discrimination and the defenders of excellence and high standards.[12]

There is a related aspect of the Plowden thesis that has been more recently enlarged upon by the National Child Development Study and in the research of Dr Halsey and his colleagues in regard to educational priority areas. This is the view – implied in the title of the National Child Development Study's Report – that the crucial years in determining a child's capacity are those from birth to age 7. This view has evident implications for national educational policy and the allocation of resources. It has led to a questioning of the wisdom of giving priority to the development of postschool education, which was a characteristic of national education policy in the late 1960s, and to an increasing conviction that higher priority should be given to extending provision at the primary and the preschool levels.

THE DEMAND FOR PARTICIPATION

A word also needs to be said about another idea that has gained wide currency in the educational world in this period and that concerns the organisation and control of education rather than its aims – the idea of participation. In a sense, of course, this idea is built into the public system of education in England and Wales, in so far as it is administered by local democratic bodies, answerable to local electorates.

But in recent years there has been a demand that the idea of participation should be more generally applied, and that all who are involved in the educational process – whether as teachers, parents, students, even pupils – should have a voice in the day-to-day running of the institutions in which they work and in educational policies generally.

New organisations have grown up: bodies concerned with particular educational interests, such as federations of parent-teacher associations, associations of governing bodies and managers of schools, or bodies with a more general concern for public education, such as the Council for Educational Advance. Some of the major reports of the period have been sympathetic to these aspirations. Thus the Plowden Report[13] paid particular attention to the question of parental attitudes and the need to associate parents with the work of individual schools.

Successive governments too have shown themselves aware of these aspirations. The 1944 Act itself allocated certain powers to managers and governors of individual schools. A later Act – the Education (No. 2) Act 1968 – extended similar provisions to technical colleges and colleges of education, and has favoured the inclusion on governing and managing bodies not only of teachers but also – in the case of establishments catering mainly for those aged 18 or over – of students.[14] The Department is usually ready to receive representations from organisations of the kind just described, and not infrequently consults them when new policies are in preparation.

SCARCE RESOURCES

It would be a serious omission to conclude this chapter without referring to one feature of the background to the Department's work in the last three decades that in many ways has been most important of all: the limitation of resources. Despite what has been said earlier about the growth of GNP, the expansion of the country's educational system which will be described in later chapters has had to be undertaken at a time when the country was impoverished by war, was frequently in economic difficulties and even in prosperity was achieving only modest economic growth. It has thus had to be carried through with strictly limited resources of money, of skilled manpower, particularly teachers, and of bricks and mortar and other capital equipment. It has been a period, moreover, in which there have been competing demands on resources for reform in other fields: housing, health and other social services arising from the development of the welfare state, as well as the cost of defence. In the 1970s all these difficulties have been compounded by the high level of inflation.

Limitation of resources is of course a fact of life which looms large in the work of any government department – or for that matter of any local authority – at any time. It loomed particularly large in the work of the Department during the three decades after the war, because this was a period when the national aim of achieving major educational advance coincided with a period of rapidly increasing numbers and of large movements of population.

There can be few who have been engaged in the administration of education in this period who have not sometimes felt condemned to work forever in a Looking Glass country, where it was always necessary to run faster and faster to stay in the same place.

NOTES AND REFERENCES

1 Lord Butler, *The Art of the Possible* (London, Hamish Hamilton, 1971); see in particular p. 109.
2 *The Health of the School Child: Fifty Years of the School Health Service*, report of the Chief Medical Officer of the Ministry of Education for the years 1956 and 1957 (London, HMSO, 1958), p. 7. It is revealing, by way of contrast, to recall the conditions that were familiar to HM Inspectors a century earlier. Matthew Arnold, after a visit to one of the poorer parts of London, could write of 'children eaten up with disease, half-sized, half-fed, half-clothed, neglected by their parents, without health, without home, without hope' (*Culture and Anarchy*, London, Smith Elder & Co., 1869, p. 244).
3 *The Health of the School Child in 1964 and 1965*, report of the Chief Medical Officer of the Department of Education and Science for the years 1964 and 1965 (London, HMSO, 1966).
4 *Adult Education: A Plan for Development: Report of the Committee on Adult Education* (the Russell Report) (London, HMSO, 1973), para. 2.
5 Largely as a result of *Children and their Primary Schools: Report of the Central Advisory Council for Education (England)* (Chairman: Lady Plowden, JP) (the Plowden Report) (London, HMSO, 1967).
6 *Half our Future: Report of the Central Advisory Council for Education (England)* (the Newsom Report) (London, HMSO, 1963).
7 *Primary Education in Wales: Report of the Central Advisory Council for Education (Wales)* (the Gittins Report) (London, HMSO, 1967).
8 *Hansard* (19 January 1944), vol. 396, col. 210–11.
9 See White Paper, *Educational Reconstruction*, Cmnd 6458 (London, HMSO, 1943), para. 1 and elsewhere.
10 National Children's Bureau, *From Birth to Seven: Second Report of the National Child Development Study on the 1958 Cohort*, by Ronald Davie, Neville Butler and Harvey Goldstein (London, Longmans, 1972).
11 Particularly in DES, *Educational Priority: Report of a Research Project Sponsored by the Department of Education and Science and the Social Science Research Council* (ed. A. H. Halsey), *Vol. I, EPA Problems and Policies* (London, HMSO, 1972).
12 The views of the more vigorous spokesmen of the latter point of view have appeared in such publications as the *Education Black Papers* and in Rhodes Boyson (ed.), *Education: Threatened Standards* (Enfield, Churchill Press, 1972) and later volumes.
13 Plowden Report, op. cit., ch. 4, 'Participation by parents'.
14 See DES and Welsh Office, *A New Partnership for our Schools* (London, HMSO, 1977).

CHAPTER 3

The Department and its Partners in the Education Service

A NATIONAL SERVICE LOCALLY ADMINISTERED

It is a basic feature of the public service of education in England and Wales that, while it is a national service, it is locally administered. Except at university level it is, in the words of Selby-Bigge, a decentralised service 'conducted by representative local bodies which are not the agents of the central authority'.[1] Unlike the ministries of education in, say, France or Italy, the central department itself takes virtually no direct part in running educational institutions. It maintains no schools or colleges; it employs no teachers; it does not control the curriculum.

The authorities that maintain the great majority of the schools and colleges in the public sector, other than universities, are elected local government bodies: the non-metropolitan county councils and the metropolitan district councils in the large conurbations, together with the Inner London Education Authority (ILEA) and the Outer London boroughs. These have the function of providing education along with other local services. In their exercise of their educational functions they are known as local education authorities (LEAs). These authorities also provide most of the schools in the public sector; that is, they are responsible for building as well as maintaining them.

They are not the only providers of schools in the public sector. A substantial proportion of schools in the maintained sector are 'voluntary' schools, that is, schools provided by voluntary bodies, notably the churches. Rather less than one-third of the schools within the maintained system, containing rather over a fifth of the pupils, are voluntary schools.[2] But it is the LEAs that maintain them and are generally responsible for planning development on the ground.

Thus the education service, except at university level, is operated as a partnership between the central authority and the LEAs – with the teachers through their national organisations increasingly involved as a third element. The framework of the partnership between the Department and the local authorities is provided by statute – by successive education and local government Acts, which define the respective duties and powers of the local authorities and of the central department. This chapter is mainly concerned with the framework. Subsequent chapters will have more to say about the working of the partnership in practice.

ORIGIN OF LOCAL EDUCATION AUTHORITIES

The first secular education authorities of a local and democratic character in England and Wales were the school boards created by the Forster Act 1870. These were *ad hoc* bodies created solely for the purpose of providing schools. Originally intended to provide only elementary (or what would now be called primary) schools, many of them by the end of the nineteenth century were extending their activities into post-elementary education. But it was widely doubted whether they were competent to do so.

By that time informed opinion was coming to the view that, if an adequate system of secondary education was to be developed, the responsibility must be given to the major local government bodies which by then existed in all parts of the country. This was the solution proposed by the Bryce Commission in 1895, and it was the solution adopted in the Education Act 1902 (the Balfour Act). This Act 'embodied the idea that the service of public education should be a specific function of ordinary local government as reorganised by the Act of 1888, that in every area there should be a Local Authority primarily responsible for the provision, organisation and administration of public education, amenable, through electoral processes, to the influence of rate-payers'.[3]

The county and county borough councils were not the only local bodies given education functions by the 1902 Act. Borough and urban district councils with populations above a certain figure (known as Part III authorities) were given powers to provide elementary education only.

By the time the Education Act 1944 was in preparation, it had become apparent that these Part III authorities were too small and deficient in resources to provide an effective service. Their perpetuation would have defeated one of the main aims of the new Act, which was to achieve a unified administration of the local education service over the whole range from primary to further education. The 1944 Act therefore allocated the education function to the county and county borough authorities (at that time there were 144 in England and Wales), and the Part III authorities disappeared as such. This general pattern of administration by county and county borough authorities continued in operation until 1974.

In the mid-1960s the whole system of local government in England and Wales (and also in Scotland) came under review. Local government in England was the subject of a Royal Commission under the chairmanship of Lord Redcliffe-Maud.[4] In Wales there were successive reviews by *ad hoc* bodies. These formed the basis of the Local Government Act 1972, although this enactment by no means followed them in all respects.

With the coming into operation of the 1972 Act the number of LEAs was substantially reduced, and the differentiation between 'county' and 'county borough' disappeared. The education authorities today are the councils of the 39 new non-metropolitan counties in England and 8 counties in Wales and of the 36 metropolitan districts in the major conurbations, together with the Inner London Education Authority and the 20 Outer London boroughs in the London area (which were not affected by this reorganisation).

Although this reorganisation involved major changes in the pattern of local authorities, it did not radically alter their functions or their relationship with the Department, because by and large the framework provided by the education Acts remained unchanged.

These councils are elected on the same basis of universal suffrage as Parliament at Westminster. In most areas – but not all – local elections are conducted on party political lines, the seats being contested by candidates supported by the main national parties.

The councils that are LEAs have a number of other functions besides education:[5] personal social services, youth employment, libraries, transportation, and certain functions in relation to housing. But education is their major responsibility.

In their capacity as LEAs these bodies are required by law to set up education committees.[6] All that the law says about the composition of an education committee is that it shall include persons of experience in education and persons acquainted with the educational conditions prevailing in the area, but that a majority shall be members of the authority. The implication is that education committees may include co-opted members, and in practice most education committees have co-opted members chosen for their educational experience, for example, teachers and representatives of voluntary bodies concerned with education, such as the churches.

Where, as is usually the case, councils are elected on party lines, the education committee may be expected to reflect the party balance in the main council, and its chairman to be a leading member of the majority party on the council.

It is the council of the county or metropolitan district, not the education committee, that is the LEA and that has the final voice (subject, of course, to the policy of central government) in determining educational policy, for the reason, amongst others, that it holds the purse strings. But it is common practice for councils in their capacity as LEAs to delegate some or all of their functions, other than the power to borrow money or raise a rate, to their education committees. As a rule it is the education committee or its sub-committees that take the initiative in formulating educational policy, and there is a requirement that LEAs should normally consider reports from their education committees before exercising their education functions.[7]

Each LEA is required (Section 88) to appoint a 'fit person' to be its chief education officer, and this officer is the council's chief executive officer in respect of the education function. He has a permanent staff including specialist advisers and local inspectors, varying in number according to the size and policy of the authority.

The chief education officer and his staff are appointed under the local government Acts, and are thus in the authority's service. Their primary responsibility is to the education committee. But they are also members of the staff of the local authority as a whole, working closely with its other chief officers. And while local authorities are within limits free to organise the operation of their services as they think fit, there is a body of opinion that holds that all chief officers, including the chief education officer, should operate as members of a management team, responsible under the leadership of the authority's chief executive for planning the authority's services. In practice chief education officers have usually had in the past, and are likely to continue to have, a fair degree of independence. As permanent officials, having as a rule first-hand experience of teaching and having at their disposal the advice of a specialist staff, they tend to have unusually wide knowledge of their field. They are key figures in the day-to-day operation of the education service on the ground.

The revenue of local authorities concerned with education comes mainly from two sources: partly (about 40 per cent or less) from the rates and partly (about 60 per cent or more) from contributions from central funds, now known as rate support grant, which are channelled through the Department of the Environment (or in Wales through the Welsh Office). The ultimate financial responsibility for the work of the education committee and its officers rests with the LEA itself.

THE DEPARTMENT AND THE
LOCAL EDUCATION AUTHORITIES

The statutory duties and powers of the Secretary of State

The statutory duties and powers of the Secretary of State in relation to the LEAs derive from successive education and local government Acts, but first and foremost from the Education Act 1944. Part I of this Act deals with the Secretary of State's[8] functions. The key phrase, as noted earlier, appears in Section 1(1), which lays on him the duty 'to promote the education of the people of England and Wales[9] . . . and to secure the effective execution by local authorities, under his control and direction' of national policy for providing a varied and comprehensive educational service in every area.

The significance of this phrase, which had no counterpart in previous educational legislation, is that it charges the Minister of Education or Secretary of State not only to oversee the LEAs in the discharge of their obligations, but in effect also to take the initiative in framing national policies for education. (The role of the Department in formulating national policies is dealt with in Chapter 4.)

Part II of the Act, which deals with the statutory services provided by the LEAs, specifies the particular duties or powers of the Secretary of State in relation to each of the main stages of education within the statutory system. Thus it requires the Secretary of State to make regulations prescribing the standards of school premises – a provision that, operated in conjunction with administrative control over capital investment in the public sector, has enabled the central department to exercise a continuing influence over educational building throughout the postwar period. It lays down the procedures for establishing new schools and closing old ones, which require the Secretary of State's approval in each case. Section 13, as extended and amended by the Education Act 1968, extends the procedure to cover changes in the character of a school. (See Chapter 6.) The Act gives him regulation-making power to ensure adequate provision of schools for handicapped children. It gives him powers with regard to the management and government of schools, the health of children in school,[10] the transport of children to and from school and the provision of school meals and milk.

Similarly the Act gives the Secretary of State specific powers in relation to further education, as a result of which LEAs were for the first time required to secure the provision of adequate facilities for further education as one of the three statutory stages of education.

Section 62,[11] dealing with the training of teachers, gives the Secretary of State the initiative in making such arrangements as he thinks are needed to secure facilities for teacher training. Mention must also be made in this context of the powers given to the Secretary of State (Section 89) to appoint a committee or committees to consider the remuneration of teachers and to require LEAs to adopt the scales recommended. This, until 1965, was the legal basis of the 'Burnham' machinery for determining teachers' salaries. (Since 1965 teachers' salaries have become the subject of separate legislation. See Chapter 7.)

The Act contains important provisions for the financing from public funds of grants to university and other students (Sections 81 and 100). In the eighteen years after the passing of the Act grants to students were made both by the Minister and by LEAs. With the passing of the Education Act 1962 virtually all grants to students, other than those to postgraduate students, are made by LEAs, but in all cases where the awards are mandatory the amounts and conditions of grants are governed by regulations made by the Secretary of State.

This is not intended to be an exhaustive list of the Secretary of State's specific powers in relation to the LEAs, but rather an indication of their range. Some will be considered in more detail in later chapters. The very important subject of the provisions, now mainly contained in local government Acts, that determine the financial relationships between the Department (and central government generally) and local authorities will be dealt with in Chapter 5.

The Secretary of State's general powers
In addition to these specific powers, the 1944 Act gives the Secretary of State certain general powers or duties in relation to LEAs. Thus he is given not merely the power but also the duty of inspecting educational establishments of all kinds (other than universities), and he is empowered to appoint – or, more precisely, to recommend Her Majesty to appoint – inspectors for this purpose (Section 77). HM Inspectorate has a role of key importance in the relationship between the central Department and the LEAs (see p. 31 and following).

Another section (92) requires LEAs to make to the Secretary of State 'such reports and returns and give him such information as he may require for the purpose of the exercise of his functions under this Act'. This provision complements that giving the Department powers of inspection. The information it obtains through HM Inspectors needs to be supplemented by information obtained directly from LEAs. This is not only needed to enable the Secretary of State to keep himself informed about the work of the LEAs; no less important, it is needed for the purposes of compiling national statistics and of assembling the data required for the formation of national policies for education.

Of special importance are two sections giving the Secretary of State powers in the event of unreasonable action or default by LEAs (or other providing bodies). Section 68 says that if the Secretary of State is satisfied, 'either on complaint by any person or otherwise', that any LEA 'has acted or are proposing to act unreasonably' in the exercise of any power conferred or the performance of any duty imposed by or under the Act, he may give 'such directions . . . as appear to him to be expedient'. Section 99(1) empowers the Secretary of State, in similar terms, to direct an LEA that he considers to be in default of some duty imposed on it by the Act.

It may be useful to note two points about the extent, and the limits, of the powers that these provisions confer. First, Section 68 gives to an aggrieved individual a recourse against unreasonable exercise of functions by LEAs (or other educational bodies) that he would not have under the ordinary law. But the Secretary of State can intervene only where an authority is exercising a power or performing a duty 'under this Act', that is, under the education Acts. He cannot invoke it in cases where an authority is acting under other Acts, for example, where it is acting in pursuance of its contractual obligations towards the teachers it employs.

Secondly, the power conferred by Section 68 is exercisable only if the authority has acted or is proposing to act 'unreasonably'. This does not entitle the Secretary of State simply to substitute his own judgement in a particular situation for that of the LEA. He can intervene only where he is satisfied that there are no tenable grounds for the authority's action.

It is thus not surprising to find that the power has been relatively rarely used. The records show that since 1944 it has been used not much more than a dozen times (except in cases involving choice of school). Section 99(1) has been used on only one occasion, and its use was a direct consequence of the failure of the body concerned (the governing body of a school) to comply with a Section 68 direction.

The existence of a power may, however, be as important as its use. Examination of the records would undoubtedly bring to light a number of cases in which an offending authority, confronted with the possibility of its use, chose discretion as the better part of valour.

Legislation

In considering the powers of the Department and its relationship with LEAs, it is important to bear in mind that, while the Department no less than the LEAs is subject to the law as it is, the law is not immutable. Governments, acting through Parliament, can and do legislate, and new legislation may materially affect the relations between the central department and the local authorities. Indeed it may be said that in some ways the most important of all the functions of the central department, and of central government generally, in relation to the education service are those of providing the organisational framework and of modifying it from time to time to meet new needs and circumstances. In the period since the 1944 Act there have been a number of education Acts, which in one way or another have affected the relations between the Department and the LEAs, and also a number of local government Acts, which have had substantial implications for the financial relationship between the central government and local authorities generally.

Limitations of the Secretary of State's statutory powers

A mere enumeration of the Secretary of State's statutory powers vis-à-vis the LEAs, starting with Section 1 of the 1944 Act, could easily leave the reader not familiar with the working of the system with the impression that the Secretary of State and the Department are virtually omnipotent and that the LEAs are no more than the Department's subsidised agents. The reality is otherwise.

In the first place, the Act itself, as already implied, is so framed as to preserve a fair measure of autonomy for the LEAs, and thus a balance of power between the central and the local bodies. While it gives a number of powers and duties, both specific and general, to the Secretary of State, it allocates others to the local authorities. Thus it is the duty of LEAs to secure the provision of sufficient schools and further education in their areas, and the initiative in planning the provision rests with them. It is they who employ and pay teachers. It is they who (subject to certain provisos) determine the curriculum or leave their schools to do so.

Secondly, the Department has not normally been hungry for power, or for detailed control. Although it is always conscious of its responsibilities for maintaining national standards of provision and for taking the initiative in framing national policy, it also has a tradition of respect for the autonomy of LEAs and of reluctance to become directly involved in the detailed running of the service. It has usually welcomed measures to increase local autonomy.

Thirdly, the LEAs themselves are not slow to assert their autonomy and to resist encroachments, and they have various means of doing so. They have a considerable measure of financial autonomy. Being democratically elected bodies, they have an appeal to public opinion. They have their associations, which are influential and well-informed bodies, and whose representations ministers and officials treat with respect.

Moreover, they have recourse to the courts, for the relationship of the central department to the LEAs, and their respective powers and duties, are defined by law; and while ultimately the central government can, through Parliament, change the law, the Department, like any other organ of central government, is subject to the law as it is. If the Department in its dealings with an authority is judged to have exceeded its powers, it is liable to an action in the courts.[12]

The role of HM Inspectors

It would be wrong to conclude this chapter without some further reference to the role of HM Inspectors. HM Inspectorate is one of the oldest parts of the machinery of central oversight of public education. The first HM Inspectors were appointed in 1839, the year in which the Education Committee of the Privy Council was established. Originally they were intended to perform the function of 'watchdogs' for the expenditure of taxpayers' money on education; and although from the outset their role has been wider than this, it is as well to recall their watchdog role. 'Historically and logically,' as Selby-Bigge observes, 'this [the inspectorial] function of the Board rests on the necessity both of supervising and safeguarding the expenditure of public money and of getting the largest possible return for it.'[13] Although the ways in which the Inspectorate works have radically changed, it is inevitable that, in a period when education claims a larger share of national resources in money, materials and manpower, than it has ever done, a concern for the wise use of resources and the related task of safeguarding standards must be two of its main preoccupations.

But they are far from being the only ones. In this century, and particularly since 1944, one of the main functions of HM Inspectorate has been to serve as a body of professional advisers and consultants on education who, by virtue of their specialist knowledge, their collective experience and their familiarity with the working of the education service in all parts of the country, possess as a body a unique understanding of the practice of education.

The primary responsibility of HM Inspectors is to ministers and the Department. They are there to provide the information and professional advice that the Department needs to carry out its functions of supervising the service and shaping national policies for education. As a field force whose members are in touch with every type and size of educational institution, with teachers and with LEAs, they are exceptionally well placed to help in providing information that the Department requires about the needs of the service and the way in which policies work out on the ground. The importance of their contribution in helping to shape national policies is recognised by the inclusion of the senior chief inspector in the policy-steering group, which is the senior body charged with the Department's policy planning, and of senior inspectors on a number of the policy groups set up within the departmental planning organisation. (See Chapter 5.)

In addition HM Inspectors have responsibilities in relation to individual LEAs. In every area of the country individual HM Inspectors are assigned as 'district inspectors' to each LEA – usually one for schools and one for further education. These have representational or liaison functions. It is their task to familiarise themselves with the needs, views and policies of the authority they are assigned to, as well as to interpret to the authority the views and policies of the Department. From knowledge of practice and standards across the country they can advise LEAs about the performance of their own institutions.

HM Inspectors also provide an advisory service to schools and colleges and to teachers, by visits, short courses and publications. Every educational institution in the country has access to HM Inspectors operating within the local network or forming part of national specialist teams or working parties. Since HM Inspectors are mostly recruited from the teaching profession or from work in industry, business and the public service that has to do with teaching and training, they have a natural affinity with the teachers, which gives them a ready insight into the teachers' point of view.

They also have important regional assignments. Unlike other major departments of central government, the Department does not have regional offices staffed by officials. It looks to senior members of the Inspectorate, which is organised on a geographical basis, to represent its interests, for example, on regional planning councils. A number of HM Inspectors are assigned as liaison officers with various professional bodies or serve as assessors on examining and other bodies.

Thus collectively HM Inspectors have at all times a close working knowledge of all types of institution, of the problems and thinking of every LEA in the country, and of a wide range of other educational and professional bodies.

This combination of functions gives HM Inspectorate a role of peculiar importance within the education service. HM Inspectors remain the guardians of national standards. They are also available to explain and interpret departmental policies to those who have to implement and adapt them. But above all they convey to the Department the complexity of the national picture and the range of issues, general or particular, arising from local variation. To what might otherwise appear the impersonal interaction of official machinery, they bring an element of direct personal relationship.

Their ability to perform these services derives largely from the recognition by all the partners in the service of their experience and professional competence, and of a certain independence of mind and detachment that goes with these qualities. Their advice 'appears to be valued mainly because it is generally accepted as being informed and disinterested'.[14]

NOTES AND REFERENCES

1 Sir Amherst Selby-Bigge, *The Board of Education*, Whitehall Series (London and New York, Putnam, 1927), p. 175.
2 There was until recently another small but important category of schools in the public sector, the direct grant schools, which were not maintained by LEAs. (See Chapter 6.)
3 Selby-Bigge, op. cit., p. 18.
4 *Report of the Royal Commission on Local Government in England 1966–69* (Chairman: Lord Redcliffe-Maud), Cmnd 4040 (London, HMSO, 1969). Local government in the London area had been reorganised by the London Government Act 1963.
5 Except the ILEA.
6 Part II of the First Schedule of the Education Act 1944 (Local Government Act 1972), Section 101.
7 Section 7 of Part II of the First Schedule, Education Act 1944. Exceptions are allowed if the matter is urgent.
8 The 1944 Act is drafted throughout in terms of a Minister of Education. In 1964 the functions of the Minister of Education were transferred to the newly created Secretary of State for Education and Science. The designation Secretary of State is therefore normally used here.
9 As noted earlier, responsibility for primary and secondary education in Wales was, subject to minor exceptions, transferred to the Secretary of State for Wales in 1970 (Transfer of Functions (Wales) Order 1970).
10 A later Act – the Education (No. 2) Act 1968 – lays down requirements for the government of colleges of education and establishments of further education. (See Chapters 7 and 8.)
11 The regulations governing the provision and conduct of teacher-training establishments are now made under local government Acts.
12 Since 1967 the Department has also, in common with all other departments of central government, been subject to the scrutiny of the Ombudsman or Parliamentary Commissioner for Administration (Parliamentary Commissioner Act 1967).
13 Selby-Bigge, op. cit., p. 121.
14 DES, *HMI Today and Tomorrow* (London, DES, 1970), p. 20.

CHAPTER 4

National Policies for Education

The previous chapter, in giving an account of the legal framework of the relationship between the centre and the local education authorities (LEAs), drew attention to the role of the Department in formulating national policy for education – a role that was for the first time given explicit recognition in the Education Act 1944.

It is undoubtedly true to say that this Act, with its emphasis on the centrality of the Minister of Education's role in formulating 'national policy', and on securing its 'effective execution' by local authorities under his control and direction, began a new phase. Moreover, the circumstances of the postwar period favoured the development of this function, indeed made it inevitable.

The rapid growth of the system in this period, as a result both of deliberate policies and of the growth in numbers, combined with the continuing limitation of resources, of buildings, of teachers, as well as of public finance, have made it inevitable that the central authority should increasingly concentrate on the role of long term planning of the system which it alone can perform, and on the task of relating resources to plans. (This is dealt with in the next chapter.)

In view of the central importance of this policy-making function in the work of the Department, it may be useful here to make a few introductory remarks about what is meant by 'national policy' – or rather, 'national policies' – for education: what they consist of, how they originate, how they are processed to the point at which they become agreed policies for the service as a whole, and how they are communicated so that they can be effectively implemented on the ground. Subsequent chapters will look in more detail at some of the more important policy developments in particular sectors of education in the postwar period.

WHAT IS MEANT BY 'NATIONAL POLICIES' FOR EDUCATION?

There are of course no rules for determining what kinds of issues or objectives take shape as 'national policies' for education. At any given time this depends not only on the needs of the system and the development of educational thought but also on the interplay of politics.

Broadly it may be said that the major issues that feature in national policies for education are: first, certain basic aims or objectives of the system on which there is in practice a fair measure of consensus (expansion of educational opportunity, mitigation of underprivilege); secondly, issues concerning the framework and organisation of the system (the duration of compulsory schooling, the availability of preschool education, the organisation of secondary or further education, and the development of higher education); and thirdly, issues concerning what may be called the logistics of the system (the supply and training of teachers, the scale and standards of educational building, and related issues about priorities in the use of resources).

For the benefit of readers familiar with the more centralised systems of many European countries, it may be remarked that there is one respect in which, in the English context, the concept of national policies for education is restricted. The debate is not, or at any rate until recently has not been, primarily concerned with issues about the school curriculum or the content of education generally. This limitation arises from a traditional feature of the English system, which gives responsibility for determining the curriculum of the schools to the LEAs and teachers and not to the central department. (See Chapter 6.) This limitation applies even more rigorously in the university sector, where individual institutions have virtually complete autonomy in academic matters.

HOW NATIONAL POLICIES FOR EDUCATION ARE EVOLVED: THE ROLE OF MINISTERS AND OF THE DEPARTMENT

It is ministers and ministers alone – that is, the Secretary of State and, where major issues of policy or resource allocation are involved, ministers collectively – who are ultimately responsible to Parliament for national policies for education, civil science and the other functions that are the subject of this volume. Any survey of the ways in which national policies are formulated needs to be prefaced with this remark.

It does not follow that all new national policies for education originate with ministers. In many instances they may do so. Individual ministers may come to office with their own considered ideas on policy. Moreover, it is increasingly common for new educational policies to feature in the election manifestos of the main political parties. It has been noted that the political parties that are the protagonists in national politics at Westminster are also active in local politics, where education is one of the main issues. The experience of party workers at local level, and their appreciation of local needs, are likely to be fed through to the central offices of the national parties, to emerge as new national policies for education.

The Department's senior permanent officials also have a role in policy making. 'We should ignore the old saw about Ministers being concerned with policy and officials with administration. It is officials' business to advise their Ministers on policy.'[1] This applies particularly to the Department, which is essentially a 'policy-making' department with few 'administrative' functions (in the sense implied in this quotation). The Department's permanent staff has in recent years become increasingly equipped, through the departmental planning organisation, to undertake systematic thinking about national policy objectives and their resource implications, and to identify longer term issues that may require policy decisions by ministers. In this context the role of HM Inspectorate must also again be referred to. HM Inspectors have in recent years come to be more closely associated with the formulation as well as the implementation of policy.

ADVISORY MACHINERY

From the time when the creation of an effective central department with a minister responsible to Parliament came to be seriously considered, it was recognised that there was a need for some form of national consultative machinery representative of the educational world to advise the Minister on national policy for education. The Bryce Commission of 1895 had emphasised the point, and the 1899 Act which created the Board of Education provided for a consultative committee.

This proved to be a valuable device. The Haldane Committee on the Machinery of Government, which reported in 1918,[12] commented favourably on the practice of the Board and of certain other central departments in this respect, and *Education 1900–1950*, the Ministry's annual report, probably did not say too much when it claimed that in this area the Board had made a special contribution to the art of government.

Some of the reports that this body produced during the forty or so years of its existence, notably its 1926 report which came to be known as the Hadow Report,[3] had a far reaching influence on contemporary educational thought and policy. Both this and the Spens Report[4] of 1938 did much to shape the thinking that went into the Education Act 1944.

The 1944 Act both extended and modified this machinery. It provided for two central advisory councils for education, one for England and one for Wales. These were to be appointed by the Minister and were to include 'persons who have had experience of the statutory system of public education as well as persons who have had experience of educational institutions not forming part of that system'. The Secretariat was to be provided by the Department. Unlike the consultative committee these councils were free to advise the Minister 'upon any matters connected with educational theory and practice as they thought fit'.

In practice the central advisory councils have not functioned as standing bodies, and they have not, except in the early years, chosen their own subjects for inquiry. Since the 1950s they have been given specific remits by ministers, and they have been reconstituted on each occasion to include members particularly suited to advise on those remits.

These councils have had an immense influence on educational policy and practice in this country – and far beyond it – and the names of the chairmen of some of the councils have become almost household words in the educational world: Crowther and Newsom for secondary education, Plowden for primary and preschool education, Aaron and Gittins for education in Wales. Some of them have injected new concepts into the educational thinking of the time, such as that of the educational priority area which was formulated by the Plowden Council.

SPECIALISED ADVISORY BODIES

In this period there has also been a development of advisory bodies for particular sectors of education, and these have come to have growing influence. Of major importance have been: the National Advisory Council on Education for Industry and Commerce (until its demise in 1977); that on the training and supply of teachers; the National Advisory Council on Art Education; the Advisory Committee on Handicapped Children; the Secondary School Examinations Council up to 1964, and thereafter its successor body the Schools Council for the Curriculum and Examinations;[5] and the National Council for Educational Technology, now reconstituted as the Council for Educational Technology for the United Kingdom.

All of these are standing committees, with varying constitutions which usually in various ways provide for representation of the local authorities and other educational bodies. In most cases (although not in all) their secretariats are provided by the Department. Their main purpose has been to advise ministers on needs and policies for the sectors with which they are concerned. Their recommendations may in many cases also be addressed to LEAs, teachers and others concerned in implementing policies on the ground.

Besides advising ministers, these bodies serve another purpose which is of peculiar importance because of the decentralised nature of the service. They serve what may be called a parliamentary function, acting as a forum for bringing together the partners involved in operating the service: local authorities, teachers, churches, and so forth, as well as the Department. They thus help to ensure a measure of consensus amongst all concerned with the implementation of policies.

With the development of these more specialised bodies, and with the enlargement of the Department's responsibilities to include the university sector, ministers have tended to resort less frequently to the use of the general advisory machinery of the central advisory councils, which is not appropriate for examining issues involving the university sector, and to opt for special inquiries by *ad hoc* bodies. Familiar examples are the Robbins Committee on Higher Education[6] and the James Committee on Teacher Education and Training.[7]

Moreover, invaluable though many of the reports of the central advisory councils have been, they sometimes have a disadvantage that is the obverse of their excellence: their period of gestation may be considerable. Some of the best-known reports of the 1950s and 1960s took upwards of three years to complete. In a society in which educational needs and the policies required to meet them are changing fast, the findings of a major committee are liable to be less relevant after three years than at the time when it began its work.

Ministers have thus come to see increasing advantage in *ad hoc* inquiries which can come to speedy conclusions. In the case of the James Committee members were invited to serve full-time (or in some cases part-time) so that they could complete their report within twelve months – an arrangement that is likely to prove attractive to ministers in the future.

THE ROLE OF THE DEPARTMENT'S PARTNERS IN POLICY FORMATION

It has been noted that one of the purposes served by these advisory bodies, both general and specialised, is to perform a 'parliamentary' function. It is worth enlarging on this point, because it draws attention to the part that LEAs and the other partners in the education service play in the process by which educational policies are formulated, and thus to the fact they are partners in the making of policy as well as in its implementation.

In the discussions that take place in these bodies in the preparation of a major report, it is frequently the representatives of the local authority or teachers' associations, or individual chief education officers or teachers, who make major contributions. 'If we look to the past,' a past president of the Society of Education Officers has remarked, 'we must certainly recognise that during the course of this century most of our major educational advances have been due to the initiative and experiment of individual Authorities.'[8] This is probably no exaggeration, and indeed is what might be expected, since it is individual chief education officers and individual teachers who have the experience that comes from working 'at the coal face'; and this experience is reflected in the contributions that their representatives make as members of advisory bodies.

The involvement of the local authority world and the teachers and their representatives by no means ends at the stage at which a major report is completed. When such a report – for example, a report of one of the central advisory councils – is presented to ministers, it is the Department's usual practice, before reaching conclusions on the government's attitude, to publish it, to allow opportunity for discussion in the press and the educational world, and to ask for formal comments from the associations.[9] These usually take the form of considered memoranda of evidence, which may have no small influence on the Department's policy for implementing the report.

Similarly it is the almost invariable practice of the Department to consult the educational and teachers' associations, and in some cases other national bodies with more specialised interests, when new departmental policies are being prepared in the form of legislation, or new regulations, or departmental circulars, or in other ways.

This consultation of the bodies concerned may thus be said to be an integral part of the process by which educational policies are formed, and since the reasons for it are not always well understood, it may be useful to say something here about its rationale.

The existence of interest groups, and the part that they play in the formation of government policy, are familiar matters to students of government. It is common practice amongst departments of central government here and in other Western countries, in the process of evolving new policies, to consult with the interests that will be affected. 'Each Department's contact with the various bodies within its own fields of business must be one of its most important tasks. It is here also that Government can best refute the charge of "remoteness".'[10]

In education there are compelling reasons for the government to involve the bodies concerned in the framing of policies. The Department's partners in the education service are much more than 'interested' bodies, in the sense that, say, trade associations are interested bodies in relation to the activities of the Department of Trade. They exist not to pursue their own material interests but to operate an essential public service, which they have a statutory duty to provide.

The LEAs, which are the main providers of public education (except at university level), have a special status in that they are democratically elected bodies, relying for a substantial proportion of their resources on local rates for which they are answerable to local electors.

There is another point. Because the LEAs are local, they have experience at first hand of local needs, of what is possible in terms of the local situation and of what will be the problems of implementing new policies on the ground. They have the 'feel' of the locality.

The reasons for associating the teachers' organisations with national policy making are essentially similar, although their role in the partnership is different. Even more directly than the LEAs, the teachers are working 'at the coal face'. An obvious reason for consulting them is that policies involving action by teachers are more likely to be effectively implemented if they have the teachers' understanding and goodwill. Moreover, they enjoy a considerable degree of autonomy in such matters as the organisation and curriculum of schools and colleges, and they have a professional concern in all that happens in the educational world and thus rightly expect to be consulted on the broader issues of national policy for education.

There is of course, and no doubt always will be, criticism of the Department on the grounds that its consultations are not sufficiently wide or timely, or that it pays too little attention to the comments it receives; and fears of this kind have tended to grow in recent years, with the introduction of more systematic central planning of educational strategy associated with the Public Expenditure Survey Committee (PESC) and with Programme Analysis and Review (PAR), which are described in the next chapter. It is here relevant to quote from a memorandum that the Department submitted to the

House of Commons Expenditure Committee (Education, Arts and Home Office Subcommittee) in November 1975:

> The Department . . . recognises the importance of associating . . . other parties and the local authority associations closely with the planning process, the results of which are often vital to their interests. There are difficulties about this – not least the fact that decisions arising from the need to reduce the rate of growth of public expenditure often have to be taken on a short time-scale. This points to the importance of developing further the process of consultation, whether formal (e.g. through the Consultative Council on Local Government Finance established in 1975, and the Council of Local Education Authorities), or informal (e.g. through involvement in the Rate Support Grant negotiations).[11]

It is probably fair to say that the Department is as conscious as any department of central government of the need to promote continuous consultation with its local authority and other partners on all major issues of policy and resource allocation.

THE ANNOUNCEMENT AND COMMUNICATION OF NEW POLICIES

Major new developments of policy involving legislation are of course first announced by ministers in Parliament. Even where legislation is not involved, ministers may in many cases think their plans of sufficient importance to justify the laying of a White or Green Paper, or a statement in the House of Commons. As a rule this is at the earliest opportunity sent to all LEAs and other educational bodies concerned. New policies may also be announced in ministerial speeches at conferences or on other occasions.

The traditional medium for communicating new policies that are for one reason or another not embodied in a White Paper or in draft legislation is the departmental circular. The Department's circulars are issued over the signature of the permanent secretary. They are not directives. They are statements of government policy on particular developments or aspects of education, usually containing explanations of the policies proposed and indications of what the LEAs and other organisations are expected to do about them. They carry an assumption, implicit if not explicit, that the Department will consent to the use by authorities of the resources needed to implement the policies. As already explained, these circulars are usually agreed statements, in the sense that they will have been the subject of consultations between the Department and the associations involved before issue. They are public, and in some cases priced, documents.*

There are a number of other channels used by the Department for communicating guidance, advice or information of a more specialised character. There is the administrative memorandum, which is used for statements of a more technical nature. Some policy branches have their own media of communication for specialised policy statements or advice. Thus Further Education and Teachers' Branches issue 'circular letters' or 'college letters' on new policies affecting these sectors. The Department's Architects and Building Branch issues periodic Building Bulletins and Design Notes to inform LEAs of the best current practice and the results of the most recent research in educational building. HM Inspectorate issues pamphlets on various subjects including aspects of the curriculum. These are designed for individual teachers and parents as well as for LEAs.

Information about educational policies and the background to them is not something which is of concern only to members of parliament, LEAs and teachers. It has been remarked earlier that there has in the last three decades been something little short of an explosion in public interest in education, and that in consequence the media devote much more attention than ever before to educational matters.

To meet these needs the Department has built up a range of services through its Information and Statistics Divisions. In addition to its annual reports, which the Secretery of State is required by law to publish, the Department publishes an increasingly comprehensive range of statistics of education. Seven volumes of these, including one for the United Kingdom as a whole, are now published annually. These are supplemented from time to time by special series, and much further statistical material is available on request.

The Department's Information Division issues a range of publications, both for the general public and for the educational world. There are monthly Reports on Education which deal with particular developments or phases of education of topical interest. There is a quarterly publication, *Trends in Education*, produced by an editorial board consisting of senior officials of the Department and HM Inspectorate. There are other periodical publications of a more specialised character. Within the last few years the Department has also published occasional Planning Papers, designed to provide a

* Prior to 1944 these appeared as Board of Education Circulars; from 1944 to 1964 as Ministry of Education Circulars; and from 1964 onwards as Circulars of the Department of Education and Science. Since November 1970 they have as a rule been issued as Joint DES/Welsh Office Circulars. In referring to particular Circulars in the text it will normally be convenient to refer simply to 'Circulars' and (in the case of Circulars issued since November 1970) to give only the DES Circular number.

framework of facts and figures for public discussion of some important issue of educational policy.[12]

Like other ministries, the Department through its Information Division keeps in close touch with the media, arranging ministerial conferences for the press, television and radio, issuing press notices, briefing correspondents and dealing with inquiries.

This information work is of particular importance in education. It helps to ensure that in educational policy making all concerned – Parliament, LEAs, teachers, universities, as well as the general public – have available to them current statistical data and the results of recent research, so providing a common universe of discourse within which debates on national educational issues can be pursued.

NOTES AND REFERENCES

1 Sir Richard Clarke, *New Trends in Government*, Civil Service College Studies (London, HMSO, 1971), p. 100.
2 Ministry of Reconstruction, Report of the Committee on the Machinery of Government (Chairman: Viscount Haldane of Cloane), Cd 9230 (London, HMSO, 1918), paras 34–7.
3 Board of Education, *The Education of the Adolescent: Report of the Consultative Committee under the Chairmanship of Sir Henry Hadow* (the Hadow Report) (London, HMSO, 1926).
4 Board of Education, *Secondary Education, with Special Reference to Grammar Schools and Technical High Schools: Report of the Consultative Committee on Secondary Education under the Chairmanship of Sir William Spens* (the Spens Report) (London, HMSO, 1938).
5 See Chapter 6. As there explained, the Schools Council is more than an advisory body and is independent of the Department.
6 This was appointed by the Prime Minister, not the Minister of Education. The universities were not at that time the responsibility of the Minister of Education.
7 DES, *Teacher Training and Education*, report by a Committee of Inquiry appointed by the Secretary of State for Education and Science (Chairman: Lord James of Rusholme) (the James Report) (London, HMSO, 1972).
8 J. C. Brooke, presidential address to the Society of Education Officers (January 1973); published in *Education*, 26 January 1973.
9 The bodies usually consulted are:
  (1) The main local authority associations concerned with education: namely the Council of Local Education Authorities, the Association of County Councils, the Association of Metropolitan Authorities, the Association of Education Committees (until 1976) and (where matters affect Wales) the Welsh Joint Education Committee. Some of these have a statutory role in relation to rate support grant negotiations. (See Chapter 5.)
  (2) The national teachers' organisations: namely, the National Union of Teachers, the National Association of Schoolmasters/Union of Women Teachers, the 'Joint Four' Secondary Associations and the National Association of Head Teachers. (Further Education, Teacher Education and other bodies are brought into consultation where appropriate.)

10 Clarke, op. cit., p. 31.
11 House of Commons Expenditure Committee (Session 1975–6), 10th Report, *Policy Making in the Department of Education and Science*, HC 621 (London, HMSO, 1976), memorandum by the DES.
12 See p. 159 for UGC publications.

CHAPTER 5

The Financing of Education

The arrangements for the financing of the educational system are of
central importance for this volume, for two reasons in particular.
The first and most fundamental is that education now accounts for a
substantial proportion of all public expenditure. As earlier noted,
expenditure on education in the public sector accounts for some 12
per cent of all public expenditure, and about 7 per cent of the gross
national product (GNP).

The second arises from the decentralised character of the education
service. Over 80 per cent of expenditure on education in the public
sector is incurred by local education authorities (LEAs), but as their
expenditure is grant aided from central funds the arrangements by
which this financial assistance is provided have an important bearing
on the working of the partnership between the central and the local
authorities in the educational field.

ORIGINS OF CENTRAL GOVERNMENT AID TO LOCAL EDUCATION AUTHORITIES

From the time of their creation by the Balfour Act 1902 the LEAs
have depended mainly on two sources of revenue. One is the rates, a
form of local tax on owners and occupiers of property. But these are
inadequate by themselves, at any level of incidence that is likely to
be politically acceptable, to finance more than a proportion of the
expenditure involved. From the time they came into being the LEAs
have depended on aid from central funds for something like half
their expenditure on education, sometimes rather less, recently
considerably more.

Up to the end of the First World War this aid largely took the form of *ad hoc* subsidies for particular activities or institutions. The first serious attempt to rationalise the financial relationship between the centre and the LEAs was embodied in the Fisher Act 1918, which, in place of a hotch-potch of separate grants, established a system of annual grants on a percentage basis related to expenditure, payable under regulations and dependent on the maintenance of an efficient service by the LEA.

THE EDUCATION ACT 1944 AND LOCAL GOVERNMENT ACT 1948

The percentage grant represented an important advance. But a coherent system of unified grants for the education service as a whole could not be achieved until the Education Act 1944 brought into being a unified pattern of LEAs covering the whole range of functions from nursery to further education.

The grant settlement associated with this Act, which with minor modifications governed the financial relationship between the centre and the LEAs until 1958, retained Fisher's principle of a percentage grant. It provided for an education 'main grant', together with certain special grants for ancillary services, carried on the vote of the newly created Ministry of Education. The main grant was based on a formula that related the amount of grant to the number of children to be educated and the capacity of the area to pay.[1] There were 'grant regulations' for various sectors of LEA activity – schools, further education, and so forth – laying down standards and other conditions to be fulfilled before grant was paid.

An authority's grant under the main grant formula was calculated on its expenditure 'allowable' for grant purposes. This meant that each authority had, before undertaking new educational expenditure, to ensure that it would be 'recognised for grant' by the Ministry. This, together with the fact that the Ministry could deduct particular items of grant if its requirements were not complied with, meant that it exercised fairly detailed control over the expenditure of individual LEAs.

THE LOCAL GOVERNMENT ACT 1958: GENERAL GRANT

With the Local Government Act 1958 a new system of central subvention of local authority expenditure was introduced, the main aim of which was to give local authorities greater autonomy in operating their services as a whole. The specific education grant made to LEAs by the Minister was discontinued (except for grants for school meals and milk, which continued until 1967–8), and education was included amongst the services aided by a general grant towards a range of the main services provided by local authorities. This, as its name implied, was a general subvention in aid of local finance, and no part of it was earmarked for a particular service. The total was fixed on the basis of a detailed examination of each of the services, together giving rise to 'relevant expenditure': the current load of expenditure, foreseeable variations in cost, probable fluctuations in demand and the need for development. It was then distributed amongst all county and county borough authorities by reference to objective factors, such as population and numbers in school, which were 'readily ascertainable' and afforded 'a fair and reasonable measure of the relative needs of each authority'. The government also continued to pay a 'rate deficiency' grant to authorities whose rate resources were below the national average.

The amount of the general grant was determined for a period of two years ahead. The grants were carried on the vote of the Ministry of Housing and Local Government (as the department concerned with local government was then called); but the calculations to arrive at a forecast of educational expenditure, which formed by far the largest item of total 'relevant expenditure', were made by the Ministry of Education in consultation with the LEAs and on the basis of information provided by them. Other central government departments concerned with local authority expenditure provided similar forecasts for the services within their purview. The final determination of the aggregate amounts of the general grant was issued in the form of an order made by the Minister of Housing and Local Government, with the consent of the Treasury, after consultation with the main local authority associations, and subject to an affirmative resolution of the House of Commons. There was provision for interim increases, or 'increase orders', to meet unforeseen increases in pay and prices of such magnitude that they could not reasonably be carried in full by the local authorities without assistance.

One consequence of the change to general grant is that the subsequent history of education finance, so far as the local authority sector is concerned, needs to be viewed in the context of the history of local government finance in general.

The introduction of general grant involved important changes in the arrangements for the Ministry's control of LEA expenditure. The grant regulations made under Section 100 of the Education Act 1944 were now replaced by substantive regulations. These still prescribed standards as before, but LEAs no longer had to ensure that individual items of expenditure were 'allowable' for grant; and the Ministry's power of enforcement no longer rested on the possibility that in the event of default it might deduct grant for a particular item. It now rested on a general provision[2] that, if an authority failed to achieve or maintain reasonable standards, the amount of its general grant might be reduced, subject to a report to and a resolution of the House of Commons.

THE LOCAL GOVERNMENT ACT 1966: RATE SUPPORT GRANT

By the mid-1960s it had become clear that general grant as conceived by the 1958 Act made little contribution to resolving what, over this period of rising expenditure on education (and other local services), was becoming one of the most intractable problems of local finance: the growing burden on the rates. It was an attempt to deal with this problem that underlay the next reform of local government finance, affecting the financing of education as well as other local services, namely, the introduction of rate support grant.

While there has, at any rate until recently, been general agreement about the social and political advantages of financing localised services partly out of local funds, there are snags about the rates as a source of local revenue. They are regressive, bearing little relationship to the ratepayers' capacity to pay, and they lack 'buoyancy'; that is, their product does not automatically increase with rising costs. Thus any attempt to increase the rate income of local government is liable to be unpopular with those whose burden it increases.[3]

But rating reform is only one aspect of the reform of local government, and by the mid-1960s the government had decided to set up a Royal Commission on Local Government (the commission under the chairmanship of Lord Redcliffe-Maud which reported in 1969). Meanwhile an interim arrangement was needed which would provide for a higher, and annually increasing, Exchequer contribution to local authority spending; and it was reckoned that this was best achieved by lessening the impact on domestic ratepayers of increases in rate poundages.

The new system, which was embodied in the Local Government Act 1966, was called 'rate support grant'. This replaced both the general grants and the rate deficiency grants, as well as the schools meals and milk grants. It differed from the general grant in that it was related to all the main revenue expenditure of local authorities except housing and trading services, accounting for more than 80 per cent of the total Exchequer contribution to local funds. It comprised three elements, the first of which, the needs element, roughly corresponded to the previous general grant but covered a wider range of services. The second, the resources element, corresponded to what was previously the rate deficiency grant and was payable to any local authority with rate resources per head of population below the national average. The third element, the domestic element, was an innovation. The Act required rating authorities to reduce the rate levied on dwelling houses by a national amount in the pound specified each year by the Minister; the domestic element was intended to compensate for the reduction in rate income brought about by this provision. In effect, this element represented a government subsidy to the domestic ratepayer.

The intention of the new system was progressively to increase the level of Exchequer contribution towards local authority expenditure. This did in fact rise from 54 per cent in 1967–8 (under the old system it would have been less than 53 per cent) to 55 per cent for 1968–9. By 1973–4 the proportion had risen to 60 per cent and by 1975–6 to 66 per cent.[4]

Under these arrangements the needs element (the largest element, accounting for over 80 per cent of the total) is distributed in much the same way as under general grant – that is, by reference to a range of objective factors that give a reasonable indication of the services provided, and also allow for circumstances that affect the relative costs of provision between one authority and another. The needs element comprises a basic payment calculated by reference to population, together with certain supplementary grants. The basic population grant constitutes Exchequer assistance towards the provision of average levels of the various local government services, including education. To the extent that the demand for a local authority's education service, measured in terms of 'education units', exceeds a certain threshold level in relation to its population, the authority qualifies for a share of the education supplementary grant. (Other supplementary grants recognise other special circumstances, such as above-average proportions of very young or old people in the population of an authority's area, high or low density, and declining population.) Provision for interim increase orders is retained.

THE LOCAL GOVERNMENT ACTS 1972 AND 1974

As a complement to the reform of local government embodied in the Local Government Act 1972, the government undertook a review of local government finance, in consultation with local authorities. A Green Paper, *The Future Shape of Local Government Finance*, published in July 1971, examined alternative sources of revenue for local government. But further discussion with local authorities, and consideration within government, led to the conclusion at that time that none of these was a practicable supplement to, or substitute for, the normal rating system. The consultation paper *Local Government Finance in England and Wales*, issued by the Department of the Environment and the Welsh Office in June 1973, confined itself to proposals for modification to the rate support grant system and to the rating system. These were embodied in the Local Government Act 1974.

Under this Act biennial negotiations for rate support grant were replaced by annual settlements. Relevant expenditure was redefined to include additional items. The three elements of rate support grant were retained, but more flexible procedures for their distribution were provided, since the formulae to be used in any given settlement were now to be laid down by regulations made by the Secretary of State for the Environment and could be varied from time to time. Amongst the changes relating to the needs element was the abolition of supplementary grants, including the supplementary grant for education. However, education units still continued to play an important part in the formula for the distribution of the needs element as a whole, and the 1974 Act extended the scope for making increase orders to cover the situation where legislation is passed after the making of a main order and its coming into effect entails a substantial increase in the level of expenditure not originally taken into account.

The Act also included another important change relating to education expenditure. This was the institution from 1 April 1974 of a 90 per cent specific grant towards expenditure incurred by local authorities on mandatory awards to students and on teacher-training awards. In consequence, local authority expenditure on these services is now excluded from relevant expenditure for purposes of rate support grant.

NEGOTIATIONS ON RATE SUPPORT GRANT

The Department, together with other departments concerned with local government services, supports the Department of the Environment in the annual negotiations with the local authority associations that lead to a rate support grant settlement. The current practice is that these negotiations rest on expenditure forecasts for education, and for the other services, prepared centrally by working groups of officials from each department concerned and from the local authorities. When the forecasts for the different services have been completed, they are aggregated, and the government forms a view on whether the resulting level of local authority expenditure is acceptable in the light of economic and other relevant considerations. The government may find it necessary to impose some reduction on this aggregate, which may or may not be allocated amongst the forecasts for individual services.

Once the total of rate support grant has been determined, the government does not control the spending of individual local authorities on any of the relevant services, or the aggregate expenditure of all authorities on a particular service. But the expenditure forecasts clearly influence local authorities preparing their budgets for the years concerned; and the actual expenditure of local authorities, both in the aggregate and also in its distribution amongst the various services, has usually conformed quite closely to the forecasts.

DEPARTMENTAL ESTIMATES, PUBLIC EXPENDITURE SURVEYS AND PPB

Up to 1973–4 the annual supply estimates covering educational expenditure submitted by the Department comprised two votes. One was the universities and colleges vote, which comprised grants to universities under quinquennial settlements (including capital expenditure), and grants to certain other institutions of comparable standing. The other was the Department of Education and Science (DES) vote, which, apart from the administrative expenses of the Department itself, covered: grants and loans to voluntary bodies (mostly church bodies) towards the costs of colleges of education and voluntary schools provided by them; payments to direct grant schools; grants to miscellaneous further education establishments and bodies providing adult education; and awards to certain groups of students.

In consequence of a general revision of supply estimates undertaken by the Treasury in 1973, two new votes for DES expenditure were instituted in 1974–5: one comprising the main grants to educational research and other minor items, together with the running costs of the Department; the other covering grants to the research councils and other scientific bodies and activities, and grants for the arts, museums and libraries.

Here the point must be emphasised – as it is essential to an understanding of the Department's functions and its relations with LEAs, universities and other providing bodies – that the control of public expenditure on education on the basis of annual estimates submitted to the Treasury, which was the traditional method of control of government spending on education up to the end of the 1950s, is not the only mechanism by which control is now exercised by central government over public expenditure on education. Indeed it has ceased to be the most important.

To explain this, it may be helpful briefly to rehearse the history of developments in government control of public expenditure since the Report of the Plowden Committee[5] in 1961. This Committee advised that the weakness of the traditional system of decision making and control by central government was that it handled public expenditure in a piecemeal way, on an inadequate time scale and without relating it to the resources available. It recommended that machinery was needed for reviewing public expenditure as a whole, including expenditure by local government and nationalised industries as well as central government, over a period of years and in relation to prospective resources.

The government of the day accepted the main recommendations of the Plowden Report and instituted a system of public expenditure surveys on the lines it proposed. An official committee, the Public Expenditure Survey Committee (PESC), was established under Treasury chairmanship. The main annual task of this committee has been to prepare a report that offers a projection over five years of public expenditure programme by programme, covering both capital and current expenditure, whether incurred by central government, local authorities or nationalised industries. These forecasts, intended to represent the future cost of the policies existing at the time at which the survey is made, are prepared through discussion between the Treasury and individual departments. As the survey is concerned with the resource costs of different programmes, each year's set of forecasts is made at the prices ruling at the time (on a 'constant price' basis) and accordingly makes no allowance for future inflation. The price base for each survey is changed annually, to reflect changes in prices over the year since the last survey. The projections of expenditure are linked, for purposes of managing the economy, with annual forward assessments of economic prospects, generally extending over the same five-year period. These reports thus make it possible to explore the interaction between public sector demands and other major elements in the economy, and to relate the total pattern of demand to a forecast of resources likely to be available.[6]

These PESC reports, as they have come to be known, are prepared during the early months of each year and are then submitted to ministers, as a basis for their annual collective review of public expenditure. Since 1969 the outcome of each annual review by ministers has been published towards the end of the year in a public expenditure White Paper, which sets out the government's assessment of the acceptable levels of total public expenditure during the review period, and contains detailed figures and conventions for each individual expenditure programme. Each White Paper has made it clear that the figures printed, especially for later years, are open to subsequent modification as circumstances require, and a comparison between successive expenditure White Papers enables modifications of this kind to be traced.

The PESC surveys have come to provide the standard framework within which ministers take their regular annual decisions on the future level of public expenditure. These usually involve a number of specific decisions about items in particular programmes, which will be recorded in the end-year public expenditure White Papers. Circumstances may, however, require ministers to make fresh decisions on the general level of public expenditure outside the normal timetable provided by the review; and particular questions with resource implications may come before ministers at different times of the year for decision and cannot always wait for the public-expenditure review process. For this reason, and to provide for unforeseeable new expenditures, the projected totals of public expenditure include a contingency reserve over and above the aggregate of the sums provided for particular programmes.

By the end of the 1960s it had come to be recognised that the PESC surveys, although they represented an important advance for the purpose of providing forecasts of what would be likely to happen on stated assumptions, were defective in certain respects, especially when viewed as an instrument of longer term planning. As they were based on the assumed continuation of existing policies, they did not require departments to review and justify these policies, which thus had an in-built advantage over new proposals for additional expenditure. Nor were departments required to define their objectives in relation to the government's general strategy, and to indicate how far either their present or their prospective policies forwarded the achievement of these objectives. Further, no useful way was provided for measuring the claims on resources of one programme against those of another. And the surveys were in general limited to a period of not more than five years ahead, which for many planning purposes, particularly in the education sector, is insufficient.

From these and other criticisms the conviction developed that the PESC surveys needed to be supplemented by more sophisticated management tools if long-term forward planning of resource allocation was to be carried out more effectively. One of the most widely favoured of these during the 1960s was the approach known by a number of titles, of which the most common is Planning Programme Budgeting (PPB). This derived originally from wartime techniques of operational research, and was systematised and applied in the defence field by the federal administration in the USA, and in many other public enterprises there. In this country it was first adopted within government by the Ministry of Defence in the mid-1960s.

What this approach essentially involves is: a methodical analysis of objectives in a particular area of policy; an accurate measuring of both the inputs of resources provided to achieve these objectives and the outputs obtained; and cost and other relevant information arranged in a way that makes possible the presentation of costed options, with supporting information about the implications of each course.

As the system had been introduced in the United Kingdom in a defence context, there were doubts whether the approach could be applied to civil expenditure. To test whether this could be done the Department, in association with the Treasury, undertook in 1967 a study of the feasibility of developing a PPB system for educational expenditure, and an examination of some of the problems that would arise. The results were published in 1970.[7]

SOME PROBLEMS OF APPLYING PPB TO EDUCATION

In this study a number of problems in the application of a systematic resource-planning approach to educational expenditure were identified and discussed, particularly in relation to the measurement of output, a cardinal feature of the PPB approach. Experience has confirmed the reality of these problems, but some progress has been made in tackling them.

One obvious difficulty arises from the decentralised character of the education service, with its diffusion of responsibility and decision making to local authorities, governing bodies and others. In practice this problem is less formidable than it may appear at first sight. Although the Department's statutory powers in relation to long-term strategic planning are limited, it has, as earlier chapters have suggested, well-tried and generally accepted means for influencing national policies and priorities in education, and the scale and pattern of expenditure.

A second difficulty arises from the nature of the education service in an advanced community. The dynamics of a developed educational system themselves impose important limitations on the scope that exists at any given time for policy changes. Freedom of manoeuvre is restricted not only by statute and by public expectations but also by the consequences of earlier decisions, which take time to work their way through the system. For example, most of the decisions of central government that involve educational building take several years to implement.

Another problem arises from the peculiar difficulty in education of defining objectives in clear-cut terms. In virtually every field there are either activities or inputs that contribute to more than one objective, and that cannot be broken into costable elements contributing to just one objective. This difficulty is compounded by the existence of differing views about the aims of education, or at any rate about the relative emphasis to be given to generally accepted aims.

Then there is the difficulty that surrounds attempts to assess the outputs of an educational system in quantitative terms. These arise particularly in attempting to quantify the benefits to the individual. Many of these consist of intangibles such as self-fulfilment, enrichment of experience, quality of life; and the difficulties of anything like a Benthamite 'calculus of pleasure' are familiar to students of philosophy. Moreover, many of the benefits of education to the individual accrue after a long time lag, some over a whole lifetime.

The problems of quantifying the social benefits of education (the 'rate of return' and 'manpower' approaches) are scarcely less intractable. These, as the Plowden Report on Primary Education pointed out, particularly beset attempts to assess the benefits of primary education; but they also arise in attempts to put a value on those forms of secondary and postschool education that are not directly geared to a specialised vocation.

The existence of these problems is admitted by those who have been attempting to apply a PPB approach to education. What the feasibility study and subsequent experience have suggested, however, is that they do not preclude all progress. Thus it has become clear that a reordering of the Department's information systems so as to relate costs to objectives rather than to institutions (which was the traditional basis for forecasting expenditure, even within the PESC framework) itself has considerable value in helping to cost policy options and in other ways.

Secondly, it is possible to single out certain medium-term objectives ('intermediate outputs') that can provide useful yardsticks of educational advance, for example, the number of school places built, teacher–pupil ratios, and the number and proportion of pupils above compulsory age in school.

There are also well-recognised yardsticks of individual attainment. The most obvious is examination results. The majority of school leavers now take either General Certificate of Education (GCE) or Certificate of Secondary Education (CSE) examinations, and while there must be reservations about using examination results in isolation as a measure of 'output', it would be generally agreed that they provide one measure amongst others that cannot be ignored.

There are other measures that have been or are being developed. These include the periodic surveys that the Department has arranged for since 1948 into the reading ability of children in school.[8] A mathematical attainment survey is also planned. As regards the social benefits of education, new ground has been broken by recent studies of the effect of education on the earning power of individuals, although much work remains to be done in this field.

Even where quantitative data are not available, there is often other objective information, such as surveys by HM Inspectors, which are of value in arriving at choices. As Planning Paper No. 1 observed, 'the key to the objective assessment of performance is not necessarily quantification'. Many would argue that the ultimate value of the PPB approach lies less in the development of specific techniques of measurement than in its encouragement of a rational, systematic and analytic approach to resource problems, and in the provision of a common framework for their discussion.

PAR AND ITS IMPLICATIONS FOR THE DEPARTMENT: THE DEPARTMENTAL PLANNING ORGANISATION

The Administration that came into office in the summer of 1970 was pledged to effect further improvements in central government's machinery for policy formulation and decision making. The new arrangements were foreshadowed in a White Paper of 1970[9] which stated that, as a natural extension of the public-expenditure survey system, there would be regular reviews of departmental policies designed to provide ministers with an opportunity to identify and discuss alternative policy options, which could then be explored in greater depth before final decisions were taken on expenditure programmes. These would involve greater emphasis on the definition of objectives, and the formulation of programmes as far as possible in output terms, with ample scope for the examination of alternative programmes. There was to be 'a capability at the centre for assessment of policies and projects in relation to strategic objectives', in the form of a small multidisciplinary central policy-review staff (CPRS) in the Cabinet Office, working for ministers collectively under the supervision of the Prime Minister. This system became known as Programme Analysis and Review (PAR) and was brought into general operation early in 1971. Since then all the main spending departments, including the Department, have undertaken programme reviews for various areas of their activities in conjunction with the central departments, including the CPRS.

The PAR system was not intended to replace the annual public-expenditure reviews, and has not done so. Its object rather has been to secure that over the course of time the main expenditure programmes are more thoroughly examined, in relation to their own objectives and to the general objectives of government policy, than is possible within the PESC timetable, and to promote forward planning on a longer time scale. The expenditure consequences of decisions arising from the consideration of reviews by ministers are embodied in the appropriate PESC reports and public expenditure White Papers.

These developments have had important implications for the Department's own planning activities. A Planning Branch already existed within the Department; it had been set up in 1967. This drew together much of the statistical and other numerate work of the Department, and laid the foundations for some of the Department's forward planning, for example, the construction of a statistical model for higher education.[10]

It came to be recognised, however, that there were serious limitations on the effectiveness of a Planning Branch that acted alongside policy branches but separately from them. Accordingly, towards the end of 1970 the Department's planning activities were reorganised with the objective of integrating them with the existing structure for the consideration of policies and the administration of the Department's functions. A policy steering group was established under the chairmanship of the permanent secretary, with a membership which included the deputy secretaries, the under-secretaries charged with central responsibilities within the Department and the senior chief inspector. This has come to operate as the senior body charged with policy planning, establishing policy groups under the chairmanship of deputy secretaries to cover specified fields, drawing their membership from the heads of policy branches within the Department and appropriate senior HM Inspectors. From its inception this planning structure was serviced by a planning unit headed by an under-secretary. More recently there have been important modifications in the structure of the Department's planning organisation.

It so happened that this organisation, originally conceived in relation to the Department's own needs for a more effective planning capacity, came into existence at about the same time that the government introduced the PAR system, and it has proved a suitable instrument for discharging the Department's contribution to the working of that system.

THE EDUCATION PROGRAMME BUDGET

An important innovation in line with this new thinking about planning was an attempt to construct a 'programme budget' for education expenditure on the lines recommended in the feasibility study referred to above. This task was undertaken primarily by the group of professional economists who were originally members of the Department's Planning Branch and who, subsequently, became part of Finance Branch. (The task is now the responsibility of the Financial Services Division.)

An important function of an educational programme budget is to show the extent to which educational expenditure is susceptible to policy choice. It is a characteristic of educational expenditure that the bulk of it is to all intents and purposes predetermined by basic demographic factors: existing numbers, expected population growth, and so forth. At any given point in time the residue is small and leaves little room for manoeuvre. However, the further ahead that this distinction between basic expenditure and the remainder is projected within the programme budget, the larger the area of choice is seen to be within the uncommitted element, which covers such factors as increased participation in education by age groups outside the period of compulsory attendance, and improvements in standards of staffing, buildings and non-teaching expenditure. Outside this area the scope for improvements, or for reductions in overall expenditure, depends on whether ways can be found, by cost-effectiveness studies or other means, of carrying out more economically the activities covered by the basic expenditure block.

Improvements in the system have been made since its introduction. Of particular importance has been the extension of the expenditure projections to ten years ahead instead of five. This carries the projections even further ahead than is immediately apparent. Even on the previous time scale it was necessary to consider place requirements eight or nine years ahead in order to project building starts for five years. This extension is highly desirable in view of the technology and management needs of the service. Improvements are also constantly being made in information systems and cost analysis, thus making possible experimental comparisons of past forecasts with actual out-turn. Work is going on all the time in attempts to clarify both 'intermediate objectives' and longer term objectives in terms of which the benefits of educational provision at various levels can be assessed.

The main value of the programme budget so far has been to generate more sophisticated figures, especially on unit costs, for use in the Department's longer term planning, and to stimulate new ways of looking at educational expenditure. Examples are the identification of total expenditure on the 16–19 age group, whether provided in the schools or further education sectors, and a clearer appraisal of demographic factors, of changes of standards, and of new policy developments and their relative influence in determining future expenditure levels.

A major product of the Department's enhanced planning capacity

and the more sophisticated thinking about the educational programme budget was the education White Paper of December 1972.[1]
Covering as it did some three-quarters of total public expenditure on
education, this was a far more comprehensive survey than had ever
been previously attempted of the future resource needs of the
service; and its breadth of coverage was matched by the length of its
time scale, which extended up to 1981. Perhaps even more important,
it represented a deliberate attempt to tilt the balance in the disposition
of resources between different sectors, but to do so in a way that
allowed all the sectors reviewed to continue expanding, as well as
introducing new developments, notably in the education of the under-
fives. This attempt to view the future of the different sectors of
education in relation both to each other and to a judgement of an
acceptable overall rate of development, rather than to consider each
one piecemeal, has perhaps been the most distinctive stamp of the
contribution made by the Department's planning organisation.

SOME IMPLICATIONS OF RECENT INNOVATIONS
FOR THE DEPARTMENT'S WORK

There has thus in recent years been a major development of the
Department's forward-planning capacity, through a combination of
organisational changes and new methods of handling and presenting
relevant statistical and financial data. These changes reflect the
growing recognition that an essential function of the Department,
over and above the performance of specific practical and administrative duties deriving from the education Acts, is that of resource
planning for the education service as a whole: that is, the formulation of objectives, the framing of national policies best calculated
to meet these objectives, the undertaking of long term costings of
policies in a way that enables ministers to choose their priorities, and
the task of effectively presenting the consequential resource needs
within central government.

But the very extent and speed of developments in the system of
central government management of the public sector has brought
in its train certain 'problems of success', in education as in other
fields. The increasing comprehensiveness and sophistication of the
techniques employed, and the extension of the time scale over which
they operate, have given rise to problems in the financial relations
between central government and local authorities, in education as in
other sectors.

Thus questions have been asked, particularly in regard to the
education section, as to whether central government's longer term
forecasts are consistent with longer-term rate support grant pro-

jections, and whether they provide adequately for the implementation within local government of policies announced by ministers. There are fears that local authorities might find themselves committed to policies for which adequate resources were in the event not provided. More generally, there have been fears that the new developments may result in a strengthening of central government control at a time when the declared aim of governments is the revitalisation of local democracy.

Undoubtedly there is a dilemma here, of which both the Department and central government as a whole are well aware. As the Green Paper of July 1971, *The Future Shape of Local Government Finance*, observed: 'the Government wish to give greater freedom to local authorities, but they cannot evade their own responsibility for management of the national economy, nor can they evade their duty to ensure minimum standards for essential services throughout the country. The problem for central government is how to resolve this dilemma within these constraints.'[12]

A good deal has already been done towards resolving this problem. As regards current expenditure, there is a close linkage between rate support grant settlements and public expenditure White Papers. This connection operates reciprocally. Central government enters negotiations for a given settlement against the background of expenditure projections accepted by ministers and published in the latest public expenditure White Paper for the different programmes in which local authorities are concerned. The forecasts of relevant expenditure accepted by the government during the course of rate support grant negotiations are themselves incorporated into the subsequent public-expenditure White Paper figures and in turn form a new starting point for the next round of negotiations.

The local authorities attach great importance to their role in the procedures for negotiating rate support grant settlements, and accept that these have been much improved in recent years, representing a significant movement towards better co-operation and a freer exchange of information between central and local government. In particular they have welcomed the arrangements for the consideration of rate support grant forecasts under which, although a settlement is made for only one year ahead, provisional forecasts are made for two further years, thus looking as far ahead as does the current public-expenditure White Paper.

As to capital expenditure, which is not covered by rate support grant negotiations, central government has undertaken, in response to local government approaches, to provide opportunities for informative discussions of the local authority components of White Paper projections for each of the services concerned. Growing interest has developed in assessing the prospective recurrent-expenditure implications of capital programmes. And the development of the longer-range forecasting capacities of central government are to some extent being paralleled by developments by individual local authorities in the direction of systematic forward planning, often based on some form of programme budgeting.

On the more general issue it is, as the previous chapter emphasised, a traditional feature of the partnership between the central department and the local authorities that operate the education service that there is extensive consultation, usually from the early stages in the inception of major new policies; and it is increasingly common for the announcement by central government of new directions in the development of the education service to be coupled with indications of the scale and pace of developments and of their longer-term resource implications.

NOTES AND REFERENCES

1 The Local Government Act 1948 established the Exchequer equalisation grant in aid of the total expenditure that would otherwise have had to be met from the rates, including education expenditure not met by Ministry grants. The principle embodied in this device has been applied, although in differing ways, in all subsequent local government Acts. One effect is that the proportion of authorities' expenditure that is grant aided from the centre varies from one area to another.

2 Section 3 of the Local Government Act 1958. Subsequent local government Acts contain similar provision. This sanction has in practice never been used in relation to an authority's educational expenditure.

3 This point was emphasised in the White Paper *Local Government Finance in England and Wales*, Cmnd 2929 (London, HMSO, February 1966). A number of ideas have been mooted at that time and since for reform of the rating system, or for replacing rates by some form of local tax. See in particular the Layfield Report (*Local Government Finance*, Cmnd 6453, London, HMSO, 1976).

4 In 1977–8, as a result of government measures to reduce public expenditure, it fell to 61 per cent.

5 *Report of the Committee on the Control of Public Expenditure* (the Plowden Report), Cmnd 1432 (London, HMSO, July 1961).

6 For fuller accounts of the origins and development of PESC see Sir Richard Clarke, *New Trends in Government*, Civil Service College Studies (London, HMSO, 1971); also Sir Samuel Goldman, KCB, *Public Expenditure Management and Control*, Civil Service College Studies (London, HMSO, 1973).

7 DES, *Output Budgeting for the Department of Education and Science: Report of a Feasibility Study*, Education Planning Paper No. 1 (London, HMSO, 1970).

8 See *Standards of Reading 1948–1956*, Ministry of Education Pamphlet No. 32 (London, HMSO, 1957); *Progress in Reading*, Ministry of Education Pamphlet No. 50 (London, HMSO, 1966); K. B. Smart and B. K. Wells, *The Trend of Reading Standards* (London, NFER, 1972).

9 White Paper, *The Reorganisation of Central Government*, Cmnd 4506 (London, HMSO, 1970), especially paras 16 and 46.
10 This was published (in a revised form) in DES, *Student Numbers in Higher Education in England and Wales*, Education Planning Paper No. 2 (London, HMSO, 1970).
11 White Paper, *Education: A Framework for Expansion*, Cmnd 5174 (London, HMSO, 1972). The policies proposed in this White Paper are discussed in more detail in subsequent chapters.
12 Green Paper, *The Future Shape of Local Government Finance*, Cmnd 4741 (London, HMSO, 1971), para. 40.

PART TWO

The Department's Main Responsibilities Under the Education Acts

CHAPTER 6

The Department and the Schools

THE GENERAL FRAMEWORK

The natural starting point for a survey of the Department's work is to see what it does in relation to the schools. The schools are the foundation on which all later stages of education are built; and while there has been a massive expansion of postschool education in the last three decades, the schools still account for more than half of total public expenditure on education.

Starting at 5 and continuing to 16, compulsory schooling begins sooner in England than in most advanced countries, and lasts longer. A large and growing proportion of children continues in full-time education beyond 16, many of them in schools; and a beginning has been made with a nationwide development of preschool education for 3 and 4-year-olds, although this will not be compulsory.

In the decentralised system that exists in this country the central department does not itself build or run schools, and has at no time done so. In the public sector it is the local education authorities (LEAs) and the various church and other voluntary bodies that provide schools. It follows that the school system is not the tidy creation of central authority working to a logically conceived national plan. It is the product of the country's educational history.

In the public sector the school system is the result of the fusion, over more than a century, of three main elements. First, there are the schools provided by voluntary bodies, mainly the churches, and now called 'voluntary' schools. Up to 1870 these were the only schools assisted from public funds. They still account for about a third of the schools in the public sector and about a quarter of the pupils.

The second element consists of the schools provided from 1870 onwards by secular authorities – the school boards until their demise at the beginning of this century, and thereafter the LEAs. These are now called 'county' schools. Originally intended simply to 'fill the gaps' in the provision made by the churches, these now account for over three-quarters of all pupils within the maintained sector.

The third element – in point of time the oldest – consists of the 'grammar' schools, many of them ancient endowments, which were brought within the public sector as a result of the Education Act 1902 to provide the nucleus of a national system of secondary education, although from that time the newly created LEAs were encouraged to augment their number by creating county grammar schools.

One other category of school within the public sector needs mention here, namely, the 'direct-grant grammar' schools, since it has been of special concern to the Department. When the endowed grammar schools were brought within the public sector after 1902 they could obtain assistance both from LEAs and from the Board of Education. After the First World War it was decided that they could not continue to be aided from both sources and must choose one or the other. Rather fewer than 200 chose to be grant-aided by the Board, and these came to be known as direct-grant grammar schools. These were run by their own governing bodies, established in accordance with their trust deeds and with statutory regulations. The governors were required to offer a substantial number of free places, either directly or through LEAs, to pupils educated for two years in maintained primary schools; and there were also pupils whose parents paid fees, subject to an income scale.

The direct grant list was terminated in 1975, and most of the direct-grant grammar schools were either assimilated into the maintained school system or became independent.

Out of these diverse elements central government has sought by successive enactments to create a coherent and developing school system. The Forster Act 1870, by creating secular school boards to supplement the work of the churches, laid the foundations of a universal system of compulsory, and eventually free, elementary education. The Balfour Act 1902, by providing for the incorporation of the endowed grammar schools in the public system, created a basis and a framework for expansion for public secondary education. The Fisher Act 1918 for the first time laid on the major authorities a duty to provide education other than elementary, including secondary education, and required them to submit 'schemes' showing how they proposed to make such provision.

But the greatest advance towards a coherent school system, with inbuilt mechanisms for development, was achieved by the Butler Act 1944. This Act, which still largely determines the shape of the school system in the public sector today, laid down that the statutory system of public education was to be provided in three progressive stages, to be known as primary, secondary and further education. Secondary education, like primary, was to be free for all. The period of compulsory schooling was extended to 15 forthwith and was to be extended to 16 when circumstances allowed. Authorities were also to 'have regard' to the need for nursery provision for children below compulsory school age.

The Act laid on LEAs the duty to provide, or secure the provision of, sufficient schools to meet the needs of their areas. It also concentrated responsibility for primary and secondary education, as well as further education, in the hands of the same authorities: namely, the county and county borough councils (and after 1974 the county and metropolitan district councils) together with the Inner London Education Authority (ILEA) and the Outer London boroughs. This, and the new settlement of the relations between the LEAs and the church and other voluntary providers brought about by the Act, afforded a more coherent framework within which the school system could develop.

The Act further gave the Minister of Education powers to see that the LEAs carried out their responsibilities, and in effect to initiate national policies both in the schools and in other sectors. Thus, while much of the initiative in developing the school system has all along rested, and still rests, with the LEAs, the central department has to an increasing extent been in a position to shape developments; and the massive expansion that has taken place since 1944 has thus tended to show the marks of a coherent national pattern.

The account given so far has covered the schools in the public sector, which contain over 93 per cent of children of compulsory school age. Outside the public sector there are over 2,000 schools run by independent governing bodies or proprietors with no direct assistance from public funds. These range from the well-known 'public' schools such as Winchester, Eton and Harrow to small, privately owned schools. Although they are still a significant element in the educational life of the country, particularly in respect of boarding education for which they provide about three-quarters of the facilities, independent schools account for a relatively small proportion of the total school population.

With the coming into effect of Part III of the Education Act 1944, all schools of this type are subject to inspection and supervision by the Department. (See p. 114 following.)

Categories of school
For historical reasons the nomenclature of schools is apt to be

confusing. It may be of help to say something about the main categories into which the 33,000 or so schools in England and Wales fall.

Let us start with the 'maintained' schools, that is, those whose costs of maintenance are borne by LEAs. First there is a classification by age. Within the category of 'primary' schools there are 'nursery' schools for children under compulsory school age – although many children of this age are to be found in nursery classes attached to primary schools. Primary schools for children between 5 and 11 may be either separate 'infants' schools for children from 5 to 7 and 'junior' schools for those from 7 to 11, or they may be combined 'infant-and-junior' schools.

Schools for children from about 11 upwards are 'secondary' schools. But a number of areas in recent years have established 'middle' schools for children in the age range 9 or 10 to 12 or 13. (In these areas the schools attended by children before they enter middle school are known as 'first' schools.) Primary and middle schools in the maintained sector are almost invariably mixed sex; secondary schools may be mixed or single sex.

Within the category of secondary schools there are three broad types. First, in areas where selection at 11+ still operates, there are 'secondary grammar' schools (and in some areas 'technical' schools), which are 'selective'; that is, they take a proportion of the school population of the area that is selected as being suitable for this type of education. Secondly, there are 'secondary modern' schools, which are 'non-selective', taking all the pupils not selected for grammar (or technical) places. Thirdly, there are 'comprehensive' schools, which take all children of secondary age in the area, or at any rate take children of all or most ability ranges. (The term 'high' school is found with varying meanings in different areas.)

In some areas there are 'sixth-form' or 'junior colleges' (schools despite their name), which take only children staying on beyond 16 for a sixth-form course. In a few areas all children over 16 are provided for in colleges of further education.

There are maintained 'special' schools for children suffering from physical or mental handicap. These may accommodate children of both primary and secondary age, and a substantial proportion of them are boarding schools. Usually they provide for children suffering from a particular handicap, for example, deafness or partial sight or maladjustment. There are also 'hospital special' schools; and since the Education (Handicapped Children) Act 1970 came into effect in 1971, LEAs have become responsible for the education of mentally handicapped children who were previously regarded as unsuitable for education at school and were often cared for in junior training centres run by local authorities.

Within the maintained sector there is also a differentiation which reflects the continued existence of the dual system. There are 'county' schools, which are provided as well as maintained by LEAs, and 'voluntary' schools, which are provided by church and other voluntary bodies but maintained by the LEA. For the most part the providers are Church of England or Roman Catholic bodies, although there are a few Methodist and Jewish schools and schools provided by bodies with no religious affiliations.

As a result of the recasting of the dual system effected by the 1944 Act, voluntary schools may be of three kinds. Where the providing body has agreed (with the help of grant from the Department) to bear certain financial costs in relation to the premises, they are called 'aided' schools. Where the providing body has opted to hand over all financial responsibility to the LEA, they are 'controlled' schools. Almost all the voluntary schools in the controlled category are Church of England schools; the Roman Catholics were generally unwilling to accept this type of arrangement. There is also a third, relatively small, category of 'special agreement' schools, which are similar to aided schools except that the financial assistance towards the provision of premises originally came from the LEA.

Outside the public sector there are the independent schools, which again are of two kinds. Rather more than half, including most of the better-known 'public' schools, have been 'recognised as efficient' under the Department's Rules 16. The remainder, which are not so recognised, are 'registered' (or 'provisionally registered') schools. Independent schools are not always differentiated between the primary and secondary age ranges. A number, known as 'preparatory' schools, take pupils between 8 and 13. Most 'public' schools admit only pupils aged 13 and over. There are also schools for handicapped children in the independent sector.

The Department's functions in relation to the schools
In relation to the schools in the maintained sector and their maintaining authorities, the Department exercises what is perhaps best described as a general influence which is effected through a variety of controls and devices: some specific, some general, some having a statutory basis, others administrative.

The statutory controls derive mainly from the 1944 Act and subsequent education Acts, and regulations made under them. The following are some of the more important.

A provision that was of importance in the minds of the authors of the 1944 Act was one (Section 11) requiring LEAs to submit to the Minister 'development plans' for schools in their areas, showing how they planned to discharge their obligation to secure the provision of sufficient schools, and other related matters. In the decade after 1944 this provision enabled the Department to exert a good deal of influence on the pattern of new development, particularly in the secondary sector.

More recently the development plan procedure has fallen into abeyance. The provision that has come to assume primary importance as the mechanism enabling the Department to influence changes in school provision is that for the establishment, closure or change in the character of county and voluntary schools (Section 13).[1] Any LEA that wants to close a school or enlarge it or significantly change its character, or to establish a new one, must submit a proposal to the Minister. (Managers and governors of voluntary schools have similar responsibilities.) After a statutory period of two months during which objections may be made, the Secretary of State decides, taking into account any objections he receives, whether or not to approve the proposal. If the proposal is for the establishment of a new school or involves a changed use of premises, and the Secretary of State approves it, the promoters must also submit detailed plans for the premises. This procedure gives the Secretary of State a watching brief for the interests of those affected by the proposal: the managers or governors of any voluntary school affected, any local authority concerned, or local government electors for the area. In this way the wishes of parents are taken into account.

Another provision that has been of key importance in the postwar period is one (Section 10) that requires the Secretary of State to make regulations prescribing standards for the premises of maintained schools. The regulations made under this provision, taken in conjunction with the Department's control of educational building and costs, have given the Department a continuing influence on school building in the maintained sector since 1944. (See p. 73 and following.)

There are important provisions concerning the management or government of schools (Sections 17ff.). It is a traditional feature of the English educational system that schools have bodies of managers (in the case of primary schools) or governors (in the case of secondary schools), consisting of people of standing in the local community with experience of education, who in consultation with the LEA and head teacher have responsibility for the conduct of the school. The 1944 Act provides that every school in the maintained sector, county as well as voluntary, shall have its body of managers or governors, constituted in accordance with properly framed instruments of management or articles of government, and that the managers or governors shall operate under rules of management or articles of government.

These provisions involve the Department in a number of ways. Thus the arrangements for the government of all types of voluntary school require the Secretary of State's approval. He also has a general duty to see that bodies of managers or governors are properly constituted, and that schools are conducted in accordance with their approved rules or instruments. This may on occasion involve the Department in making searching inquiries into the conduct of an individual school; and although occasions of this kind are rare, the possibility of such an inquiry acts as a safeguard to ensure that schools are run according to the approved rules.

In fulfilling their duties to provide sufficient schools for the needs of their areas, LEAs are required to have regard to the needs of handicapped pupils. They must make arrangements for ascertaining which children from 2 years of age in their areas are in need of special education, so that arrangements for their education in an appropriate school can be made. The Secretary of State is required to formulate regulations defining the various categories of handicap and making provision for the methods of education suitable for each category, and may make regulations specifying the conditions that special schools for handicapped children must satisfy. Where children have handicaps that are not serious, or where they have serious handicaps but it is impracticable for them to attend a special school, they may be catered for in ordinary schools in either ordinary or special classes.

The Act contains provisions that give the Secretary of State a specific concern with various ancillary services that LEAs provide for the schools that they maintain. These cover such matters as the transport of children to and from school, school meals and milk, and (until recently) school health.

The effect of the provisions on school transport (Section 55 together with Section 39(5)) is that LEAs have a duty to provide free transport to the nearest suitable school for all children of compulsory school age whose journey to school is greater than 'walking distance', defined in the Act as two miles for a child who has not attained the age of 8 and three miles for other children. They may also provide, or contribute towards, the cost of transporting pupils to schools outside the catchment areas of their local school for which parents express a preference on denominational or other grounds, or for shorter distances to take proper account of other factors, such as safety. The Secretary of State is given power under these provisions to issue directions to authorities in certain circumstances. (This power is in practice rarely used.)

There are important provisions on school meals and milk (Section 49). The Act puts on LEAs a general duty to provide 'milk, meals and other refreshment' for pupils at maintained schools in accordance with regulations made by the Secretary of State. The first regulations, made in 1945, required every LEA to establish a school meals service and to see that the necessary accommodation was provided in its schools. The current regulations impose on authorities a duty to provide for every pupil in a maintained school on every school day a midday dinner suitable in all respects as the pupil's main meal of the day, and give authorities powers to make similar provision on days when the schools do not meet. Authorities also have power to provide on schools days 'such other meals and refreshment' as they consider appropriate. The regulations prescribe the charge to be made for school dinners and the arrangements for remitting the charge in cases of hardship to help low income families. Authorities also have a duty to provide free milk for certain categories of pupils. Over the last three decades the provision of meals and milk has developed into a large scale operation. In 1975 nearly 6 million dinners were being served daily (780,000 free of charge), and about 2 million pupils were receiving free milk daily.

Up to 1974 LEAs had a duty to provide for periodical medical and dental inspections of the children in their schools, and to secure the provision of free treatment for those found to be in need of it. This they might either arrange through the national health service or provide themselves. These provisions formed the basis of a major expansion of the school health services, under the guidance of the Department's medical and dental staff, between 1947 and 1974.

Under the National Health Service Act 1973 these responsibilities were transferred to the national health service. That Act gave the Secretary of State for Social Services a duty to provide for the medical and dental inspection and treatment of pupils in maintained schools (and of certain other specified categories of pupil), and thus in effect incorporated the school health services as part of an integrated child-health service within the national health service. LEAs continue to have a duty to encourage and assist pupils to take advantage of the school health services and to make available appropriate accommodation. In certain circumstances they may provide supplementary services under their general powers under the Local Government Act 1972.

Schools regulations

Schools regulations, now made under local government Acts, give the Secretary of State power to supervise standards and conditions in a wide range of practical matters relating to maintained schools, such as school years, terms and holiday periods, hours of attendance and entry of pupils for external examinations. They also contain important provisions about the qualifications of teachers, arrangements for their appointment, and so forth.

The Secretary of State's general powers in relation to schools

In practice, if not in law, the Secretary of State's concern with the maintained school system extends beyond matters for which he is given specific statutory powers. In the maintained school system as in other sectors of the local-authority-operated service, he has the responsibility for framing national policies, for making available resources both financial and other, and for ensuring the supply of teachers, to enable the LEAs to implement them.

The Department also has an important means of keeping in touch with the work of the schools through the operations of HM Inspectorate. This is more fully discussed elsewhere.

The law on school attendance and choice of school

It is the duty of parents of children of compulsory school age to see that their children attend school (or receive other suitable education) and do so regularly (Education Act 1944, Section 36). The responsibility for seeing that parents comply with their duty rests with LEAs, not with the Department. The administration of the law of school attendance has always been a local matter since compulsory attendance was first introduced in 1876.[2]

The LEAs are also responsible for the allocation of school places in their area, but there are certain circumstances in which the Secretary of State may become involved. An important, if somewhat general, section of the Act (Section 76) says that in the exercise and performance of their powers and duties the Minister (or Secretary of State) and LEAs shall have regard to the general principle that, so far as is compatible with the provision of efficient instruction and training and the avoidance of unreasonable expenditure, pupils are to be educated in accordance with the wishes of their parents.

This section does not confer a specific right on parents. It merely lays down a general principle to which LEAs and the Secretary of State shall have regard (amongst others). Moreover, it sets specific limits to the extent to which this principle shall be applied; LEAs' arrangements must be compatible with the provision of efficient instruction and training, and must avoid unreasonable expenditure. In practice the range of provision made by LEAs, and thus the choice available to parents, is strictly limited.

SCHOOL BUILDING SINCE THE WAR[3]

By any standards the achievements in the field of educational building in England and Wales since the war have been remarkable, in both scale and quality, standing comparison with those of any other advanced country in this period. Between 1945 and 1973 over 6 million new school places have been provided in the public sector. Postwar school buildings in England and Wales have been widely acclaimed as setting new international standards in design and cost-effectiveness.

It must again be emphasised that because of the decentralised nature of the education service it is the LEAs and other educational bodies, not the Department, that build schools and colleges. But throughout the postwar period the Department has been closely involved.

This was a period in which there was a need for new educational building on an unprecedented scale. In the immediate aftermath of war there was an urgent job to be done in making good wartime damage and deterioration. Over 5,000 schools, or over a sixth of the country's stock of schools, had been destroyed or seriously damaged. The backlog of seven years in which there was virtually no school building had to be made good.

The 1944 Act itself contained new policies which involved extensive building: secondary education had to be provided in separate premises, which meant converting or taking out of use nearly 9,000 all-age schools. The school leaving age was to be raised immediately to 15 and eventually to 16. The implementation of the policy of free secondary education for all meant a large increase in the numbers staying on voluntarily after the statutory leaving age. Eventually (although this did not come till later) there would be need for substantial building to provide for the expansion of nursery education that the Act envisaged.

Places had to be provided for the large increase in school population as the birth groups of the 'bulge' years 1944–8 reached school age and moved through the primary schools into secondary schools, and thereafter for the increase resulting from the continuing and unexpectedly high level of births in the 1950s and early 1960s. The school age population in England and Wales increased between 1947 and 1977 by over 4·4 million.

On top of this, places were required to meet the needs of families moving as a result of the large population movements in this period consequent on industrial change, slum clearance and new house building. Between 1945 and 1970 some 6 million new houses were built privately or by local authorities and some 4 million children moved with their families into new housing.

Sooner or later, too, a start had to be made with systematic replacement or remodelling of obsolescent schools. As late as 1962, by which time much new building had already taken place, it was estimated that over half of all maintained schools in the country were housed in premises mainly dating from before 1903. It was not only new schools that were needed. As the larger age groups moved up into further and higher education, and as the provision of secondary education for all became effective, there was need for a massive increase in the number of places in technical colleges and universities; and the continuing shortage of teachers called for a large programme of building for colleges of education.

All this had to be achieved against a background of continuing shortages of resources, not only of money but also of materials and manpower – of bricks and cement, steel and timber, professional and skilled men. In the immediate postwar period these shortages were acute. But long after the immediate postwar crisis was over, limitations of capital investment resources continued to be one of the main constraints on educational advance.

The Department's concern with educational building
From the early years of the century the central department had exercised some control over educational building by local and voluntary bodies. The Board had a set of 'Rules to be observed in the Planning and Fitting up of Public Elementary Schools', which in 1905 were converted into statutory regulations, subsequently also applied to secondary schools. At this time, and indeed right up to the Second World War, central control was essentially regulatory. The Board had a 'blacklist' of defective school premises and did what it could to get schools on the list closed, replaced or improved.

Another device for the regulation of development by the centre, which first made its appearance in the interwar period, was the building programme. From 1925 onwards authorities were encouraged by the Board to think of their school-building needs in terms of a 'well-considered plan of orderly advance', covering at least three years ahead.[4]

The circumstances of the immediate postwar period called for greater central control, to ensure that national educational policies were carried out within the severely limited financial and material resources available, but also for greater co-operation between the centre and the local providers of schools. A simple administrative framework was needed which would concentrate the LEAs' resources on the most urgent jobs and then leave them free to get schools built with the minimum of control from London. The framework devised at that time by the Ministry consisted of three elements: building regulations, cost limits and annual building programmes.

Building regulations

As earlier explained, the Education Act 1944 required the Minister to make regulations prescribing standards for the premises of all types of school maintained by LEAs.

The first 'Standards for School Premises Regulations' came into operation in April 1945. Their importance at that time was that they gave LEAs a clear idea of the standards that would be accepted by the Ministry in considering authorities' development plans. Taken in conjunction with the Ministry's cost limits they ensured, and continue to ensure, a reasonable degree of uniformity in school building throughout the country, while allowing flexibility.

These are necessarily complex and technical regulations, laying down in some detail, for various types of school, the minimum standards of essential accommodation, physical performance and amenities. They are intended to safeguard standards and not to restrict them. They are revised from time to time in the light of experience, recent research and new needs; and on the whole, the tendency on each revision has been towards greater flexibility.

Cost limits

Before 1944 there was no general control by the centre on school and other building costs, each proposal being considered on its merits. As prices were then relatively stable this system – or lack of it – sufficed. But in the period of rising costs that followed the war, further measures were needed to ensure that the best use was made of scarce resources. The Ministry therefore in 1950 started fixing 'cost limits' for various types of school and other educational buildings. LEAs and other bodies erecting educational buildings had to show, as a condition for the approval of their plans, that each individual project could be built within the cost limits fixed for that type of building, the cost allowed for any given project being the cost per place multiplied by the number of 'cost places' to be provided.

The cost limits for any given period were determined in the light of research going on all the time in the Ministry's Architects and Buildings Branch into building costs and techniques, comparison of the costs of different kinds of building, and collation of the experience of LEAs. The aim was to enable designers of average ability to produce acceptable buildings, while leaving some margin for skilled designers to achieve something more than the minimum standard required. The system also gave authorities considerable freedom to balance the area per place against the cost per unit area – in other words, to choose between quantity and quality.

Cost limits were kept under continuous review and adjusted as necessary, such changes coming into the same category as 'pay and prices' adjustments in the forecasting by LEAs of their educational expenditure.

This system served three purposes. First, it acted as an inducement to economic building. For example, between 1949 and 1952 the average cost per place of both primary and secondary school building was actually reduced in real terms by almost half despite rising building costs, and was maintained at almost the same level for most of the next two decades notwithstanding a further rise in costs and the increasingly sophisticated demands of school organisation and curriculum. This was achieved partly by a more efficient use of space, partly by the development of cost-planning techniques and partly by research into the components of school-building costs. Secondly, cost limits became a major element in the system of programming of educational building (described later). Thirdly, cost limits have provided a convenient means of arriving at costings of the building element in national education policies – a matter of growing importance in view of the developing techniques of decision-making by central government.

The Department's aim in successive revisions of building regulations and cost limits has been to secure the best possible return on public investment in educational building. This has been broadly successful in that systematic development work over the years has produced radical improvements in design, and as a result the schools and other educational buildings of today are undoubtedly better suited to changing needs than those of forty years ago. At the same time a far higher level of building has been achieved than would have been possible without such a system.

Educational building programmes

The third control introduced, or rather developed, in this period was an administrative one: the educational building programme. Up to 1969 this control was operated on an annual basis. Having agreed with the Treasury the global amount of 'public investment' resources that could be permitted in a given year for each sector (schools, further education and teacher training, special schools etc.) and having settled the policies and priorities that were to govern the resources to be made available, the Department invited all LEAs to submit bids in conformity with these policies for projects on which they would like work to start during the year in question, supported by detailed justification in terms of expected growth of school population, new housing, and so forth, and by a costing for each project. The weaker claims were then weeded out during discussions between authorities and the Department before a final programme was submitted to ministers for approval. The approved programme was announced in the form of a list of projects that each authority or school governing body was authorised to proceed with in the relevant starts year, at an agreed cost. The amounts agreed were not grants, and no financial transactions between the Department and the authorities were involved; each authority financed the work out of its own resources, whether from revenue or, more usually, by loan.[5]

In 1969, in order to maintain the momentum of the greatly enlarged building programmes by then required, and to secure more effective control over the whole period of gestation of major projects, the Department introduced a three-year rolling programme.[6] Under this there were three lists running concurrently but relating to three successive years: a 'preliminary list' covering the starts year next but two; a 'design list' of projects on which sufficient preparations had been completed to make it reasonably certain that they could be started in the year next but one; and a 'starts list' of projects ready to proceed to tender for construction. All three lists comprised named projects.

These procedures applied only to 'major' building projects. For 'minor' works – that is, projects costing not more than a given limit, lately £50,000 – a separate programme was operated under a simplified procedure. The total sum allocated for such works was shared amongst authorities by the Department; each authority could then use its allocation without further clearance except in respect of building regulations. (Allocations for minor works projects at voluntary-aided and special agreement schools were separately administered by the Department.)

While building programme arrangements on the whole proved acceptable to the LEAs, particularly in the early postwar years when there was an acute scarcity of resources, there was by the end of the 1960s a growing feeling that the control that they gave to ministers not only to determine broad lines of policy but also to select individual projects was too detailed. Successive governments have recognised the desirability of more flexible programming arrangements.

In the early 1970s the Department started informal discussions with the local authority associations to examine the feasibility of a system of block allocations for school and other educational building, which would permit each authority to decide on individual projects within a total allocation fixed on the basis of agreed objective criteria. A pilot scheme on these lines for part of the building programme was inaugurated but, for reasons explained in what follows, was overtaken by events.

In 1973 the building sector of the construction industry became so overloaded and prices were rising so fast that tenders could often not be obtained, and those that could were at unprecedentedly high prices. The government therefore decided to rephase the programme of public building to ease the pressure on the industry, and this led the Department temporarily to suspend final approvals for building projects.[7]

At the end of 1974 a revised system of building controls was introduced, to come into effect from 1975–6 onwards.[8] The three-stage planning cycle for major projects described earlier in this section was restored, and the system of formal cost limits for individual projects was replaced by one of nationally determined cash allocations, or more precisely, authorisations to each authority within which the total value of work started in each sector must be contained. There were to be no separate allocations for minor works (except in Wales), authorities being broadly left free to decide how much of their lump sum authorisations to devote to minor works.

Development

The Department's building controls rest on a basis of intelligence and development work, and this also enables the Department's Architects and Building Branch to provide services to LEAs and thus to establish a constructive relationship with them.

There are two main ways in which the Department tries to ensure that its standards and cost limits are reasonable and economic. First, design and construction information for every major building project is collected, together with all available information about the existing stock of buildings.

Secondly, projects and investigations are undertaken by the Department's development groups. These are interdisciplinary teams set up within the Department's Architects and Building Branch soon after its formation in 1948. They include architects, quantity surveyors and others with professional qualifications, as well as HM Inspectors and administrators. Their functions are to pioneer new forms of design to meet new educational requirements, to work with manufacturers in developing new building components and techniques and to apply the results of research into building materials and techniques of cost control.

The groups have undertaken more than twenty projects acting as architects for LEAs. These may be described as prototype projects. The results are disseminated in various ways. The buildings themselves are extensively visited as showpieces. The experiences gained from them may influence subsequent revisions of the building regulations. The detailed findings are published in the Department's Building Bulletins, and shorter summaries are given in the Design

Note series.[9] These have served to create over a period of years a corpus of common ideas and information that is a distinctive feature of educational building in this country and helps to ensure constructive debate on aims and methods.

Industrialised systems and the local authorities consortia

More recently the most important technical innovation in which the Department's Architects and Building Branch has been involved is the development of industrialised systems of school building. Development projects by the groups in conjunction with the Hertfordshire Authority in the early postwar years, and later with the Nottinghamshire Authority, paved the way for the formation in 1957 of the first of the local authorities consortia. By agreeing on common design requirements for their systems the consortia are able to offer bulk orders of standardised components which can be produced economically by manufacturers in long production runs; these can thus be obtained at highly competitive prices which ensure that members get good value for money. There are also important savings in design time and increases in site labour productivity.

By 1970 there were eight consortia. Between them they had achieved virtually nationwide coverage, and about half of the school programme was being built in one or other of the consortium systems. The consortia keep in close touch with the commercial firms providing their components, to ensure optimum use of resources. Collaboration between the consortia and the development groups is also close: the groups co-ordinate work on development and carry out the major share of the programme of studies on common problems. During the 1960s a building productivity group was set up within the development group to encourage the organised development of new building systems and to facilitate 'dimensional co-ordination' and the interchange of components between different systems.

The Department has also encouraged the formation of groups specialising in particular aspects of building or equipment – such as furniture, science equipment and school meals equipment – to help get better value for money by promoting standardisation.

THE GROWTH AND ORGANISATION OF SECONDARY EDUCATION

The reform of secondary education was in many ways the most important of all the reforms that the Education Act 1944 brought about. It was of major consequence both in itself and as creating the base for the massive expansion of further and higher education described in later chapters.

In the nineteenth century, England had, for reasons touched on earlier, lagged behind leading Western countries in its provision of public secondary education.[10] At the beginning of the present century, there were less than 100,000 pupils in grant-aided secondary schools properly so called. Few of these received their education free.

There were of course much larger numbers of what would now be deemed pupils of secondary age in the elementary school system – that is, in higher-grade elementary schools or in the 'higher tops' of ordinary elementary schools – but these were all conducted under the elementary code. The provision as a whole could scarcely be regarded as a coherent system of public secondary education.

The Balfour Act 1902, by incorporating the endowed grammar schools in the public sector, and by bringing in the county and county borough councils as maintaining authorities with powers to provide new grammar schools as well as to maintain existing ones, created the framework for a developing system of secondary education, but it did not lead to a spectacular advance. The new authorities had no duty to expand their secondary provision; they were required only 'to consider the educational needs of their area and to take such steps as seem to them desirable, after consultation with the Board'.

From 1907 onwards there was an important advance in the shape of the 'free place' system, which enabled some children from elementary schools to attend secondary grammar schools free. A further advance resulted from the Fisher Act with its requirement that the major LEAs should submit schemes showing how they proposed to carry out their duties in respect of secondary and other forms of higher education; and the Fisher Act also put on the LEAs responsible for elementary education a duty to make adequate provision for post-primary education in central schools or classes or otherwise.

Eight years later the Hadow Report recommended that secondary education should be regarded as a distinct phase in the education of all children, provided in separate premises designed for the purpose, and that it should be free.

For all this, the state of public secondary education in England in the interwar years left much to be desired. When war broke out in 1939 there were still barely half a million pupils, or 10 per cent of the age group, in secondary schools properly so called. Some two-thirds of these were receiving their education free, but to obtain their places they had to undergo competitive examinations that were widely regarded as having undesirable effects. 'There is nothing to be said', the White Paper of 1943 observed, 'in favour of a system which subjects children at the age of 11 to the strain of a competitive examination on which not only their future schooling but their future careers may depend'.[11] For the remaining third of children in secondary schools the parents had to pay the fees.

The 90 per cent who failed or did not attempt admission to a secondary grammar school at 11 (except for a limited number admitted to junior technical schools) received the remainder of their full-time education in schools conducted under the elementary school regulations. While the more fortunate of these were accommodated in separate 'modern' or central schools, some 50 per cent were still housed in unreorganised all-age schools.

Except for those in secondary grammar and technical schools, the school leaving age was still for all practical purposes 14.

The Education Act 1944 and secondary education

The effect of the 1944 Act was that secondary education was no longer to be a particular kind of postprimary education for a selected minority. It was to be one of the three statutory stages of education that LEAs were given a duty to provide in a suitable form for all children in their area. All forms of secondary education were brought under the same regulations. As and when resources became available, the 'all-age' schools were to be phased out. All secondary schools were to have 'parity of esteem', enjoying the same facilities in terms of accommodation and staffing. Fees in maintained secondary schools were abolished. The school leaving age was to be raised immediately to 15, and as soon as circumstances permitted to 16.

Table 6.1, showing the growth in numbers in grant-aided or maintained secondary schools over the past seventy years, gives some idea of the magnitude of the transformation that has followed from the 1944 Act. Much of the increase in secondary numbers in the postwar period is of course attributable to the growth in the number of children of school age resulting from increased births from 1944 onwards. But much of it was the direct consequence of the Act.

Table 6.1 *Full-time pupils in grant-aided secondary schools (to nearest thousand).*

| | Secondary schools in receipt of grant from Board | | Maintained secondary | Direct grant grammar |
	England	Wales	England and Wales	
1904–5	85,000	9,000		
1913–14	170,000	17,000		
1937–8	425,000	45,000		
1959–60			1,723,158	108,663
January 1972			3,251,000[1]	119,000
January 1977			4,039,000[1]	118,000

[1] Including pupils in middle schools deemed secondary.

The organisation of secondary education

In the years following the 1944 Act, one of the first questions to which the Ministry had to address itself was: What sort of secondary education? How was it to be organised, and in what kind or kinds of school? This question arose because the Ministry had to consider the provision for secondary education that LEAs were proposing in their development plans, and in one form or another it has recurred throughout the postwar period. Although it involves issues of political controversy, a brief discussion of it is called for here, if only to put it in some sort of historical perspective.

The Act itself was not specific about how the new secondary education should be organised. All it said was that secondary provision would not be deemed sufficient unless it provided 'a variety of types of instruction and training', and in this context it referred to the 'different ages, abilities and aptitudes' of pupils and 'the different periods for which they might remain at school'. There was no requirement that authorities must establish a selective or 'tripartite' system.[12]

How then did it happen that, in the early postwar years, the new secondary education came to be organised on what was later to be known as a 'separatist' pattern?

First, there was the existing situation on the ground. LEAs were not free to plan their secondary provision from scratch. There were buildings in being, and faced with a massive increase in school numbers and an acute shortage of resources, LEAs were under pressure to devise plans that could so far as possible be accommodated in existing buildings. At secondary level these were everywhere organised on what is now called a 'separatist' pattern: there were the grammar schools; there were central or senior schools or (where the phasing-out of all-age schools had made headway) secondary modern schools; in some areas there were 'junior technical' schools; for the rest, there were the all-age schools.

No less important, there were at that time certain prevailing ideas about how secondary education should be organised, derived largely from educational reports of the prewar and war period, notably the Hadow, Spens and Norwood Reports.[13]

The Hadow Committee had favoured a variety of types of secondary school, and had elaborated a philosophy for the secondary 'modern' school. The Spens Committee, which had been asked to look at secondary education in grammar and technical schools, had been impressed with the potentialities of the latter, and had urged that the provision of such schools should be increased, to act as a counterweight to what they regarded as the excessively academic traditions of the grammar schools. The Norwood Committee, which had been asked to look at the curricula and examinations in secondary schools, had also favoured a tripartite pattern.[14]

These reports inevitably coloured the thinking not only of the LEAs but also of the new Ministry itself at this time. The Ministry's first pamphlet, issued in 1945 to give guidance to LEAs in the preparation of their development plans, said: 'We have in fact a new genus of secondary education which has already developed a variety of species . . . Three broad types . . . are intended to meet the differing needs of different pupils . . . it may be assumed that these broad types furnish the point of departure for further development'.[15]

The unqualified character of this advice may well to many now read oddly in the light of later developments (it was in fact later withdrawn). However, it is fair to point out that it reflected the prevailing, although not universally accepted, thinking in all the political parties in 1945. It was then a widely held belief that the implementation of the Act's provisions in the matter of free secondary education for all would of itself bring about a major advance towards the equality of opportunity that was one of the Act's fundamental aims, and, more particularly, that the opening up of the grammar schools, which had come to be regarded as the poor man's ladder to advancement, to all children of ability irrespective of their parents' means was a key to that advance.

As things turned out, the pattern never became effectively tripartite, because the third element in the design, the technical school, never fulfilled its promise. Most LEAs never established technical schools. Many of those which existed were assimilated to grammar schools or phased out. What came into being was essentially a 'bipartite' or 'selective' pattern.

Beginning of the comprehensive idea

There were a few LEAs that from the outset favoured what was at that time known as the 'multibias' or 'multilateral' type of school – the forerunner of what came to be known as the 'comprehensive' school.[16] There were two types of area in which, often for practical as much as for ideological reasons, this type of school was favoured. There were counties with sparsely inhabited rural areas, notably in Wales, where the existing grammar or intermediate schools were so small as to be barely viable educational units. In these areas there were cogent arguments against creating parallel and separate 'modern' schools, which were even less satisfactory as educational units. The needs of such areas were most conveniently met by 'neighbourhood' schools catering for secondary children of the entire ability range.[17]

The other type of area whose authorities tended to favour schemes of this type was the urban area where there was need for extensive new secondary building because of war damage or new housing development, for example, London, Bristol and Coventry. In such areas political and social convictions were undoubtedly a factor; but practical considerations, of educational advantage and economy in use of resources, were usually also important.

The Ministry was not at this time, or at any time later, entirely opposed to multilateral or comprehensive schools. It was prepared to consider individual proposals for such schools in certain conditions.[18] However for most of the first two decades after 1944 it regarded this type of school as being in the experimental stage, to be authorised only in specified circumstances.[19] Thus the White Paper of 1958, which inaugurated a major new drive to develop secondary education, said that comprehensive schools must not be established where this would involve the abolition of existing grammar schools, and warned about the dangers of very large schools.

Problems of the selective system: the 11+
But if there were problems about comprehensive organisation, there were also problems about the selective pattern, and during the 1950s and 1960s these became increasingly apparent to the growing number of families whose children were now benefiting from the expansion of secondary education.

The main cause of disquiet lay in the arrangements that authorities operated for selecting children for grammar schools: the so-called 'eleven-plus' (11+). The competitive examinations criticised in the 1943 White Paper had now been replaced by a system of objective testing. But this too came under criticism. There was widespread concern about the psychological stresses that it caused amongst children, and about the adverse effects on the morale of those who failed it. Criticism also arose because the proportion of children selected varied widely from one area to another. In some areas it was as low as 10 per cent; in others, for example, many parts of Wales, it might be as high as 40 per cent or more. The validity of the selection procedures was also widely questioned. By the end of the 1950s it came to be generally accepted that they were subject to a considerable margin of error, of the order of 10–15 per cent.

These might not have been serious weaknesses if there had been general and uniformly applied arrangements for 'late transfer' from modern to selective schools at 12 or 13. But although such arrangements were common, they too varied from area to area and in some areas were virtually non-existent.

In theory parents could appeal to the Minister on selection cases. In practice the Ministry commonly took the view that selection, like the curriculum, was a matter for LEAs, in which the Minister did not intervene. The apparatus of 11+ testing was left to LEAs, with such help as they might obtain from research bodies.

Behind this concern about selection procedures lay disquiet about the quality of the education provided in the non-selective schools. Although these were now operated under the same regulations as the grammar schools, and every effort was made to give them 'parity of esteem' and equal treatment in matters of accommodation and staffing, the shortages of the postwar period made this difficult. For the first ten years or more the great majority of 'non-selective' children continued to be accommodated in what were previously senior or central schools, whose facilities were far from adequate and which many parents still regarded as elementary schools. And the last of the all-age schools were not eliminated until after 1970. Some of the worst deficiencies were eliminated as a result of the White Paper of 1958,[20] which inaugurated a major drive in secondary building; and further advances in the quality of the education in the modern schools resulted from the Newsom Report of 1963.

But lack of facilities was by no means the only complaint. Parents by this time were becoming increasingly aware of 'the importance of being qualified', and for children in secondary schools the achievement of qualifications meant taking external examinations. It was a widely held view at this time – and one that the Ministry supported – that modern schools should be free from external examinations. This meant in effect that modern school pupils could not obtain a nationally recognised leaving qualification.

From the mid-1950s the official view on this issue was modified.[21] Pupils in non-selective schools were permitted and even encouraged to attempt 'O' level examinations of the General Certificate of Education (GCE). But the achievement of a reasonable number of passes at 'O' level was an exceptional achievement for any but grammar school pupils. Success at GCE 'A' level, which was required for admission to university, meant staying at school to 18, and this was almost entirely confined to grammar schools.

In this situation there was a growing momentum of support for secondary reorganisation on comprehensive lines.

The development of the comprehensive idea
Some of the attractions of the comprehensive solution were noted by the Crowther Council.[22] The role of comprehensive schools, they observed, is 'to play Theseus to the Procrustes of the tripartite system'. 'One of their great strengths is that it is much easier to change forms than to change schools.' Another 'lies in the range of options that a large organisation can offer 15 year olds. There is, or

ought to be, something for nearly everybody. Find it by 14 and there will be no need to transfer at 16.'

The Crowther Council also believed that such schools could fulfil a social role: 'The different social backgrounds from which the pupils come, and the different kinds and levels of employment to which they are going, more closely correspond to the national pattern than in other schools. This width of experience in a common life is surely of great value.' A comprehensive school could act 'as an effective symbol of that unity in society which our age covets'.

The Crowther Council saw very clearly the objections that could be urged against the comprehensive school. They singled out two in particular: size, and the threat to existing schools. As regards size, they shared the common belief of that period that to throw up an adequate sixth form a comprehensive school would have to have between 1,200 and 2,000 pupils. 'Some would argue that that is too many anyhow. Some would say that, since no school is better than its headmaster, we stake the future of too many boys and girls on one man's strength.' They thought that there might be devices, such as two-tier systems, that might circumvent this objection.

More serious, they thought, was the effect that comprehensive policies might have on existing schools in areas where a comprehensive school could only be brought into being by harming long-established schools that were doing a good job. Moreover, it was not in their opinion wise 'to have only one place in which a 17-year-old can get full-time education. Freedom to choose the institution as well as freedom to choose a course is important to teenagers and their parents.'

The Crowther Council, reporting in 1959, regarded the comprehensive school as being still in the experimental stage, and did not recommend its general adoption. But it could be argued that by the early 1960s the time had come when experimentation in limited areas should lead to nationally applicable conclusions about the structure of secondary education. The first chairman of the Central Advisory Council (England), Sir Fred Clark, observed that a diagnostic period of twenty years would show whether a particular structure of secondary education was likely to be beneficial.[23]

By about the middle of the 1960s a growing number of authorities had concluded that a new pattern was needed and were introducing comprehensive schemes of various types; and the Ministry was becoming more favourably disposed to such schemes, although there was as yet no major change of policy.

One variant of comprehensive organisations that attracted attention in this period was the 'Leicestershire experiment'. This provided 'common high' schools from 11 to 14, followed by 'common grammar' schools from 14+ onwards for all whose parents agreed that they should stay at school for at least two years. This had the advantage that it eliminated the 11+ without requiring the creation of very large schools or making heavy demands on building resources. From this grew the idea of the 'middle' school – that is, a school catering for children from 8 or 9 to 12 or 13, which, like the primary school, would be comprehensive. An Act (the Education Act 1964) making possible this type of organisation was passed in July 1964, and it is a type of organisation that has found increasing favour in recent years.

By 1963 more than half of all LEAs in England and Wales had either (in a few cases) completed, or were working on, schemes of comprehensive reorganisation for all or part of their areas. But the policy was that of individual authorities.

Comprehensive reorganisation as a national policy
The Labour Administration which took office in October 1964 had a mandate to promote reorganisation on comprehensive lines as a national policy. A circular issued in July 1965[24] requested all LEAs that had not already done so to submit plans for reorganising secondary education in their areas on comprehensive lines.

The circular gave guidance on how this could be done. It suggested a variety of patterns that reorganisation might follow. In addition to the orthodox pattern of 'all-through' comprehensive schools for the age range 11–18, it permitted various forms of two-tier organisation, with a break at 13 or 14; or a pattern of comprehensive 'middle' schools, to which children would transfer from primary schools at 8 or 9, subsequently transferring to comprehensive schools at 12 or 13; or comprehensive schools for the age range 11–16, with sixth-form colleges for those over 16. (The latter was regarded as an experimental arrangement, which would be permitted only in a limited number of cases.)

This choice of patterns for reorganisation was important, because in many areas it offered the only prospect of carrying through reorganisation within a reasonable cost and time scale. In most areas secondary school buildings, both old and new, were on a 'separatist' pattern. Even if resources had been unlimited, it would have been unthinkable that all these schools, new as well as old, should be taken out of use to make way for new comprehensive schools. As it was, resources were far from unlimited, and the circular made it clear that the Department could not make resources available solely for reorganisation. All-through comprehensive schools, even of the smaller type that the circular permitted, are costly to build; and this meant that, as a rule, new comprehensive schools of the orthodox all-through type could be provided only in areas where there were large increases in school population. In other areas authorities that wanted to go comprehensive had to do so by adopting one or other of the alternative patterns allowed.

The circular also made it clear that reorganisation must not be achieved by the framing of 'plans whose educational disadvantages more than offset the benefits which will flow from the adoption of comprehensive schooling', in other words, by what came to be known as 'botched up' schemes.

Authorities were asked to have close consultations with teachers in the preparation of their plans, and to ensure that parents were informed.

It is noteworthy that, despite the far-reaching and, in many areas, controversial character of the changes involved, and the continuing shortage of resources, the great majority of authorities again followed the lead from the centre – as they had done in the period after 1944 – and proved willing to undertake the exacting task[25] of drawing up schemes, consulting teachers and voluntary bodies and explaining their plans to parents. By the spring of 1970 about three-quarters of the 162 authorities then existing in England and Wales had pronounced in favour of comprehensive policies and had reorganisation schemes implemented or approved by the Department. The churches had also taken steps to reorganise their secondary schools on comprehensive lines as resources allowed. The number of comprehensive schools in the country had increased from 262 in 1965 to 1,145 by January 1970. By that date not far short of a third of all children of secondary age were in comprehensive schools.

It has been remarked earlier that, although the 1944 Act explicitly recognised the Department's role in formulating national policies for education, the departmental circular is an administrative device with no statutory force. For this reason, the wording of Circular 10/65 made it clear that what was involved was a request, not a direction, to LEAs to submit plans for comprehensive reorganisation. As noted above, it was a request with which the great majority of LEAs complied.

But there was a sizable minority that did not accept the policy. At the end of 1969 there were still over twenty authorities that had either formally declined to submit comprehensive plans at all, or had submitted plans that were not regarded as complying with the circular.

The reluctance of this minority to conform with the national policy caused serious concern to ministers. They concluded that the only way to ensure that all authorities adopted the comprehensive pattern was to legislate, and in the spring of 1970 Labour government introduced a Bill that would have made the submission of plans of comprehensive reorganisation mandatory on all authorities. But before the Bill got through Parliament, a general election had returned a Conservative Administration to power.

Circular 10/70 and its sequel

One of the first acts in the field of education of the new Administration which assumed power in June 1970 was to issue a new circular[26] superseding Circular 10/65. This did not reverse the policy recommended in Circular 10/65, but it made clear the Conservative government's view that a uniform pattern should not be imposed on LEAs by legislation or otherwise. LEAs were to have greater freedom themselves to determine the shape of secondary provision in their areas, and ministers would exercise greater discrimination in approving particular projects. The Secretary of State would expect educational considerations, local needs and wishes and the wise use of resources to be the main principles determining the local pattern.

It was later indicated that authorities would no longer be expected to submit reorganisation plans for approval in principle, as they had been required to do by Circular 10/65. Each individual proposal for the establishment, closure or change in character of a school would be considered on its merits under the statutory procedures of Section 13. Guidelines were given on the points at which ministers would look in considering LEAs' proposals under Section 13. There was emphasis on the drawbacks of very large schools and the advantages of small ones. Ministers had strong reservations about schools in split premises, and about two-tier schemes, particularly those involving transfer at 14. One consideration to which they attached particular importance was that parents' choice should not be eroded and should wherever possible be extended.

In the period immediately following the issue of this circular very few authorities that had had comprehensive schemes approved or had already submitted proposals asked to modify or withdraw them. There was no indication of any general wish to go back on approved plans, and there was a continuing flow of new proposals.

While in some cases LEAs' proposals were rejected or modified for reasons such as those indicated above, the great majority received ministerial approval. In 1972 and 1973 the pace of reorganisation was gathering momentum as plans that had been under discussion were put into effect, and the allocations of resources to provide for the raising of the school leaving age to 16 gave a further impetus. By January 1975 some 70 per cent of pupils of secondary age were in comprehensive schools. Of the 163 LEAs then in existence, 72 had received approval to reorganise wholly on comprehensive lines and 76 had reorganised in part; only 15 had received no approval to reorganise.

With the return of a Labour Administration to office early in 1974 there was again a change of policy. Circular 10/70 was withdrawn and replaced by a new circular[27] broadly reverting to the policy of Circular 10/65: that is, the development of a fully comprehensive system and the ending of selection at 11+ or any other stage. This emphasised the urgency that ministers attached to early progress being made towards these objectives, and required LEAs to submit information on the measures that they were taking to complete the process of reorganisation.

Like Circular 10/65 it left LEAs considerable freedom to choose, in consultation with local interests, between various types of comprehensive reorganisation, while drawing attention to those which experience had proved to be most satisfactory.

It made clear, as had been done in 1965, that building projects for non-comprehensive schools would not in future be included in building programmes except where these were necessary to enable the schools to become comprehensive.

It also – and this was new – gave an important indication of ministers' views about the role of voluntary schools. It noted that, while in many instances the governors of voluntary schools and diocesan authorities had responded constructively in the matter of comprehensive plans, there were some cases in which governing bodies had stood out against the wishes of their maintaining LEAs to achieve a full comprehensive system in their area. Such governing bodies were invited to reconsider their attitude; and it was indicated that, if the governors of voluntary aided schools were not prepared to co-operate with their LEAs in this matter, they could not expect to continue receiving their financial support.

In a statement made at the time at which the circular was issued[28] the Secretary of State explained that the circular was a clear statement of national policy, and that ministers would use their full power, including control over building programmes, to secure the co-operation of LEAs and voluntary bodies. It was not his intention at that time to ensure compliance by legislation, but he made it clear that he would propose legislation if and when it became necessary. Such legislation was in the event introduced, reaching the statute book as the Education Act 1976. This required all LEAs to have regard, in all their duties relating to secondary education, to the principle that such education should be provided in schools that admitted students without reference to ability and aptitude, and empowered the Secretary of State to call for proposals to complete reorganisation in cases where he felt that progress or further progress was necessary. The Act also gave the Secretary of State power to require the managers or governors of voluntary schools to submit proposals for comprehensive reorganisation where this had not already been done, and to control authorities' arrangements for the support of education in non-maintained schools.

RAISING THE SCHOOL LEAVING AGE

An important feature of the plans of successive administrations for expanding secondary education since 1944 was the progressive raising of the school leaving age, and since the raising of the age to 16 has been the subject of controversy, it may be helpful to say something here about the historical background to this measure.

When the Board of Education came into being in 1900 the school leaving age was 12; it had been raised from 11 the previous year. In 1944 it was still for all practical purposes 14. The Education Act 1936 had provided for it to be raised to 15, but with effect from 1 September 1939. With the country on the brink of war, the implementation of this provision was postponed for the duration.

The Education Act 1944 provided for the age to be raised without exemptions to 15 in 1945 (with the proviso that it might be postponed for two years), and to 16 as soon as the Minister was satisfied that it was practicable. This provision was not included in a fit of wartime exuberance. It had been regarded as ultimately inevitable by the Spens Committee,[29] because it was in their view essential if there was to be effective parity amongst the various types of school at the secondary stage.

The provision to raise the age to 15 was put into effect in 1947. It was aptly described at the time as an act of faith. An additional 400,000 children had to be accommodated in the schools in conditions of acute shortage of buildings, staff and equipment and dislocation due to war.

The raising of the age to 16 was to prove a scarcely less formidable task because of the massive increase in school population during the 1950s.

The Crowther Council in its Report presented in 1959[30] reviewed the proposed reform at length, considering whether it was still justified, whether it should take priority over the implementation of plans for county colleges and if, so, when it should be undertaken. They reached the unqualified conclusion that it should be implemented at the earliest possible date, and should take precedence over plans for county colleges.

Their conclusion was based primarily on educational considerations: 'A boy or girl of 15 is not sufficiently mature to be exposed to the pressures of the world of industry or commerce,' they argued. 'He needs an environment designed specifically to develop his powers'. The promise of secondary education for all contained in the Education Act 1944 could not in their view be redeemed unless it was continued for all to 16.

They thought that the educational case was powerfully reinforced by economic arguments: the national interest in tapping all the available supply of talent, and the need to provide for what they called 'the universal up-grading of jobs'. They were clear that increased voluntary staying was too haphazard to be depended upon to achieve the same results as compulsion.

They thought that the most favourable time, if the reform was to be achieved without an unacceptable deterioration of staffing standards, was some time in the years between 1965 and 1969, when there would be a temporary decline in the size of the 15–16 age groups.

Because of the continuing teacher shortage this reform still remained unimplemented in the early 1960s. In 1963 another Central Advisory Council (England) reverted to the subject. Their conclusions were even more forthright:

There are still too many boys and girls who . . . leave at the earliest possible moment, whatever their potential abilities, because outside pressures are too much for them. Again and again teachers confirm that the pupils with whom we are especially concerned stand to gain a great deal in terms of personal development as well as in the consolidating of attainments from a longer period of full-time education – but it is just these boys and girls who most readily succumb to the attractions of the pay-packet and the bright lights it commands.[31]

The Newsom Council's first recommendation was that an immediate announcement should be made by the government that the age would be raised to 16 for all pupils entering secondary school from September 1965 onwards.

The government's decision was announced in a debate on the Newsom Report in the House of Commons, in January 1964. The government, said the then Minister, regarded the carrying through of this reform as a test of our national commitment to secondary education for all. The teacher supply position was by this time improving; the buildings could be provided without disturbing existing programmes; and there now existed in the Schools Council a body that could tackle the curriculum problems involved. Plans were being made to raise the age in the educational year 1970–1.

These preparations were continued by the Labour Administration that came into office in autumn 1964. The financial crisis of 1967–8 imposed a temporary postponement. But during 1968 the government reaffirmed its determination to go ahead with the reform, and in 1969 restored the necessary provision in building programmes.

The Conservative Administration that came into office in June 1970 took over the plans already made. An order in council raising the upper limit of compulsory schooling to 16 was made in March 1972, and came into operation that September.

Because of the continuing increase in the numbers staying on voluntarily, the number of additional children to be accommodated was now barely 250,000. The number of teachers was by now increasing at a rate of almost 20,000 annually. Extensive work had been undertaken by the Schools Council to ensure that the raising of the school leaving age did not simply take the form of 'tacking on an extra year', but that the years up to 16 represented a coherent educational experience for all pupils.[32] There now existed in the Certificate of Secondary Education (CSE) an examination well suited to many of the pupils involved. When the school leaving age became 16 in September 1972 the additional places needed in the schools were, with very few exceptions, ready.

Thus was brought to completion what the White Paper of December 1972 described as 'a great reform'.

THE DEPARTMENT'S CONCERN WITH THE SCHOOL CURRICULUM AND EXAMINATIONS

The Department's role in relation to the school curriculum has traditionally been strictly limited. The Education Act 1944 specifically provided that 'secular instruction' in the schools – that is, the teaching of all subjects other than religion – shall be under the control of the LEA.[33] As a rule LEAs delegate this responsibility to heads of individual schools. In practice this has meant that the teachers have been within limits free to determine their own curricula.

There are of course practical constraints on the teachers' freedom: there are those imposed by limitations of staff and resources; there are the wishes of parents and governors; there are the constraints of external examinations.

Moreover, the Department is by no means entirely unconcerned. Although the Act gives responsibility for the curriculum to the LEAs, this does not take it entirely out of the Department's purview, in so far as the Department has a general concern with everything that the LEAs do under the education Acts, and has a general duty to keep Education Ministers informed of developments in the curriculum and their relationship to other interests outside the schools.

In practice, the Department has traditionally been reluctant to intervene in curriculum matters. There are, however, two ways in which it has had, and continues to have, a general concern with what is taught in the schools. The first is through the work of HM Inspectors. One of the essential roles of HM Inspectorate today, as earlier explained, is to serve the schools – and the LEAs which maintain them – as advisers and consultants; and much of the advice that they give, whether on visits to schools, or on the short courses that they conduct for teachers, or in the pamphlets that they publish from time to time, concerns the curriculum. However, this advisory activity is something far removed from direct control of the curriculum by the Department, which is a feature of many national systems of education. HM Inspectors, in offering advice, do not act as agents of the Department, conveying departmental policies on curriculum matters. They act essentially as consultants, who advise by virtue of their specialist knowledge and their membership of a professional body with wide collective experience. Their advice is no more than advice.

The second way in which the Department is involved with the curriculum is through its concern with secondary school examinations. 'The question of the use and abuse of examinations', observed Selby-Bigge, 'will probably be debated till the end of the educational world.' The debate is still very much alive, and is of close concern to the Department because major examination policy questions are decided by the Secretary of State.

In the nineteenth century public examinations were seen by enlightened opinion in England as an instrument of reform, substituting merit for patronage as the basis of recruitment for the public services and the liberal professions. More recently, examinations have come to have a less favourable image. Yet they persist, and the numbers offering themselves as candidates grow from year to year. It is difficult not to conclude that they perform some essential function in society.

In any advanced industrial society, where there is a developed system of higher education and a large demand for men and women with specialised or professional skills, some system of public attestation is needed to select individuals for entry to higher education and to skilled and professional occupations. Examinations perform what has been described as the 'allocative' function, the importance of which increases as the educational system tends to become the main source of recruitment for qualified people. And because success in examinations offers a passport to higher education and the more sought-after careers, the examination syllabuses tend to exert a strong influence on the school curriculum, particularly if, as in England, this is not subject to control by the central department.

The Secondary School Examinations Council

In such a situation there is always a danger, as the Taunton Commission pointed out more than a century ago,[34] that examinations will disrupt the work of the schools. In 1911 another commission[35] repeated the warning. By this time there was a Board of Education, and in 1917 it acted. It decided to undertake 'the functions and responsibilities of co-ordinating Authority for secondary school examinations'.[36] To advise it in this task it set up a Secondary School Examinations Council (SSEC), consisting of representatives of the university examining bodies, the LEAs and the teachers. The main function of the SSEC was to approve secondary school examinations and the boards that ran them. Two public examinations were approved by the Board: the First or School Certificate taken at 16, and the Second or Higher School Certificate (HSC), taken at the end of a sixth-form course. These were the only officially recognised secondary school examinations.

After 1944 the functions of the SSEC were extended. The Minister was no longer merely to co-ordinate, but assumed 'full responsibility . . . for the direction of policy and general arrangements'[37] for secondary school examinations, although the day-to-day supervision needed to ensure efficient administration, comparability of standards, and so forth was still delegated to the SSEC. The SSEC was reconstituted, with increased local authority and teacher representation and the addition of representatives of further education. The eight examining boards continued in operation as agents of the Ministry.[38]

The General Certificate of Education

The first major task that the reconstituted SSEC was asked to undertake was to devise and launch new secondary-school examinations to take the place of the old School and Higher School Certificates. These, and particularly the former, had come under growing criticism, notably by the Spens and Norwood Committees, because they were 'group' examinations, that is, the candidate had to achieve success in subjects chosen from amongst a specified group of subjects, the object being to ensure that pupils received education in a range of subjects. These requirements had been found to have restrictive effects on the schools, particularly for less able pupils who might have been able to succeed in one or two subjects only.

The SSEC now devised a new examination, the General Certificate of Education (GCE), which was to be entirely a 'subject' examination with no built-in grouping requirements. For the 16-year-olds an 'Ordinary' or 'O' level was designed, to provide a test in a subject for pupils taking it at the end of a five-year secondary course. The 'O' level pass standard was set at the 'credit' standard of the old School Certificate; in other words, the standard of the examination at 16 was raised. It was intended that as a rule the 'O' level examination would be accessible only to pupils of the secondary grammar schools or comparable types. (For the 'newer secondary schools' the SSEC envisaged various types of internal examinations. They did not believe that any formal or nationwide external assessment of such examinations was either possible or desirable.) For the 18-year-old leaver an 'Advanced' or 'A' level was designed, with a standard roughly equivalent to that of principal subjects in the old HSC, to provide a test of attainment in a subject for pupils who had taken it as a specialist subject for two years in the sixth form. This was also intended to serve a 'qualifying' function for university entry and other purposes. [39]

The first examinations for the GCE were held in 1951. The examination quickly established itself; and GCE results came to be generally accepted by university and technical colleges, by professional bodies and by employers. [40]

In the early years the new arrangements undoubtedly had a liberating effect on the schools, because of the greater freedom afforded by a subject examination. They also had the effect of encouraging further education colleges to offer GCE courses, since they enabled young people who chose to continue their education in such institutions – and also older students – to take individual papers in subjects suited to their needs. By 1962, about a sixth of all candidates taking GCE at 'O' and 'A' levels came from further education establishments, and the proportion has since increased. But by the late 1950s difficulties began to appear, both in the examination arrangements at 16 and in those at 18.

Examining problems at 16
One of the main difficulties about the examination at 16, or 'O' level, was that it failed to meet the examination needs of the rapidly increasing numbers in the newer secondary schools. The 'O' level was designed for the top 20 per cent of pupils completing a five-year secondary course of a 'grammar' type. It followed that it was not suitable for the 80 per cent of children in 'modern' schools and streams, even those staying on to 16. The theory was that these schools should have the freedom to develop a type of education

specially suited to the children in them, unencumbered with external examinations.

During the 1950s it became clear that this theory was difficult to sustain in practice. As 'O' level came to be generally accepted, it acquired, as the old School Certificate had acquired, a social function and prestige. It became a passport, or at any rate a prerequisite to obtaining a passport, to higher education and the better-paid careers. Modern school pupils and their parents became restive at finding that they were in effect debarred from entering for it, particularly as, during the 1950s, more pupils in modern schools stayed on to 16.

In 1955 the Ministry abated its objections to modern schools entering their pupils for examinations. Pupils in all kinds of schools, modern as well as selective, who 'were suited' to 'O' level were encouraged to have a go,[41] and there followed a striking growth in the proportion of modern school leavers gaining some success. At the same time, despite departmental discouragement, there was a proliferation of other external examinations, both at 16 and at 15.

Origins of the Certificate of Secondary Education
The growth of unrecognised examinations caused increasing concern to LEAs and teachers, and in 1958 the SSEC appointed a committee under the chairmanship of Mr Robert Beloe to advise them on whether there should be publicly recognised examinations other than the GCE. This committee's report was published in 1960. While strongly condemning all external examinations at 15, it concluded that there were good practical and educational arguments in favour of examinations at 16 for pupils not in selective schools and streams.

The Beloe Committee took the view, however, that, for all but a small minority of pupils in such schools, 'O' level was not a suitable examination. They also saw very great dangers for the schools in the proliferation of privately operated examinations that were not subject to public supervision.

Their solution was a new national examination to be taken at the end of a five-year secondary course which, while officially recognised and supervised and thus having national currency, would be organised on a regional basis and mainly teacher controlled. It would be designed not for the top 20 per cent of the ability range who normally took 'O' level in several subjects, but for the next 20 per cent below these, or rather more. Like the GCE it would be a subject, not a group, examination. To ensure that the new examining bodies were in touch with new developments in examination practice, and to safeguard standards, they proposed that there should be co-ordination and research by a central body with the necessary staff and resources.

These proposals were endorsed by the SSEC,[42] and were accepted, although with certain reservations, by the then Minister. It was decided to call the new examination the Certificate of Secondary Education (CSE). There were to be between ten and fifteen regional examining bodies,[43] all substantially teacher controlled. The standard of the examinations was to be such as to make it suitable for pupils of roughly the second fifth of the age group at 16. There was to be a variety of modes of examination. Schools might either submit candidates for the regional body's examinations, or put up their own examination scheme for approval by the body, or ask the body to examine candidates on their own syllabuses.

The SSEC was reconstituted to include members with knowledge of non-selective schools, and provided with staff to undertake research and development work. A structure for the new examining bodies and the scope and standards of the examination were worked out in more detail in two further reports.[44] It was proposed that the results should be recorded in terms of grades, and there was an important suggestion that the pass–fail concept might eventually be superseded altogether.

The first examinations for the CSE were held in 1965. By 1966, when all the new examining bodies were in operation, the number of candidates was over 140,000; and thereafter numbers built up rapidly, reaching nearly 600,000 in 1976. By the end of the 1960s a pass at Grade 1 of the CSE was coming to be widely accepted as equivalent to a pass at GCE 'O' level, for such purposes as entry to further education courses. Table 6.2 gives GCE and CSE passes for 1965–76.

The launching of the CSE examination, which was the last major task undertaken by the SSEC, represented an innovation in school examinations, notably in three respects: it provided for an effectively teacher-controlled examination, with flexibility in examination arrangements; it gave general currency to the idea of recording results as grades of attainment rather than in pass–fail terms; and it provided for the first time that the central supervising machinery should be supported by continuous research and development.

But it bequeathed to the Schools Council certain problems. The most obvious was that there were two recognised examinations at 16. Their continued existence side by side undoubtedly created difficulties for pupils and teachers. And there remained a fundamental problem which the very success of the new examinations brought into prominence, namely, that of defining curricular aims for the large number of secondary school pupils for whom national examinations are not a suitable objective. This was a problem that could only be tackled by a body with a wider remit than the supervision of examinations.

Table 6.2   *Secondary-school examination results and school leaver achievements.*

GCE examinations	1954[1]	1964[1]	1974[1]	1976[1]
'O' level				
(a) All passes[2]	603,236	1,061,514	1,622,129	1,614,198[4]
(b) School leavers with five or more passes[3]	61,100	97,900	159,320	164,010[4]
(c) (b) as percentage of age group	11	15	23	22
'A' level				
(a) All passes	88,747	174,896	342,662	378,325
(b) School leavers with two or more passes	23,600	40,800	83,530	90,980
(c) (b) as percentage of age group	7	11	12	13
(d) School leavers and students in further education with two or more passes	24,600	43,300	95,600	106,040
(e) (d) as percentage of age group	7	11	14	15
CSE examinations		1965	1974	1976
(a) All grades, 1 to 5		216,339	1,982,495	2,324,321
(b) School leavers with five or more Grade 4 or better		12,490	150,410	180,110

[1] Academic year for items (b) and (c).
[2] Covers further education establishments and privately entered candidates as well as schools.
[3] Includes 'O' level passes on 'A' level papers, and CSE Grade 1 from 1965 onwards.
[4] Grades A to C.

Some problems of examinations at 18

The difficulties with the examination arrangements at 18 have been of a different kind. They have arisen largely from the intensified competition for university places resulting from the very large increase in the output of well-qualified leavers from school sixth forms. GCE 'A' level had been designed on the assumption that what was needed for most sixth formers (other than those aiming at scholarships) was a test of attainment, which would also 'qualify' for university entry. This presupposed that most of those who so qualified (roughly those with two or more 'A' level passes) would obtain university places if they wanted them; and in the early 1950s this assumption was a reasonable one.

But in the later 1950s the situation altered radically. Between 1958 and 1965 the numbers leaving sixth forms with two or more 'A' levels were increasing much faster than the numbers that could be admitted to universities. In these circumstances 'A' levels came increasingly to be used by universities not as a qualifying examination but as a means of selection. The universities' general matriculation requirements ceased to be of significance. What came to matter were the detailed requirements of particular colleges, departments and faculties, and the marks that candidates achieved in 'A' level examinations. Sixth formers were thus under pressure to specialise to an extent that left little place for more general studies. Furthermore, there were pressures on pupils to start specialising before they reached sixth form. The difficulties were compounded because, as the sheer volume of knowledge increased, syllabuses became more and more overloaded.

During the 1960s some relief was afforded by the expansion of the universities which resulted from government action on the Robbins Report, and by the development of degree and comparable courses in polytechnics and other non-university institutions. But the examination problems at 18 proved intractable; and as time went on it came to be widely realised that these were inseparable from the more fundamental issues of the sixth-form curriculum, and the proper extent of the universities' influence upon it, and that they could be resolved only in the context of a major review of sixth-form curricula as a whole.

Origins of the Schools Council
By the early 1960s there was growing awareness both in the Department and in the educational world generally of the need for a new approach both to school examinations and to the more fundamental problems of the school curriculum. It was becoming evident that the development of the curriculum required to keep it abreast of the growth of knowledge and of changing needs was a task that could not be left to take care of itself or be adequately tackled through changes in examinations alone.

It came to be widely agreed that what was needed was the systematic application of research and development over the whole range of the school curriculum, of the kind that was at that time being pioneered in the natural sciences by the Nuffield Foundation and the Science Masters' Association. It seemed clear that it was only in this context that the influence of examinations could be contained, and coherent development achieved.

In 1962 a 'curriculum study group' was set up within the Department, to explore the possibilities. In the event this unit did not prove acceptable as a permanent agency for curriculum development. It became apparent that, to obtain the active support of teachers and LEAs, an agency must be created that was independent of the Department and whose constitution reflected the primacy of the teachers in the curriculum field.

In 1964 the then Secretary of State, acting on the recommendation of a widely representative working party under the chairmanship of the late Sir John Lockwood, who was at that time chairman of SSEC, decided to establish a new independent body called the Schools Council for the Curriculum and Examinations. The new Schools Council met for the first time in the autumn of 1964.

The essential function of the Schools Council, as expressed in its original constitution, was the promotion of education by carrying out research into, and keeping under review, the curriculum, teaching methods and examinations in schools, including the organisation of schools so far as it affected curricula, this function to be performed with regard at all times to the general principle that each school should have the fullest possible measure of responsibility for its own work, with its own curriculum and teaching methods based on the needs of its own pupils and evolved by its own staff. The Schools Council was specifically charged with assuming the work in relation to school examinations that had up to that time been performed by the SSEC.

The constitution of the Schools Council provided for a chairman and seventy-five persons representative of the teachers' organisations, LEAs, the churches, the universities and examining bodies, and including representatives of both sides of industry, parents and the Department itself. The Department and the Welsh Office were represented not by assessors but by full voting members. It also provided for co-options and for four *ex officio* members: namely, the chairmen of the steering committees and of the committee for Wales (mentioned below).

Under the direction of the governing body, there was provision for a structure of committees: a programme committee to perform the function of a senior policy committee, three curriculum-steering committees and a committee for Wales, together with a number of subject and examination committees. A basic feature of the constitution was that, on the Schools Council itself and on all the committees (except those concerned with finance and staffing), there must be a majority of serving teachers.

By the early 1970s there was a staff of about a hundred and twenty, forty of them at senior levels, under the direction of three joint secretaries (at least one seconded from the Department and one from local authority service) and a director of studies. Initially the Schools

Council was provided with staff, accommodation and services by the Department; some of the key staff were drawn from the curriculum study group.

The Department also initially made available a proportion of its own funds for sponsoring research. In 1967–8 the LEAs began to contribute. In 1970 agreement was reached that the Department and the LEAs should each pay to the Schools Council one half of its approved annual budget, to be used as the council saw fit.

The establishment of the Schools Council, as the Department's annual report for 1964 remarked, was an event of major importance for the education service. But this is not the place to attempt a detailed review of its work, which is available in its own reports and publications.

It is, however, perhaps relevant to give some indication of the main fields with which the Schools Council concerned itself in the early stages. Many of its major projects or areas of activity arose logically from what has been said about its origins. Thus it has undertaken two important inquiries about secondary school examinations. First, there has been an attempt to devise a unified pattern of examining at 16+, suitable to the greatly increased numbers and varied abilities of those in the secondary schools wishing to take a public school-leaving examination. Secondly, there has been an attempt to assess whether a new course and examination should be introduced for sixth formers not likely to go on to higher education, and, subsequently, an inquiry into the possible revision of the 'A' level examination. Associated with these undertakings is an extensive programme of research into examinations.

In the curriculum field the Schools Council is engaged in many subject areas, notably continued work on major projects in science, mathematics and modern languages inherited from the Nuffield Projects; and it has developed major projects in the humanities, in English and (through its committee for Wales) in Welsh. There are projects related to specific reforms of the educational system. Of special importance has been work on the curriculum requirements for raising the school leaving age to 16, and the Schools Council has established a working party on nursery education. There are projects related to specific problems central to the educational system, for example, reading and oracy; or to new developments, for example, teachers' centres and new aspects of educational technology; or to the needs and problems of particular groups, for example, handicapped children, gifted children and the children of immigrants.

More recently, further thought has had to be given to the relationship between the Department and the Schools Council, largely as a result of growing public insistence that the Department should involve itself more directly in curriculum and examination questions. This whole matter was the subject of an important Green Paper issued by the Department in 1977,[45] designed to stimulate public discussion of the issues involved.

Some indication of the Department's thinking at this time may be seen in this statement in the Green Paper:

> At national level the Secretaries of State (i.e. the Secretary of State for Education and Science and the Secretary of State for Wales) are responsible in law for the promotion of the education of the people of England and Wales. They need to know what is being done by the LEAs, and through them what is happening in the schools. They must draw attention to national needs if they believe the educational system is not adequately meeting them.

RELIGIOUS TEACHING AND WORSHIP IN SCHOOLS

An unusual feature of the Education Act 1944 is its provision with regard to religious teaching and worship in schools. (Sections 25 and following.) This requires that, subject to certain safeguards for parents and teachers, religious instruction shall form part of the curriculum of every maintained school, both county and voluntary, and that on each day there shall be a collective act of worship.

This was a provision to which great importance was attached by the authors of the Act. It was not of course a complete innovation. Many of the schools within the maintained system, as explained earlier, are provided by church bodies, and in these it had long been the practice to provide religious instruction. And when after 1870 secular bodies were created to fill the gaps in school provision, it was usual for the schools that they provided to give religious instruction, although there was no legal requirement that they should do so; the only requirement was that, if such instruction were given, it had to be non-denominational.

What the 1944 Act did was to put on a statutory basis what was by then a general practice in the schools. The broad intentions of its authors in this matter were made clear in the White Paper of 1943.[46] 'There was a very general wish, not confined to representatives of the churches, that religious education should be given a more defined place in the life and work of the schools, springing from the desire to revive the spiritual and personal values' in society.

It is not specified in the main body of the Act what religion is to be taught. The intention was that both the teaching and worship should normally be Christian. There are, however, now several 'agreed syllabuses' (see below) that also provide for pupils to receive instruction in religions other than Christian, and for some study of non-religious attitudes to life. In voluntary schools instruction and worship can be in other religions; and county and other schools may make arrangements, at the request of parents, for pupils of non-Christian faiths to receive appropriate instruction.

The provisions are detailed and complex, reflecting the experience of a century of controversy over the place of religious teaching in schools; and the safeguards for parents and teachers are important.

In county schools it is laid down that the teaching must not be distinctive of any particular denomination and must be in accordance with the 'agreed syllabus' adopted for the school. In voluntary controlled schools also the teaching is normally non-denominational, but parents may opt for their children to have denominational teaching in accordance with the trust deed of the school. In aided and special agreement schools the teaching is denominational, but parents may opt for non-denominational teaching.

A parent of a child at any maintained school, whether county or voluntary, may ask for his child to be wholly or partly excused from religious teaching and worship.

There are safeguards for teachers. They are protected from disqualification by reason of religious opinion, or for attending or omitting to attend religious worship; and no teacher, except certain categories of teachers in voluntary schools, can be required to give religious instruction or be discriminated against for declining to do so.

A schedule to the Act (Fifth Schedule) provides for machinery for the preparation by LEAs of 'agreed syllabuses' of religious instruction to be used in their county schools. They are required to appoint constituent bodies, composed of representatives of the Church of England (except in Wales), the main religious denominations in the area, the teachers' associations and the LEA, whose responsibility it is to convene conferences for the purpose of drawing up or revising agreed syllabuses. The recommendations of the conference must be unanimous, and in the event of a conference failing to agree it falls to the Secretary of State to appoint a representative body of persons with experience in religious education to prepare a syllabus. The agreed syllabuses, as approved by LEAs, are published documents. LEAs may appoint standing advisory councils to advise them on religious matters connected with the religious instruction to be given in accordance with an agreed syllabus – in particular as to methods of teaching, the choice of books and the provision of in-service training for teachers.

These provisions of the 1944 Act have continued in operation substantially unchanged during the past three decades. Although there have from time to time been proposals for reform, these have not reached the point at which legislation has been brought forward.

It is to be noted that, in this area as in that of secular instruction, the main responsibility and initiative rest with the LEAs and voluntary bodies. However, religious instruction in county schools and agreed syllabus instruction in other schools are subject to inspection by HM Inspectors.

PRIMARY EDUCATION: PRIORITY
FOR THE UNDERPRIVILEGED

During the 1950s and early 1960s the emphasis in policy making was on secondary and postschool education. It was in these sectors that the 1944 Act had set the stage for major reforms. And from the mid-1950s the larger age groups of the 'bulge' were arriving in the secondary schools, and thereafter were reaching the age of further and higher education.

From the later 1960s there was a shift of attention to the primary sector, and within this sector the Department came to be specially concerned with the needs of two groups: the underprivileged, and children below compulsory school age.

Educational priority areas: the Plowden thesis
A major factor in bringing about this shift was the appearance of the Plowden Report.[47] This contained a chapter on 'educational priority areas';[48] and although this was far from being the report's only contribution to new thinking about primary education, it may be helpful here briefly to recall its thesis, in view of its influence on national policies.

The Plowden Council paid particular attention to the home and social environment of children in school. Comparing the home backgrounds of the primary school children of the 1960s with those of the 1930s, they noted great changes: unemployment had been reduced; incomes had risen; nutrition had improved; housing was better; the health and social services brought help where it was needed. Most of the children were now 'physically healthy, vigorous, curious and alert'. They noted too that the primary schools were 'more and more a cross-section of the nation'.

But they found that there was a minority of families who trailed behind. They found neighbourhoods – inner city centres and declining industrial communities – that had 'for generations been starved of new schools, new houses and new investment of every kind'. Being areas of static or declining population, these had scarcely benefited from postwar school-building programmes, which gave priority to areas of population growth. In these neighbourhoods they saw a vicious circle developing. There was an outflow of the more successful young people, and the schools were particularly affected. Conditions were such that teachers competent to do a decent job in ordinary schools were liable to be defeated. This made it difficult to attract teachers, and there was a high turnover of staffs.

The Plowden Council pointed out that industrial development and the social services provided by the state could not be relied on automatically to ensure increasing opportunity to every child. Whether or not they did so depended on the pattern of public services, and of school provision in particular. While there had been some improvement in the living conditions of deprived groups and areas, there had not been an appreciable narrowing of the gap between the least well off and the rest, and the gap was most evident amongst children, particularly in large families.

They made a further point. While accepting that many of the things that needed to be done to achieve greater equality of educational opportunity must be done at the secondary and postschool stages, they insisted that reform at these levels would not be fully effective unless it also touched the primary schools.

'Positive discrimination' for educational priority areas
To set in train the changes needed, the Plowden Council proposed a nationwide policy of what they called 'positive discrimination' in favour of deprived areas and schools and of the children in them. The aim should be first to bring the schools in these areas up to the national average, and then to make them better – 'as good as the best in the country' – and thus able to compensate for what the children lacked in their home and social environment.

They proposed that LEAs should be invited to consider which neighbourhoods and schools within their areas suffered from deprivation, measured by certain objective criteria: large families with low family incomes, incomplete families, overcrowding and poor housing, high unemployment, a high proportion of retarded or maladjusted children or of immigrants unable to speak English.

For these 'educational priority areas' they proposed a programme of inter-related measures: steps to attract more and better teachers, and special efforts to reduce class sizes, through salary incentives and in other ways; special allocations in school-building programmes; experiments with what they called 'community schools', which would remain open beyond school hours for the use of children and their parents and in certain circumstances other members of the community. They proposed that the expansion of nursery education, which was another of the main recommendations of the Plowden Report (see following section), should begin in priority areas.

They also pressed for research to determine the relative effectiveness of the measures proposed, as a basis for longer term planning.

Government action on the Plowden proposals for educational priority areas

Government action on these proposals began soon after the publication of the Plowden Report. A circular of August 1967[49] announced a special building programme for the educational priority areas. Projects were not confined to the primary sector, but the major share of the additional resources went to primary schools. The Department gave general indications of the types of multiple deprivation that might justify authorities in selecting priority areas.

In the following year a special salary addition for qualified teachers in 'schools of exceptional difficulty' was agreed by the appropriate Burnham Committee. The criteria were the social and economic status of parents, the absence of amenities in the homes, a high uptake of free school meals and a high proportion of children with serious linguistic difficulties. Some 570 schools proposed by LEAs were formally recognised by the Secretary of State for this purpose. The Department also modified the teacher quota to help priority areas.

Also in 1968 the first phase of the urban programme was announced.[50] This was a programme sponsored jointly by the Home Office and the Departments of Education, the Environment, and Health and Social Security. Projects, both educational and other, authorised in the programme attracted a special rate of grant from central government (75 per cent on capital and current cost).

Projects that went to the roots of 'special social need', but that would not be undertaken in normal building programmes, were given priority; and priority in all sectors, including education, was given to projects designed to benefit very young children. Thus in the educational sector projects for nursery schools or classes were favoured in the initial stages because (before 1972) these could not normally be included in school-building programmes.

Arising out of another Plowden recommendation, the Department in 1968 joined with the Social Science Research Council in sponsoring a research project on educational priority areas.[51] This was designed to mobilise local initiative by teachers and others for a programme of action and research based on schools, with the objects of raising the educational performance of children, giving encouragement to teachers and increasing the involvement of parents.

The first volume of a report on this subject was published in 1972, with the title *Educational Priority*.[52] This endorsed the Plowden thesis that the concept of the educational priority area, despite difficulties of definition, was 'a socially and administratively viable unit through which to apply the principle of positive discrimination'. It also endorsed the Plowden Council's view that partnership between schools and families in priority areas was of first importance, and suggested practical ways of improving it. It wanted to see further experiments in the creation of community schools in these areas. It thought that, in the general approach to raising educational standards in educational priority areas, high priority should be given to preschooling. (See following section.)

The primary-school improvement programme
The Administration that came to office in June 1970 was committed to a policy of shifting the emphasis within the education budget in favour of primary schools. Their intention to do so was largely influenced by the Plowden thesis that all later education depends on the soundness of the foundations laid in the primary schools.[53]

Starting in the autumn of 1970 a substantial building programme was instituted, alongside that designed to accommodate increasing numbers, with the object of improving or replacing Victorian primary-school buildings, of which there were at that time about 7,500, containing $1\frac{1}{4}$ million pupils or a quarter of the total primary school population. The aim was to replace or bring up to date all primary schools built before 1903 for which there was a continuing need. In the four programmes of 1972–6 projects were included resulting in well over 2,000 of the pre-1903 primary schools being replaced or improved. Although not confined to deprived areas, this programme was to be of substantial benefit to them because a large proportion of Victorian schools were in these areas, and their continued existence was a factor tending to perpetuate deprivation.

THE UNDER-FIVES

The age at which compulsory education begins in England and Wales is lower than it is in most countries. Nevertheless, there has since 1918 been provision within the public system for preschool or nursery education, and the White Paper of 1943 attached importance to nursery provision, specially emphasising the need for it in the poorer parts of large cities, whose condition had been brought to public attention by the wartime evacuation of children.[54]

But the 1944 Act did not impose on LEAs a duty to make nursery provision. It said only that in fulfilling their duties to provide sufficient schools for their areas authorities should 'have regard' to the need to secure provision for under-fives (Education Act 1944, Section 8(2)(b)).

As things turned out, the implementation of this provision proved to be beyond the resources of most authorities in the early postwar years. Faced with large increases in school population and with acute problems of accommodation and teacher supply, authorities had to concentrate on meeting the needs of children of compulsory school age.

The Department was also primarily concerned in this period with ensuring that the needs of children of compulsory school age were met, and it was found necessary as a matter of national policy to impose strict limits on the provision for nursery education. Broadly the policy was to restrict the number of under-fives in school (other than rising-fives) to that reached in the mid-1950s,[55] and this policy continued in force, with minor adjustments, during most of the 1960s.

The Plowden Council's views on nursery education
During the 1960s there was growing concern in the educational world about the restrictions on nursery education. This found expression in the Plowden Report.[56]

The under-fives, the Plowden Council pointed out, were the only age group for whom no extra educational provision had been made since 1944. They found that in 1965 only about 7 per cent of all children under 5 were receiving education in a nursery school or class, the proportion having scarcely changed since the 1930s.

They pointed to the growing evidence that the years between 3 and 5 are crucial for the learning process.

They drew attention to aspects of modern life in cities whose effects on very young children must be a cause of concern: high-rise flats, increasing population movement, the gradual disappearance of the 'extended family', the growing number of mothers going out to work. They found that the proportion of married women in employment had doubled between 1931 and 1951, with a further rise since 1960, and that there was every prospect of the trend continuing. Many of these were mothers of young children.

They emphasised the special needs of children from deprived, broken or otherwise inadequate homes, children living in overcrowded premises and children with handicaps. They had before them research findings that indicated the extent to which nursery education could compensate for social deprivation and special handicap. They concluded that it had a major role to play in educational priority areas.

They did not overlook the arguments against nursery education, such as the danger of children being separated at too early an age from their mothers. Their view was that this was not an argument against nursery provision as such, but one for ensuring that it should not normally start before the age of 3, and that for most children it should be part-time rather than full-time.

They concluded that a large expansion of nursery education was needed. They believed that most of the needs could be met by part-time attendance, but that there might be some 15 per cent of children for whom full-time provision was desirable. They were clear that it should not be compulsory, but that it should be available for all whose parents wished their children to have it. They reckoned that provision would eventually be needed for 90 per cent of 4-year-olds and 50 per cent of 3-year-olds.

The provision should in their view be made by LEAs as part of the education service, and should be made without charge. They proposed that it should be made available in 'nursery groups' of twenty places, two or three of which groups might constitute a 'nursery centre'. Each unit should be under the authority of a qualified teacher, with help from experienced nursery assistants. Ideally all services for the care of young children, they thought, should be grouped together and sited near the children's homes and their primary schools.

They attached great importance to involving parents: 'Nursery education should throughout be an affair of co-operation between the nursery and the home and it will only succeed to the full if it carries the parents into partnership.'

Conscious that the shortage of teachers at that time would make the early attainment of their targets difficult, they proposed that until enough places could be provided in schools LEAs should be encouraged to assist nursery groups run by non-profit-making associations, which should be subject to inspection.

Government action to increase provision for the under-fives
From 1969 onwards, despite the restrictions of Circular 8/60 which were still in force, there was some increase in the number of under-fives in school, particularly where there were vacant places in primary schools as a result of a decline in primary numbers, and in areas of special need where nursery places could be provided under the urban programme. By the end of 1972 over 24,000 additional nursery places had been provided under this programme. (See previous section.)

A major advance came with the White Paper of December 1972. The Administration that took office in 1970 was committed to expanding nursery education, and plans for a nationwide expansion of education for under-fives was one of the White Paper's main features.

The government's aim, based on the Plowden and Gittins recommendations, was that within ten years nursery education should become available to all children of 3 and 4 whose parents wished them to have it, within the limits of demand estimated by the Plowden Council. It was to be available without charge.

The objectives of nursery education, the White Paper made clear, should be both educational and social. But while the value of nursery education in promoting the social development of young children was acknowledged, the government's main objective was to improve educational opportunities for the under-fives.

The educational case that influenced the government's thinking was that, given sympathetic and skilled supervision, children may make great educational progress before the age of 5, particularly in the use of language, in thought and in practical skills, which give a sound basis for subsequent stages of education. The extension of nursery education would also make possible the earlier identification of children with special difficulties, either social, psychological or medical.

The White Paper accepted the Plowden thesis that an important aspect of the new policy would lie in the opportunities that it could offer for families living in deprived areas. LEAs with substantial areas of social deprivation were to be given some priority in the initial allocation of resources.

The responsibility for expansion, the government believed, must rest with LEAs. They thought that most of the additional provision should take the form of classes for under-fives forming part of primary schools – an arrangement that avoids a change of school at 5. But such classes must be housed, staffed and equipped to meet the special needs of young children.

In preparing plans for expansion, LEAs were invited to take account of other forms of provision for under-fives, particularly the voluntary playgroups, which by 1972 were providing for over 250,000 children with substantially increased government support.

The government accepted the Plowden view that for most children part-time attendance was preferable until they reached compulsory school age, but that there would be some children, perhaps 15 per cent, who for educational reasons or because of home circumstances would benefit from attending full-time.

They stressed that provision for the under-fives, whether in deprived areas or elsewhere, should build on and not supplant parents' own efforts. Authorities were urged to profit from the experience of playgroups, the most successful of which had derived much strength from the support of parents. They pointed to the opportunities that nursery education offers for enlisting parents' understanding and support for what the schools are trying to achieve, which is vital to successful education at subsequent stages.

The White Paper accepted the need for research to monitor the effectiveness of the programme, and announced the government's intention to set up a research programme in conjunction with other departments concerned with social policy.[57]

Implementation began early in 1973 with the issue of a departmental circular,[58] superseding Circular 8/60, giving detailed guidance on the nature and scale of the expansion, the staffing and building implications, and related matters – such as arrangements for an increase in the output from colleges of education of teachers trained to teach the younger age groups, and for a substantial expansion in the number of trained nursery assistants.

While, as in other fields, progress has since been slowed by financial and other constraints, nursery education for all who need or want it remains a clear objective.

THE INDEPENDENT SECTOR

A familiar feature of the school system in England and Wales is the existence, for historical reasons peculiar to this country,[59] of a substantial independent sector, consisting of schools run by autonomous bodies of governors or individual proprietors, and financed by income from endowments and/or fees without any assistance from public funds.[60]

This sector includes the so-called 'public' schools (mainly boarding schools of the secondary grammar type), but also a considerable range of schools of other types: for example, 'preparatory' schools (many of them mainly boarding) for the 8–13 age group, local day schools and some schools for the handicapped. In January 1976 there were some 2,330 independent schools with over 414,500 pupils (about 4 per cent of all children of school age).

Before 1944 the Board of Education had no statutory powers of supervision of independent schools. From 1906 there were arrangements by which independent secondary schools that reached the standards of grant-aided secondary schools could voluntarily apply to the Board for inspection with a view to 'recognition as efficient' under what are now called the Department's Rules 16; and these arrangements were later extended to schools other than secondary. By 1938 some 750 schools in the independent sector, including most of the major public schools, had been recognised as efficient.

But there were many independent schools that were not subject to any effective public supervision, and the condition of some of these was becoming a matter of increasing public concern in the interwar years.

The 1943 White Paper announced the government's intention to introduce a system of compulsory registration and inspection of all independent schools, with provision to require the closure of any school found deficient unless the defects complained of were remedied. These proposals were given effect in Part III of the Education Act 1944, which was brought into operation in 1957.

Part III required the Minister to appoint one of his officers to be 'registrar of independent schools', and to keep a register of all independent schools. It required all such schools to apply for registration within a specified period, and it became an offence for anyone to conduct such a school unless it was registered or provisionally registered. Proprietors were required to furnish certain information, and to make their schools available for inspection at all reasonable times.

A procedure was laid down for cases where the Department's inquiries revealed serious defects. The Minister was required to serve on the proprietor a formal 'notice of complaint', specifying the matters complained of and, unless they were in the Minister's opinion irremediable, specifying the measures needed to remedy them. A school might be found objectionable on any or all of four counts: unsuitable premises, inadequate or unsuitable accommodation, lack of efficient instruction suitable for the pupils, or unsuitability of the proprietor or of a teacher.

The Act provided for the establishment of 'independent schools tribunals' to which any proprietor of an independent school receiving a notice of complaint, or any teacher judged to be unsuitable, might appeal. A tribunal might order that the complaint be annulled; it might direct that the school be struck off the register; it might order the disqualification of the premises or a part of them from use for school purposes, or the disqualification of an unsuitable proprietor or teacher.

If a school failed to meet the Minister's requirements within a given time, and the proprietor did not appeal, the Minister could make an order that a tribunal might have made had there been an appeal. Striking a school off the register in effect meant the closure of the school, since the Act made it an offence to conduct a school not on the register.

Most of the work of the registration and inspection of independent schools that were not already recognised as efficient was done in 1958. By the end of that year only 258 out of the 2,886 unrecognised independent schools in existence in England and Wales at that time remained 'provisionally registered'. The number of cases in which it has since proved necessary to serve notices of complaint has been relatively small, and the number of schools struck off the register as a result of failure to comply with the Department's requirements has been smaller still.

The effectiveness of the Part III provisions in achieving the aims envisaged in the 1943 White Paper is not to be judged solely by the number of schools struck off the register. The introduction of Part III led a number of schools whose fitness for final registration was in question to improve their standards. A considerable number closed down voluntarily, many of them no doubt because they felt unable to satisfy the Department's requirements. Between 1958 and 1977 the number of unrecognised independent schools fell from 2,886 to 1,952, while there was no corresponding increase in the number of schools recognised as efficient.

Throughout the period since 1944 it has been the Department's policy to encourage independent schools to aim at higher standards than those required for registration under Part III, and to seek to qualify for recognition as efficient.

The relationship between the independent and maintained sectors
The presence within the independent sector of a small minority of unsatisfactory schools was, and is, far from being the only cause for public interest in, and concern about, this sector. With the expansion of the maintained sector in the first four decades of the century, and with the change in public attitudes to the role of education in society, the very existence of an independent sector, and particularly the presence within it of a relatively small group of schools of high academic attainment and prestige, became, as the Public Schools Commission remarked in 1968, a 'perennial topic of discussion'. Ideas for reform have ranged from outright abolition of the independent sector to closer association of the independent schools, or some of them, with the maintained sector.

This is not the place to discuss the various proposals for reform of the independent sector in any detail, since they have remained largely unimplemented and have thus not formed part of the work of the Department. But it may be relevant to note briefly the findings of two reports about this sector by government-appointed committees or commissions.

During the Second World War, Mr Butler (as he then was) set up a committee under the chairmanship of Lord Fleming to advise on how best to extend the association between the public schools and the national educational system.[61] A number of the Fleming Committee's proposals concerned the public boarding schools, which were potentially of importance because the 1944 Act, in laying on LEAs the duty to provide or secure the availability of sufficient schools of various types in their area, specifically mentioned the desirability of boarding education.

Among the Fleming proposals was one for associating the public boarding schools more closely with the maintained system by providing that any such schools that wished to do so should take a minimum of 25 per cent of pupils from grant-aided primary schools, who would either be awarded bursaries by the Ministry or fill places reserved by LEAs (for which they would receive grant aid from the Ministry).

Little came of the Fleming scheme. The Education Acts 1944 and 1953 required LEAs to pay for boarding, without charge to the parents, if it was arranged because suitable education could not otherwise be provided for a child, as well as empowering them in other circumstances to help with the payment of fees and boarding charges. The onus of exercising these functions was left on LEAs; and although some independent school places were taken up by some LEAs, or filled with their help, the number was at no time significant, and it may be said that as an instrument of national policy the Fleming proposal became a dead letter. Fundamentally this was because, at a time when the expansion of the public sector and rising school population were making heavy demands on resources, neither the government nor the LEAs were in a position to give priority to a scheme that would have entailed large expenditure for a relatively very small number of children.

The Labour Administration that came to office in 1964 was pledged to find ways of integrating the public schools into the state system of education, and in 1965 the then Secretary of State set up a Public Schools Commission[62] to advise on the best way of achieving this aim.

This commission was also particularly concerned with the contribution that the private sector could make in helping to meet the national need for boarding education. The central feature of their scheme was a proposal that independent boarding schools that were suitable and willing to be integrated into the national system should make at least half their places available to pupils in need of boarding education. In most cases schools would be required to admit pupils from a wide range of ability. All pupils deemed to be in need of boarding education were to be entitled to free tuition, together with assistance (subject to a parental contribution based on an income scale) towards maintenance expenses.[63]

In their second report[64] the Public Schools Commission considered what should be done about the independent day schools and also the direct-grant grammar schools. Their main recommendation on the independent day schools was that LEAs should take up places and pay the full fees where a child required a particular kind of educational provision, or education of a particular denomination, that was not available in an accessible maintained school or college of further education, or direct grant school.

NOTES AND REFERENCES

1 Subsequently amended by the Education (Miscellaneous Provisions) Act 1953 and the Education (No. 1) Act 1968.
2 Sir Amherst Selby-Bigge, *The Board of Education*, Whitehall Series (London and New York, Putnam, 1927), p. 36.
3 Much of this section applies to other educational building also.
4 Ministry of Education, *Annual Report 1900–1950*, ch. 8, para. 7.
5 Loan charges for educational buildings are 'relevant expenditure' for rate support grant purposes. Loan sanction is automatic once the Department's building-programme approval has been given.
6 Circular 13/68.
7 Circulars 12/73 and 15/73.
8 Circular 13/74 of 31 December 1974.
9 Building Bulletins, Nos 1– ; Design Notes, Nos 1– .
10 Both Scotland and Wales were ahead of England at this time. In Scotland the school boards had been empowered to provide secondary education from 1872. Public secondary education had become generally available in Wales as a result of the Welsh Intermediate Act 1889.
11 White Paper, *Educational Reconstruction*, Cmnd 6458 (London, HMSO, 1943), para. 17.
12 Section 8(1). Lord Butler has pointed out that neither the 1944 Act nor the White Paper that preceded it ruled out the creation of what were at that time called multilateral schools (Lord Butler, *The Art of the Possible*, London, Hamish Hamilton, 1971, p. 123).
13 Board of Education, *Report of the Committee of the Secondary School Examinations Council appointed by the president of the Board* (Mr Butler, as he then was) *under the chairmanship of Sir Cyril Norwood* (the Norwood Report) (London, HMSO, 1943).
14 Norwood Report, op. cit., pt I, ch. 1. Both the Spens and Norwood Reports contemplated the possibility of 'multilateral' schools, but on the whole they did not favour them. They believed that such schools would have to be very large.
15 *The Nation's Schools: their Place and Purpose*, Ministry of Education Pamphlet No. 1 (London, HMSO, 1945).
16 The term 'comprehensive' only came into general use in the 1950s. Strictly speaking, a multilateral school is not the same thing as a comprehensive school; the former consists of separate types of school located on the same site, while in the latter the separate elements are integrated in a single school. In practice the former has tended to develop into the latter.
17 One such area was the Welsh county of Anglesey, whose development plan submitted to the Ministry in 1946 proposed that secondary education for the entire island should be provided in five 'multilateral' secondary schools. This plan was approved by the Ministry.

18 Circular 73 of 12 December 1945. Both the Anglesey and London plans were approved by the Ministry.
19 White Paper, *Secondary Education for All: A New Drive*, Cmnd 604 (London, HMSO, December 1958).
20 ibid.
21 Circular 289 of 9 July 1955.
22 *Fifteen to Eighteen: Report of the Central Advisory Council for Education (England)* (the Crowther Report) (London, HMSO, 1959), Vol. 1, paras 614ff.
23 Quoted in the introduction to *Half Our Future: Report of the Central Advisory Council for Education (England)* (the Newsom Report) (London, HMSO, 1963).
24 Circular 10/65 of 12 July 1965.
25 'Only those actually in the business can begin to realise how much administrative time and effort has gone into planning, reappraising, investigating, negotiating, and afterwards implementing, schemes [of reorganisation]' (Derek Birley, *The Education Officer and His World*, London, Routledge & Kegan Paul, 1970, p. 60).
26 Circular 10/70 of 30 June 1970.
27 Circular 4/74 of 16 April 1974.
28 Address to the annual conference of the National Union of Teachers, 16 April 1974.
29 Board of Education, *Secondary Education, with Special Reference to Grammar Schools and Technical High Schools: Report of the Consultative Committee on Secondary Education under the Chairmanship of Sir William Spens* (the Spens Report) (London, HMSO, 1938), ch. IX, pt V, section 19.
30 Crowther Report, op. cit., chs 11 and 12.
31 Newsom Report, op. cit., para. 20.
32 See Circular 8/71 of 24 August 1971. Subsequently legislation was passed, after consultation with the Trades Union Congress, making it possible for school pupils to have periods of work experience in factories, shops and offices as part of their studies (Education (Work Experience) Act 1973).
33 Except in aided secondary schools, and any other schools whose rules of management or articles of government provide otherwise.
34 *Report of the Schools Inquiry Commission* (Taunton Report) (London, HMSO, 1868).
35 Board of Education, *Report of the Consultative Committee on External Examinations in Secondary Schools*, Cmnd 6004 (London, HMSO, 1911).
36 Circular 996 of May 1917.
37 Circular 113 of 26 June 1946.
38 A ninth board, mainly representative of further education, was added later. The number of GCE examining bodies has since been reduced again to eight.
39 In addition there were scholarship papers (sometimes described as 'S' level) to give specially able pupils a chance to show merit or promise, and to help university selectors. Scholarship papers were discontinued after 1962, when the Department ceased to offer ordinary state scholarships. Following a recommendation in *The General Certificate of Education and Sixth-Form Studies: Third Report of the Secondary School Examinations Council* (London, HMSO, 1960), examining bodies thereafter offered 'special' papers for candidates of high ability.
40 See Circulars 227, 5/62 and the Schools Council booklet *GCE and CSE: A Guide to Secondary School Examinations* (London, Evans/Methuen Educational, 1973).
41 Circular 289 of 9 July 1955. A regulation that forbade the entering of under-age pupils for any other external examinations was kept in force.

42 *Fourth Report of the Secondary School Examinations Council* (London, HMSO, 1961).
43 In the event fourteen were approved.
44 *Fifth Report of the Secondary School Examinations Council* (London, HMSO, 1962) and *Seventh Report etc.* (1963).
45 DES, *Education in Schools: A Consultative Document*, Cmnd 6869 (London, HMSO, 1977).
46 *Educational Reconstruction*, op. cit., paras 36 and following.
47 DES, *Children and their Primary Schools: Report of the Central Advisory Council for Education (England)* (Chairman: Lady Plowden, JP) (the Plowden Report) (London, HMSO, 1967), A corresponding report by the Central Advisory Council for Education (Wales) (the Gittins Report) appeared at about the same time.
48 Plowden Report, op. cit., ch. 5, paras 131–75.
49 Circular 11/67.
50 In Circular 19/68, issued in conjunction with the Home Office, Department of Health and Social Security and Department of the Environment.
51 Directed by Dr A. H. Halsey of the Department of Social and Administrative Studies at Oxford, and undertaken by four research teams in collaboration with four LEAs, having major educational priority areas: namely, the ILEA, Yorkshire (West Riding), Birmingham and Liverpool. There was a similar project in Scotland.
52 Detailed accounts of the work of the project in five areas and attempts at evaluating their successes and failures were published in subsequent volumes.
53 White Paper, *Education: A Framework for Expansion*, Cmnd 5174 (London, HMSO, 1972), para. 37.
54 *Educational Reconstruction*, op. cit., para. 25.
55 Circular 8/60 of 31 May 1960.
56 Plowden Report, op. cit., ch 9, paras 291 and following.
57 A management committee under the Department's chairmanship was subsequently established to commission and monitor projects.
58 Circular 2/73 of 31 January 1973.
59 For the historical background see Board of Education, *The Public Schools and the General Educational System*, Report of the Committee on Public Schools appointed by the President of the Board of Education in July 1942 (under the chairmanship of Lord Fleming) (London, HMSO, 1944); DES, *The Public Schools Commission: First Report* (London, HMSO, 1968).
60 Except to the extent that in some cases fees were paid in full or in part by LEAs.
61 *Public Schools and the General Educational System*, op. cit.
62 Under the chairmanship of the late Sir John Newsom. The Commission was later reconstituted under the chairmanship of Professor David Donnison and given new terms of reference.
63 DES, *The Public Schools Commission: First Report* (London, HMSO, 1968).
64 DES. *The Public Schools Commission: Second Report* (London, HMSO, 1970).

CHAPTER 7

Teachers and Teacher Training

THE FRAMEWORK

The main problem of any service of public education is to provide an adequate staff of well-educated and skilful teachers, working under conditions favourable to the effective and zealous performance of their duties . . . The corps of teachers occupies the key position in the strategy of education.[1]

In this country the Department, as earlier explained, does not itself employ teachers. Within the maintained system the teachers are employed either by the local education authorities (LEAs) or by the governing body of schools and are therefore not civil servants.[2] However, the Department is concerned, both statutorily and in other ways, with the qualifications, training, supply, salaries and superannuation of teachers in the maintained system, both in schools and in further education. This chapter is concerned with teachers for the schools.

The Department has a further concern with the arrangements for training teachers. The colleges in which most intending teachers receive their professional education and training form part of the higher education system, along with the universities and the colleges providing advanced further education, and the courses they offer are amongst the options open to school leavers wishing to continue their studies.

Teachers' qualifications and arrangements for training

The Secretary of State lays down by regulation the basic qualifications required of teachers in the schools. All teachers employed in a full professional capacity in maintained and special schools, except for certain very small categories, must achieve the status of 'qualified teacher', which is conferred by the Secretary of State.

Normally this is obtained in one of two ways: by successful completion of an initial course of professional training at a college of education or other such establishment, or by possession of a special qualification approved for the purpose, the most common being a degree of a university in the British Isles. Although both graduates and others using the latter route have long been encouraged to take in addition a one-year course of professional training, they were during most of the 1950s and 1960s able to obtain qualified teacher status on the strength of their specially approved qualification alone. The regulations, however, now normally require those graduating or obtaining other specially approved qualifications to have successfully completed an initial course of professional training before they become eligible to be qualified teachers.[3]

All qualified teachers on first appointment are required to serve a probationary period (of one year for trained teachers and two years for others) to demonstrate their practical proficiency.

Training colleges were first established in the nineteenth century by church bodies. The churches have maintained their interest in teacher training, and a number of the colleges are 'voluntary' colleges provided by church bodies, the running costs being in general met from the Exchequer. The Balfour Act 1902 empowered the LEAs which it brought into being to establish and maintain their own training colleges, and by 1944 a substantial majority of the colleges were LEA maintained.

Until the beginning of the 1970s almost all the colleges of education (as training colleges came to be called) were 'monotechnics', existing for the sole purpose of providing vocational training for teachers. Following the 1972 White Paper *Education: A Framework for Expansion*, colleges have been encouraged to diversify their work and, where feasible, to merge with other establishments of higher or further education.

From the 1890s the universities began to establish teacher-training departments, now usually called university departments of education (UDEs). Most universities in England and Wales now have UDEs. These provide one-year courses of postgraduate professional training for teaching. Recently a number of polytechnics have established education departments, in some cases through amalgamation with former colleges of education.

The Education Act 1944 and the McNair reforms
Almost from the time that it began to grant-aid schools, the central department has concerned itself closely with the training of school teachers.

The Education Act 1944 put on the Minister a duty to ensure the availability of sufficient facilities for the training of teachers, and empowered him to direct LEAs to establish, maintain or assist colleges or to contribute financially to other authorities providing them.

After 1944 there was a radical reorganisation of training arrangements, based on the McNair Report,[4] one of the major reports commissioned by the Board when the 1944 Act was in preparation.

One of the main McNair recommendations was that the Minister should recognise only one grade of teacher, namely, a 'qualified teacher', and that – subject to his having discretion to accord recognition to anyone with good academic or other attainments – qualified status should be obtained only by satisfactory completion of an approved course of education and training. This recommendation was accepted by the government, and one of its consequences has been that any qualified teacher can teach in any maintained school and teachers are not, as in many countries, limited to working for a particular age group or type of school. (In practice the age range and subjects in which a teacher has specialised are likely to be taken into account by his employing authority.)

Another major McNair proposal was that all training arrangements in both UDEs and training colleges should come within the scope of an 'area training service' covering the whole of England and Wales, and that in each area there should be an 'area training organisation' (ATO), based on a university but comprising all the colleges in the area, which would be responsible for college curricula and syllabuses, for the assessment of students and for other related matters. These recommendations were also, in the main, accepted by the government of the day. ATOs were established to cover the country, in almost all cases under the general direction of university institutes of education financed (like the UDEs) by the University Grants Committee. Within this framework the colleges retained their individual identity, financed by LEAs or by the central department as before.

The universities thus came to have a dual role within the system, the UDEs providing courses of training and also opportunities for research, and the university institutes of education having a wider role as the centres of the ATOs.[5] The arrangements for governing the institutes were devised to give the LEAs and the teachers in the area a substantial share along with the universities in the control of their work.

The Ministry also accepted a proposal by the committee for the establishment of a National Advisory Council for the Training and Supply of Teachers (NACTST), with representatives of the universities, the LEAs, the teachers, and the training interests. This advised on major national issues of both training and supply until 1965 when it was discontinued. In 1973 a somewhat similar committee was established entitled the Advisory Committee on the Supply and Training of Teachers (ACSTT). (See p. 128 and following.)

The McNair Committee had also wanted to see the normal course in the colleges extended from two to three years. In the situation of acute teacher shortage in the immediate aftermath of the war it proved impracticable to carry out this recommendation. It was eventually implemented in 1960.

The framework provided by the 1944 Act and the McNair proposals continued substantially unchanged up to the early 1970s. Within this framework the ATOs were responsible for supervising courses of training in their member colleges, for conducting examinations and recommending successful students for qualified teacher status, and for planning the development of training facilities in their area, including in-service training.

The role of the Department, with the advice until 1965 of the NACTST and subsequently of the ACSTT, is to supervise and plan the development of the system as a whole: the number of institutions and their size and character, the total number of students and the proportions to be trained to teach various age groups. The Department has no direct financial control, but there is indirect control through the Department's involvement in the determination of rate support grant; through the supervisory arrangements for pooling the cost of training (all expenditure incurred by LEAs on initial training in the maintained colleges and some expenditure on in-service training is chargeable to the teacher-training pool); through capital investment; and through control of the number and categories of students admitted to training. The Department directly controls the expenditure of the voluntary colleges.

All the colleges are run in accordance with regulations made by the Secretary of State, which lay down broad specifications about the suitability of premises, the nature and duration of courses, the admission and health of students, and the number and suitability of teaching staff.

HM Inspectors also have a considerable role. Each college and polytechnic department of education has an HM Inspector assigned to it, who advises on the general running of the courses, on the curriculum and on related matters such as arrangements for teaching practice. HM Inspectors organise courses for serving teachers, which along with courses organised by LEAs and other bodies are an important element in the growing provision of in-service training.

The UDEs are not subject to the controls described above. A member of HM Inspectorate acts as liaison with each university department.

Academic and other developments since 1944

A major academic development in the colleges was the implementation in 1960 of the McNair recommendation to extend the period of initial training to three years. Courses consist of a combination of advanced personal education and professional training, provided concurrently. Students take one or, in some cases, two main subjects in depth and two or three subsidiary subjects. On the professional side they study the psychology, philosophy, history and sociology of education, and a range of studies in teaching method according to the phase of education for which they are preparing. All courses include substantial periods of observation and teaching practice in schools.

As the greater part of the colleges' efforts has been devoted to training for primary teaching, there has been an emphasis on professional studies relevant to the teaching of the younger age groups, on subjects such as physical education, handicrafts and housecraft for which there is little or no provision in universities, and on other subjects for which the supply of graduates is insufficient. There are special courses for intending teachers of specialised subjects such as art and music.

Another important academic development of recent years arose out of a recommendation in the Robbins Report. The Robbins Committee thought that students from the colleges should have the opportunity of obtaining degrees related to their professional training, and recommended that four-year courses leading to both a degree and a professional qualification should be provided in the colleges for suitable students, a successful candidate being awarded a Bachelor of Education (BEd) degree by the university with which the college was linked. They thought that there should also be opportunities for serving teachers to obtain this qualification by part-time study. These recommendations were accepted by the government of the day. In 1964 universities were invited to work out arrangements with the colleges, and by 1970 nearly all colleges were providing such opportunities.

A third development, in this case of an administrative character, also arose indirectly out of the Robbins Report. The Robbins Committee had wanted to see the colleges in each area incorporated, along with the UDEs, into schools of education, responsible in academic matters to university senates. The government did not accept this proposal as it stood. They believed that, given the continuing shortage of teachers at that time and the effectiveness with which the LEAs and voluntary bodies had developed the colleges, the balance of advantage lay in retaining the then existing arrangements for the financing of the colleges, under the general supervision of the Department.

They accepted, however, that provisions for governing the colleges should be reviewed to see if they could be given more autonomy, and in December 1964 the then Secretary of State set up a study group under a senior official of the Department[6] to make proposals. The conclusions of this group formed the basis for new legislation,[7] which applied to all maintained colleges of education and also to major establishments of further education.

All maintained colleges are required to have governing bodies constituted in accordance with articles of government, which must be approved by the Department and designed to give these bodies a certain degree of autonomy. They must include members of the academic staff (amongst them the principal), of the teachers in the area and of the university concerned, as well as of the maintaining authority or voluntary body. Most governing bodies include student representatives. All colleges must have an academic board.[8]

The James Report and government action arising

For the teacher-training system, and particularly for the colleges, the 1960s were a period of massive expansion. In the ten years from 1961–2 to 1971–2 the numbers on initial training rose from fewer than 40,000 to nearly 120,000. However, by the end of the 1960s there was increasing public disquiet about the way in which the system was developing. Partly this was the inevitable consequence of the scale and rate of expansion, but there were also more specific grounds for concern.

Amongst the LEAs which employed teachers there was a feeling that the training system was in too many cases turning out teachers inadequately prepared to cope with the needs of the schools. And there were many, both in the colleges and in the educational world generally, who were becoming increasingly aware of the disadvantages of colleges devoted solely to teacher training and wanted to see the colleges associating more closely with other sectors of higher education and diversifying their activities.

Amongst teachers themselves there was disquiet about the continued existence of two avenues of access to qualified teacher status: one through the universities (often without professional training) and another through the colleges. This was felt to have a divisive effect on the profession. Although the introduction of the BEd had done something to mitigate this, there was a growing demand for an all-graduate profession, with similar pre-entry training for all.

There was thus a widespread demand for a national inquiry into teacher training. In 1969 the House of Commons asked its own recently established Select Committee on Education and Science to undertake an investigation,[9] and early in 1970 the then Secretary of

State invited all ATOs to undertake reviews of their courses and procedures.

The government which came into office in the summer of 1970 were committed to instituting a national inquiry, and late in 1970 the then Secretary of State appointed a small committee, under the chairmanship of Lord James of Rusholme, to undertake a speedy inquiry. The committee were asked to look into the content and organisation of courses and to consider what should be the role of the colleges of education, the polytechnics and the universities respectively in the training of teachers, and whether ways could be found of training a larger proportion of intending teachers alongside students not intending to teach. The committee reported in December 1972.[10]

The James Committee, while acknowledging the achievements of the system during two decades of unprecedented expansion, found that it was 'no longer adequate to its purposes'. This inadequacy, they thought, arose basically from an overdependence on initial training which was insufficient to equip teachers for a lifetime's service in the schools with their constantly changing needs. They also thought that the task of the profession was made more difficult by the existence of an 'unhelpful' distinction between two kinds of training.

Their proposals to remedy these weaknesses were based, as regards teachers for the schools,[11] on five main objectives: a large and systematic expansion of in-service training; a planned reinforcement of the process of induction of probationary teachers; progressive achievement of an all-graduate profession; the full acceptance of the colleges into the family of higher education institutions; and improved arrangements for the co-ordination of teacher training and supply both nationally and regionally. A feature of their proposals for in-service training was a recommendation that every qualified teacher should have an entitlement to periods of in-service training on full pay.

The Secretary of State's consultations on the James Report revealed general support for the committee's main objectives, and these were endorsed by the government. Some of their concrete proposals were also widely accepted; others proved controversial.

There was acceptance in principle of their proposals for in-service training, and the government in the White Paper of December 1972 announced their intention to put in hand a substantial expansion of in-service training, building up to a point at which 3 per cent of the teaching force would be released at any one time. (This was in line with the James Committee's proposal.)

There was also widespread support for the committee's view that the induction of probationary teachers needed reinforcement, although not necessarily on the lines proposed by the committee. The government's view was that teachers' initial professional training must include sufficient practical experience to enable them to take their place in the schools as teachers who were qualified although still subject to probation. The government concluded that they should have not more than three-quarters of a full teaching load and should be released for one-fifth of their time during this period for in-service training. The plans then announced for the growth of the teaching force assumed that LEAs would engage the additional teachers needed to make this possible. It was agreed that the teaching profession itself should play a major role in the induction process, and that a network of professional centres in existing training institutions and teachers' centres should be developed.

The government made clear their intention to work towards an all-graduate profession. They envisaged a new three-year course, incorporating educational studies, which would lead both to the award of a BEd degree and to qualified status. The degree would normally be an ordinary degree, but those attaining a high standard would be able to continue for a fourth year to take a BEd (Hons). The greater length of the college year as compared with that in universities would permit the inclusion of at least fifteen weeks' supervised practical experience. Since the courses would be degree courses the normal entry requirements would be two 'A' levels, but it was recognised that for a limited period the certificate courses (for which two 'A' levels are not required) would need to be continued alongside the BEd courses. The awards would be validated by the existing awarding bodies. It would be for the colleges to plan the courses and in doing so to achieve the right balance between academic and professional requirements.

Bearing in mind the interests of the uncommitted student, the government wanted to see the courses so planned that the first two years could lead to a qualification acceptable in its own right as a terminal qualification. They believed that there was a need for a qualification on the lines of the Diploma in Higher Education (DipHE) proposed by the James Committee, but with wider application – i.e. one attainable after two years of higher education, at a level as intellectually demanding as the first two years of a university degree course – and they had found that there was sufficient support to justify the introduction of such an award.

The government agreed with the committee's view that a restructuring of the organisation and administration of teacher training was needed, although they did not favour the committee's detailed proposals, which would have involved the creation of a system largely divorced from the universities.

The White Paper distinguished four functions which need to be discharged nationally in relation to teacher training: academic validation, professional recognition, co-ordination, and higher education supply (that is, in this context teacher supply).

The government took the view that academic validation should remain the responsibility of existing academic bodies: the universities and the Council for National Academic Awards (CNAA).

On professional recognition they thought it right in principle that the teaching profession (including teachers in colleges and UDEs) should have a major although not exclusive role, and that future arrangements should reflect this principle. They shared the view, expressed in a report of a working party presented to the Secretary of State in 1970,[12] that a separate body, namely, a teaching council, was desirable. But they were clear that this function must remain the responsibility of the Secretary of State unless and until the outcome of discussions in train led to the establishment of a teaching council with which it could be shared.

On co-ordination the government proposed that after further consultation the existing university-based ATOs should be replaced by new regional committees. But they made it clear that the demarcation of suitable regions would have to await decisions on other matters.

They agreed with the James Committee that improved national arrangements were needed to look after teacher supply, and announced their intention of establishing the ACSTT referred to earlier.

The closer association of the colleges with the higher education system
The government attached importance to enabling the colleges to find an assured place within the higher education system and at the same time to diversify their role, Two major considerations were involved. The first was that because of the fall-off in the rate of growth of school population there would no longer be a need for the teacher force to expand at the rate then prevailing. The second was that the government's plans for the expansion of higher education as a whole (see Chapter 10) could be achieved only if, alongside the build-up in universities and polytechnics, a substantial contribution could be made by other institutions, including the colleges. What was involved, as a subsequent circular explained,[13] was 'a major reconsideration of the future role of the colleges of education'.

Subject to geographical considerations, the government hoped to see some colleges, either singly or jointly, developing into major institutions of higher education, concentrating on the arts and human sciences, with particular reference to their application to teaching and other professions. Others might combine forces with neighbouring polytechnics or colleges of further education to fill a somewhat similar role. The possibility that some colleges might be incorporated in universities was not ruled out. It was envisaged that a number of colleges might have to close.

THE SUPPLY OF TEACHERS FOR SCHOOLS

As earlier explained, there are two main sources of supply of newly qualified teachers for the schools: the colleges of education and the universities. (A third source which has assumed increasing importance in recent years is the qualified married woman who returns to teaching after raising a family. See p. 130.) The system that the Department inherited from the prewar period was geared to circumstances in which the school population was more or less static. In 1938, when there were eighty-seven colleges, mostly with two-year courses, and twenty-two UDEs, the output of the training system (including about 1,800 from UDEs) was about 6,000 a year. The number of teachers of all categories in grant-aided schools was less than 200,000.

In the immediate postwar period, the decline in recruitment during the war years and the raising of the school leaving age to 15 in 1947 led to an acute shortage of teachers. To meet this the Ministry mounted a special operation: the emergency training scheme. This was financed from Exchequer funds and consisted of crash courses lasting thirteen months, mostly in improvised premises, for men and women returning from the Forces. In six years this scheme produced some 35,000 teachers.[14]

In 1951 when this scheme was being wound up, the newly established NACTST was already warning that the shortage of teachers was likely to continue and that an expansion of permanent training arrangements would be needed. At that time there were differing views about the probable future trend of births, but by the later 1950s it became clear that shortage of teachers would be a persistent problem. Indeed for most of the three decades following the 1944 Act the securing of an adequate supply of teachers to meet the needs of a growing school population was one of the Department's major preoccupations.

The continuing increase in births was not the only factor responsible; another was the large and continuing loss of women teachers. One of the characteristics of the teaching profession is that it is particularly suitable for women. In the postwar period a high proportion of these have been women in the younger age groups; and with the trend towards earlier marriage a growing number of these have been leaving the profession to marry within a few years of completing their training. It came to be recognised that the women who left early were not necessarily lost to teaching. Many might return to teaching when their children were old enough, and from the early 1960s the Department began to make efforts to attract 'married returners'. But recruitment from this source, although eventually to become substantial, could not be built up quickly, and in the 1950s and 1960s the outflow far exceeded recruitment.

In the 1950s the annual 'net increase' of teachers (that is, the excess of recruitment over wastage) was running at not much more than 5,000–6,000. This was barely adequate even to meet the demands of the schools in terms of numbers and was quite inadequate to provide for the improvements in quality envisaged by the 1944 Act.

By the mid-1950s the situation became so serious that several areas which had difficulty in attracting teachers were faced with short-time working or even closure of schools. In 1956 the then Minister, in consultation with the local authority and teachers' associations, instituted what was in effect a scheme of rationing of the distribution of teachers amongst authorities. The main purpose of this device, which came to be known as the 'teacher quota', was to ensure that authorities which found it relatively easy to recruit teachers held back improvement of their staffing standards so that more teachers would be available for shortage areas. The scheme was administered by the Department acting on behalf of the local authority associations. It had no statutory basis; it rested on a voluntary agreement between the Department and the LEAs. It continued in operation until 1976, when it was replaced by new arrangements for monitoring LEAs' staffing standards.

The expansion of recruitment from 1958
From the end of the 1950s the Department, as advised in a series of Reports by the NACTST, embarked on measures to step up training provision. In 1962 a new branch was created within the Department to deal specifically with problems of teacher supply. Plans were made to increase the number of places in the colleges to 80,000 by 1970, permitting an annual intake to the colleges of about 27,500.

Further expansion came as a result of proposals in the Robbins Report for the expansion of higher education. The government accepted a Robbins recommendation that the colleges should aim for an annual intake of 40,000. This involved increasing the number of places in the colleges to 111,000 by 1973–4.

At the same time the massive expansion of the universities provided for by the government in response to the Robbins Report (see Chapter 9) resulted in a greatly increased flow of university graduates into school teaching.

In 1965 further steps were taken to increase the intake into the colleges and other institutions in the maintained sector, for example, by filling spaces left empty by students on teaching practice. The combined effect of all these measures and of the expanded building programme accompanying them was that the Robbins target for 1973–4 was achieved by 1970.

By the early 1970s a 'net increase' approaching 20,000 a year had been achieved. By autumn 1972 there were over 400,000 qualified teachers in maintained primary and secondary schools (including part-timers) – something like twice the 1938 figure. Despite the very large increase in school rolls the national pupil–teacher ratio had by then improved from 24·6 in 1961 to 22·0. (A roughly comparable figure for 1937–8 was 30·1.) The proportion of primary classes with over forty pupils fell in the same period from 14·4 per cent to 2·5 per cent.[15]

Teacher supply proposals in the 1972 White Paper, and subsequent developments

A continued expansion of the teaching force, accompanied by measures to improve its quality and training, were amongst the major objectives of the 1972 White Paper *Education: A Framework for Expansion*. By this time, as a result of the measures taken to build up the sources of supply of teachers, and of the slowing down in the rate of increase of school population, there was some easing of the pressure of sheer numbers and an opportunity to pay more attention to the quality of teaching – in particular to staffing ratios. The government took the view that there should be a continuing improvement of staffing standards during the 1970s and beyond. They thought it reasonable to aim by 1981 at a teaching force that was 10 per cent above the number needed to maintain the staffing standards prevailing in 1971. Additional teachers would be needed over and above this to carry out the government's policy of implementing the James recommendations on in-service training and the induction of new teachers. Allowing for these factors, for the continued (although slowing) growth of school population and also for the additional teachers required for the nursery programme, the government saw a broad requirement by 1981 for a teaching force of some 510,000 (full-time equivalent) qualified teachers in maintained schools, representing an overall pupil–teacher ratio of about 18·5. This was the objective that the White Paper proposed as the basis of planning for the period to 1981.

Target figures of this kind for a number of years ahead necessarily involve major uncertainties and may be subject to extensive revision. These problems are well illustrated by the course of events subsequent to the publication of the 1972 White Paper. A steady decline in the birth rate, and thus in the prospective school population, created a substantially new situation, which early in 1975 made necessary a downward revision of the 1981 teacher target figure from the 510,000 proposed in the 1972 White Paper to 480,000–490,000 – a range that would nevertheless have allowed the attainment of more generous staffing standards than those contemplated in 1972.

However, because of constraints on public expenditure modified plans for school staffing, announced early in 1976, allowed no provision for improvement in staffing standards.[16] This inevitably meant sharp reductions in the intake of students for teacher training, and this in turn involved an accelerated programme of mergers or closures of colleges of education.

TEACHERS' SALARIES AND SUPERANNUATION

The Burnham machinery

From 1902, when LEAs took over the payment of teachers' salaries in the schools that they maintained, until after the First World War, there was no national machinery for agreeing teachers' salaries. Scales were fixed by individual authorities and varied widely from area to area. This was a cause of much dissatisfaction.

In 1918 the then President of the Board of Education, H. A. L. Fisher, called conferences with the local authorities' and teachers' associations which led to the establishment of a standing joint committee 'to secure the orderly and progressive solution of the salary problem . . . by agreement on a national basis'.[17] The first chairman of this joint committee, and of similar committees for salaries in secondary and technical schools, was Lord Burnham, and he has bequeathed his name to subsequent arrangements.

The Board's attitude at that time was that, in view of the decentralised nature of the service, settlements on a national basis should be agreed between the teachers and their employing authorities acting collectively. But the Board was inevitably concerned, both because of the importance of salary questions for the satisfactory working of the school system and because substantial Exchequer funds were involved. It therefore required that settlements should have its concurrence. Settlements were not then mandatory, but the Board could in the last resort withhold grant to secure compliance.

The Education Act 1944 put the arrangements on a statutory basis. The relevant section (Section 89) required the Minister to secure that there should be one or more committees approved by him, with a chairman nominated by him, consisting of LEA and teacher representatives, whose duty would be to submit recommendations on salary scales. If the Minister approved, he might make an Order which was then mandatory on employing authorities.

The Burnham Committees were reconstituted, with a single committee to deal with primary and secondary schools, a second to deal with teachers in technical institutions and a third to deal with those in farm institutes.[18] Each consisted of a local authorities' panel and a teachers' panel between whom negotiations took place with a view to submitting agreed recommendations to the Minister. The Minister could either accept or reject the recommendations put to him but could not amend them. There was no provision for arbitration, and there was also no explicit provision for retrospective settlements.

By the early 1960s it had become evident that from the government's point of view it was unsatisfactory that the Minister had no options other than those of accepting or rejecting the committees' recommendations, and no means of influencing the broad policies underlying the recommendations made. In 1963 the then Minister announced his intention to introduce legislation to ensure that each of the parties in the education service, including the Minister, should have a role in the negotiating procedure.

The consequential legislation received the Royal Assent as the Remuneration of Teachers Act 1965. This provides for committees to be constituted broadly as before, but with representatives of the Secretary of State on the management panels. The Secretary of State determines which bodies are to be represented on the two panels and the number to be appointed by each body.

The Act makes an agreement in a committee binding on the Secretary of State, who must implement it without amendment by statutory instrument. But the Secretary of State's position is safeguarded in two ways. First, a concordat within the management panel between the Department and the local authority associations gives the Secretary of State a veto on an offer if he objects to the total cost involved. Secondly, the Department's representatives have a vote weighted at about 37 per cent of the whole management panel in discussions on the distribution of the agreed amount. In practice votes are rare, but the departmental representatives take part in panel discussions.

There is provision for arbitration. Either panel can propose a reference to arbitration, but in the event of the other panel refusing to agree the independent chairman decides the stage at which the negotiations can be held to have run their full course so that arbitration has become necessary. The recommendations of arbitrators, like an agreement in a committee, are binding on the Secretary of State, but they can be set aside by a resolution by both Houses of Parliament on grounds of national economic circumstances. There have been a number of arbitrations since 1965, but the procedure for setting aside an award has never been used.

Teachers' superannuation
The central department has concerned itself with schemes for teachers' superannuation for more than a century, and from 1898 onwards it has been responsible for legislation governing teachers' superannuation schemes and for their administration.

An Act of 1918 prescribed a scheme which has remained unchanged in its basic pattern. Major revisions of the scheme were made in 1956 and 1972, and numerous other changes have been made from time to time.

The scheme prescribed by the 1918 Act was non-contributory. Acts in 1922 and 1925 required contributions from teachers and subsequently from employers. The rates of contributions were increased to meet the increased cost of benefits resulting from the major revision in 1956, and employers were in addition made liable to pay supplementary contributions to offset actuarial deficiencies. Contributions were again increased, for the same reason, following the major revision in 1972, but the teachers' contribution subsequently reverted to its former rate on the principle that it should be related to the level rather than the cost of the benefits. In other schemes with a similar level of benefits, notably the local government scheme, the employees' contribution was still at the 1956 rate.

An Act of 1965 allowed a teacher to provide for a widow or other dependant by making an additional percentage contribution, the scheme for this purpose and the fund formed by teachers' contributions being administered by the Department under the general direction of a board of management representing teachers (in the majority) and employers. The separate family benefits scheme was discontinued in 1972, since when an integrated scheme providing both personal and family benefits has obtained.

In 1967 new regulations provided for part-time as well as full-time service to count for pension purposes.

Provision to increase pensions already in payment to take account of increased living costs has been made by a series of Pensions (Increase) Acts, applicable to all public service superannuation schemes. The 1971 Act provided for a system of annual reviews.

It is worth remarking that the administration of the teachers' superannuation scheme is one of the few areas in which the Department has executive functions, employing a sizable group of executive and clerical staff for the purpose.

NOTES AND REFERENCES

1 Sir Amherst Selby-Bigge, *The Board of Education*, Whitehall Series (London and New York, Putnam, 1927), p. 247.

2 H. A. L. Fisher records that he at one time 'toyed' with the idea of making teachers civil servants: 'But on a closer view the policy disclosed such a prospect of danger to educational freedom and to a wholesome variety of experimentation, such a menace to local responsibility and so formidable an accretion of work and power to the Board at Whitehall, that I dismissed it from my mind' (*An Unfinished Autobiography*, London, OUP, 1940, pp. 96–7).

3 Circular 11/73.

4 *Teachers and Youth Leaders*, report of the committee appointed by the President of the Board of Education to consider the supply, recruitment and training of teachers and youth leaders (the McNair Report) (London, HMSO, 1944).

5 Some universities have schools of education which combine these functions.

6 Mr T. R. (later Sir Toby) Weaver.

7 Education (No. 2) Act 1968. Similar provisions relating to voluntary colleges are contained in regulations.

8 Circular 22/68 of 9 September 1968.

9 Select Committee on Education and Science (Session 1969–70), *Teacher Training*, HC 182 (London, HMSO, 1970).

10 DES, *Teacher Training and Education*, report by a Committee of Inquiry appointed by the Secretary of State for Education and Science (Chairman: Lord James of Rusholme (the James Report) (London, HMSO, 1972).

11 The Committee also had proposals on teachers for further education.

12 *A Teaching Council for England and Wales* (London, HMSO, 1970).

13 Circular 7/73 of 23 March 1973.

14 The story of this scheme was told in *Challenge and Response*, Ministry of Education Pamphlet No. 17 (London, HMSO, 1950).

15 Prior to 1969 it was the practice to measure improvement of staffing ratios in terms of the reduction in 'oversize' classes, that is, classes in excess of the numbers laid down in regulations then current, which were forty for primary schools and thirty for secondary schools. The regulations laying down these maximum sizes were, with wide agreement, amended in 1969 (Circular 16/69). It is now widely accepted that national staffing objectives are better defined in terms of national pupil–teacher ratios.

16 *Public Expenditure 1979–80*, Cmnd 6393 (London, HMSO, 1976), p. 87, para. 7.

17 Selby-Bigge, op. cit., p. 262.

18 Salaries of staffs in colleges and departments of education were settled outside this machinery by a broadly similar body known as the Pelham Committee. In 1976 the Burnham Further Education Committee was reconstituted and its remit extended to embrace farm institutes and the former maintained colleges of education. The farm institutes and Pelham Committees were accordingly disbanded.

CHAPTER 8

Further Education

THE FRAMEWORK

Further education in England and Wales is usually taken to mean all forms of postschool education other than that provided by universities and colleges of education (but see Chapter 1). It includes a wide range of vocational education, but also general education, the youth service and adult education. This has been one of the fastest growing sectors of the maintained system since 1944. Numbers of students in major establishments have more than doubled. There has been extensive new building of colleges. By the early 1970s LEAs' expenditure on further education accounted for over 18 per cent of their total expenditure, compared with about 5 per cent in 1947. This is also a sector in which there have been valuable innovations: in types of institution, in courses and in examining arrangements.

Further education before 1944

Central government was involved in the promotion of technical education and the monitoring of standards from the 1850s, and local authorities have been empowered to supply or aid technical instruction since the 1880s. But throughout the nineteenth century provision in this country compared unfavourably with that in other European countries, and at the turn of the century this was widely held to be one of the reasons why Britain was falling behind her industrial competitors.

There was only limited progress during the first four decades of this century. The LEAs had no duty to provide, and the Board had no powers to make them do so. The further education system was still largely a local service. Most of those who aimed at high technological qualifications had to come up 'the hard way' – by pursuing part-time study, usually in evening classes, while supporting themselves by employment. The technical colleges lacked both resources and prestige. There were no colleges in this country with the standing of, say, the technical high schools of Switzerland or the Netherlands.

After the First World War an attempt was made, in the Fisher Act, to bring into being a nationwide scheme for 'day continuation schools' to be attended part-time by all young people up to the age of 15 who were not in school. But the scheme was not regarded with favour by employers. It was one of the casualties of the Geddes Axe of 1921–2, and no attempt was made to revive it nationally, although in some areas where there were enlightened firms day release centres were built up by LEAs on a voluntary basis.

Further education provisions of the Education Act 1944
One of the major reforms effected by the Education Act 1944 was the translation of the LEAs' power to provide into a duty. Further education became one of the three progressive stages of the statutory system of education. A duty was laid on all authorities to secure the provision of 'adequate facilities' for it in their areas, and the Ministry was given the responsibility and the powers to ensure that LEAs carried out their duties in this sector (Education Act 1944, Sections 41 and following).

The new arrangements were to comprise two related elements. There was to be a major expansion of technical, commercial and art education, and of leisure-time cultural and recreational provision. And there was to be a nationwide provision of county colleges on the lines of Fisher's day continuation schools, which all children under 18 not in school would be required to attend part-time.

LEAs were required to submit 'schemes' of further education for their areas,[1] and these, when approved, became mandatory. In practice these schemes have ceased to be of primary importance in determining the shape of LEAs' provision. But it has come to be generally recognised that LEAs have an obligation to ensure the provision of courses in all cases where there is demonstrable and continuing demand.

LEAs are not themselves required to provide all the facilities for further education in their area. They must 'secure provision'. They may do so by assisting or encouraging various existing institutions or bodies, and other LEAs, as well as by providing themselves. Thus in the youth field it is common practice for LEAs to work through voluntary youth organisations. But systematic technical and vocational education is mostly provided in colleges which the LEAs themselves maintain,[2] and it is to the building up of these that their main efforts in this sector have been devoted.

THE DEPARTMENT'S ROLE

In further education, as in the schools sector, the Department does not itself provide and maintain establishments,[3] or employ the teachers in them. The Department's role is that of supervision to maintain standards and national planning of development. Ministers have certain specific powers, both statutory and other, for this purpose, as well as general powers and means of influence.

The need for ministerial approval of authorities' schemes has been mentioned. In addition there are regulations which lay down conditions to be met by authorities in such matters as the suitability of colleges' premises and equipment, the arrangements for employment of teachers, and the approval of new advanced courses.

Building by LEAs in the further education sector is controlled through educational building programmes operated in much the same way as those in the schools sector, that is, by means of three-year rolling programmes.

The requirement with regard to new advanced courses is important. No new course of an advanced character[4] may be started without the prior approval of the Secretary of State. Proposals by colleges for the establishment of such courses are considered in each region by a senior HM Inspector, the 'regional staff inspector', in consultation with the regional advisory council for further education in the region. Decisions on approval are taken in a regional or national context in the light of total student demand for a particular course. The purpose of this control is to ensure that advanced courses which may make heavy demands on staff and costly specialised facilities are started only where an adequate and continuing intake of students can be foreseen and there is no unnecessary duplication.

The Department does not directly control LEAs' expenditure on further education[5]; but, as in other sectors, there is indirect control through the Department's involvement in the determination of rate support grant (the forecasting of LEAs' expenditure is related, for the purposes of both rate support grant and public expenditure surveys, to the Department's forecasts of student numbers) and in pooling arrangements (the cost of advanced courses is met from a pool to which all LEAs contribute on an agreed basis.)

Every maintained college that provides full-time education is required by law (Education (No. 2) Act 1968; see previous Chapter) to have an instrument of government providing for the constitution of a governing body approved by the LEA, operating under articles of government approved by the Secretary of State. Governing bodies may not form part of the LEA's committee structure. These arrangements afford the governing bodies of individual colleges a measure of academic and administrative autonomy, the extent of which varies according to the size and level of work of the individual college.

In further education as in the schools sector the Department is involved through the Burnham machinery in the determination of national scales for teachers' salaries.

The role of HM Inspectorate

HM Inspectors have traditionally had a close concern with the curriculum in the further education sector. There is no body in further education corresponding to the Schools Council. Their role in monitoring the distribution of advanced courses has already been mentioned. And they are involved in varying degrees with the bodies controlling further education courses and examinations. Thus they have been active in helping to establish the National Certificate and Diploma courses and serving on the joint committees that administer them. They often serve as assessors for the Department on the committees of independent examining bodies such as the City and Guilds of London Institute and the regional examining bodies, on the Council for National Academic Awards (CNAA) and its subject panels, on the National Council for Diplomas in Art and Design (NCDAD), and on many others.

Advisory machinery

In planning the development of further education the Department may call on the help of a number of advisory bodies. For nearly thirty years the major advisory body was the National Advisory Council on Education for Industry and Commerce (NACEIC). Set up in 1948, this was widely representative of both sides of industry and commerce as well as LEAs and teachers, the majority being nominated by the Secretary of State on the advice of the regional advisory councils for further education (see following paragraph). This body, or committees appointed by it, produced a number of influential reports: for example, one in 1950 on the development of higher technological education which led to the establishment of the National Council for Technological Awards (see p. 145); one in 1958 on further education for commerce; one in 1964 on day release (see below, p. 141); several reports on agricultural education; and one in 1969 on courses and examinations at technician and equivalent levels (see p. 147). The NACEIC was wound up at the end of 1977.

At the regional level there is a framework of regional advisory councils for further education. There are ten such councils: nine in England and one in Wales. They operate within constitutions agreed amongst the participating LEAs and are financed by them. Their constitutions as a rule provide for a membership drawn from LEA members and officials, universities and polytechnics in the region, principals and teachers of further education colleges and co-opted members, mainly people representing both sides of industry and commerce. Each regional advisory council has its own small permanent staff. HM Inspectors serve as assessors.

Much of the work of the NACEIC was done through committees set up for particular purposes: for example, successive advisory committees on agricultural education, or the Haslegrave Committee on education at technician and equivalent levels. (See p. 147 and following.)

A separate National Advisory Council on Art Education (NACAE) was set up in 1959 and produced some influential reports. When the membership came up for review at the end of 1971 the Secretary of State decided not to reconstitute the council immediately, but to consider as future needs arose how best to draw on opinion and guidance in this sector of further education.

An essential function of these and other advisory bodies in further education is to provide a framework for continuing discussion on policies between the Department, the world of industry, commerce and the arts, and the LEAs and teachers who have to put policies into effect.

STAGES OF DEVELOPMENT OF FURTHER EDUCATION SINCE 1944

In the early postwar years progress in the further education sector was inhibited by lack of resources and the pressing demands of the schools. But there were major developments from the mid-1950s onwards. It may be convenient, if somewhat arbitrary, to single out five main stages of advance.

The 1956 White Paper Technical Education
The first came in 1956 with the government's White Paper *Technical Education*[6] and the resulting drive for new technical-college building. This reflected the widespread apprehension felt at the time that Britain was falling behind other advanced countries, particularly the USA and the USSR, in the output of highly qualified scientists and technologists and of supporting technicians.

As part of a plan to meet this need (which also included new developments at universities), the White Paper foreshadowed a five-year programme to increase by over 50 per cent the numbers qualifying by advanced courses at technical colleges. It announced the government's intention to select a small number of leading colleges for designation as 'colleges of advanced technology', which would concentrate on advanced work. It was envisaged that many of the students at these colleges would follow courses leading to the Diploma in Technology of the National Council of Technological Awards (the Hives Council), a body constituted at the end of 1954 with the object of establishing standards in technological courses in the colleges equivalent to those of honours degree courses in universities.

Other technical colleges were classified into three categories according to the level of courses offered.[7] There were to be 'regional' colleges providing a substantial amount of advanced work in full-time and 'sandwich' courses; 'area' colleges also providing advanced work, mainly for part-time Higher National Certificate (HNC) courses, along with lower-level work; and 'local' colleges providing only non-advanced and mainly part-time work. A sandwich course is one in which students spend alternate periods in college and employment, the aim being to integrate the full-time study of the theoretical principles of particular subjects with industrial practice and the student's own experience. In many cases students on sandwich courses are sponsored by their future employers. 'Day release' is the system by which employers free employees with pay, usually for one day a week, to attend courses of further education which are commonly arranged in association with the industry or commerce concerned. In recent years a number of colleges have made provision for an alternative to day release in the form of 'block release', that is, release for periods of some weeks at a time involving full-time study at a college. All colleges providing advanced courses were to qualify for a special rate of grant in respect of their advanced work.

Corresponding increases were envisaged in provision at technician and lower levels. The White Paper set as a target the doubling of the numbers of young employees given day release by their firms to obtain technical qualifications.[8]

To help to achieve these targets the government undertook to make available for technical college building in the period 1956–61 capital resources that were almost double those allocated in the previous decade.

The 1961 White Paper Better Opportunities in Technical Education[9]
The second stage of development mainly concerned students at less advanced levels, that is, those on courses for technicians, craftsmen and operatives. By the beginning of the 1960s there were already about half a million such students in the colleges, but the government wanted to see a further large increase in the opportunities open to the rapidly growing numbers coming up through the secondary schools.

The provision existing at that time was unsatisfactory in several ways. There was lack of continuity between school and technical college; courses were often not adequately adapted to the increasingly sophisticated needs of industry, particularly at 'technician' level; and wastage rates were high.

One of this White Paper's main proposals was that students should start technical college courses immediately after leaving school. A new type of 'general' or diagnostic course was instituted which students would enter straight from school. This was designed to last two years in the case of the 15-year-old leaver and one year for those leaving at 16, and to lead either to a technician course or to an Ordinary National Certificate (ONC) or Diploma (OND) course.

The standard of entry to ONC courses was raised in most cases to four appropriate General Certificate of Education (GCE) 'O' levels, and their duration was reduced from three years (part-time) to two. A new range of technician courses for particular industries was planned for those not able to reach the standard of entry to ONC. There was to be extensive development of craft and operatives' courses, and the government again looked for an increase in day release.[10]

Technical colleges and industrial training

A third major area of development has been that related to industrial training, in particular to the Industrial Training Act 1964 and the Employment and Training Act 1973. The Department was closely associated with the preparation of these Acts and with their implementation, although statutory responsibility rests with what is now the Department of Employment.

The basic aims of the Industrial Training Act, as outlined in the White Paper[11] that preceded it, were 'to enable decisions on the scale of training to be better related to economic needs and technological developments; to improve the overall quality of industrial training and to establish minimum standards; and to enable the cost to be more fairly spread'. The Act empowered the then Minister of Labour to set up industrial training boards to be responsible for all aspects of training in individual industries. A board's main statutory duties were: to provide or secure the provision of training; to make recommendations on the content and length of training for occupations in its industry and on the further education to be associated with the training; to raise a levy upon its industry; and to give the Minister such information as he required.

There was provision for education members to be appointed to boards, after consultation with the Minister of Education; and also for education members to be appointed to the Central Training

Council, which was to advise the Minister on the exercise of his functions under the Act.

By 1970 twenty-seven statutory boards (and one statutory sub-committee) were in operation, covering industries employing about 15 million people, and with a total levy income of about £200 million. About 90 per cent of their expenditure was on grants to employers, largely offset against levy due from them.

This Act, and the training boards it created, involved the further education service in two main ways. First, the formulation of recommendations on training and associated further education led to the planning of new further education courses, and the revision of existing ones, to complement industrial training. Thus the Engineering Industrial Training Board's requirements gave rise to a new scheme of engineering craft studies courses, superseding the existing craft practice courses.[12] Of particular interest also was the development of integrated courses of training and associated further education, followed full-time in colleges by first-year apprentices in engineering, construction, road transport and other industries. Formal machinery, based on the Council of Technical Examining Bodies,[13] was developed for the joint planning by boards and the education service of training and further education.

Secondly, the further education service was involved through the operation of boards' grant schemes. These were based on board recommendations covering further education as well as training, to be met by employers as a condition of grant. In 1965 the then Minister of Labour said that he would not normally approve a grant scheme unless it provided, as a condition of grant, for day release for all young people in occupations requiring substantial training, that is, training lasting about a year or longer. A considerable part of grant paid annually by boards related to education and training activities in further education colleges – day release, sandwich and full-time courses, management and supervisory courses, training of officers, and so forth.

It was hoped that these measures would result in a substantial increase in the numbers receiving systematic further education as part of their training, and more particularly in the numbers on day release. In the event these hopes were to be only partially realised. The targets for day release in 1969–70 that had been proposed in the Henniker-Heaton Report of 1964 were in the event not attained.

The Administration which took office in 1970 announced its intention to carry out a fundamental review of national arrangements for training, and in February 1972 it published a consultative document, *Training for the Future*. After extensive consultations, proposals for new legislation were set out in a Bill and an explanatory White Paper.[14] The Bill received the Royal Assent as the Employment and Training Act 1973. This established a Manpower Services Commission, responsible to the Secretary of State for Employment, consisting of representatives of employers and workers and of local government and education interests. It was to be responsible for the management and development of employment and training services previously run by the Department of Employment (other than careers services for people attending and leaving education, laid by the Act on LEAs). Two agencies, the Training Services Agency and the Employment Service Agency, were to form the executive arms of the commission. The commission would rely on the co-operation of the education service in several aspects of its work, and arrangements were made for consultation and liaison both nationally and locally. The commission came into being in January 1974.

The Training Services Agency became responsible for government training services (mainly the new training opportunities scheme announced in August 1972); it was to co-ordinate the work of the industrial training boards and to have general responsibilities for training in sectors not covered by the boards. The Act made significant amendments to the Industrial Training Act 1964, notably in replacing the levy/grant system by a levy/grant/exemption system, making the raising of a levy permissive rather than mandatory (although still subject to ministerial order), setting an upper limit to levy (normally 1 per cent of payroll), and providing grant-in-aid to meet boards' administrative expenses and to promote training through grants for key training activities such as off-the-job training of apprentices and technicians.

The training opportunities scheme was an important new government initiative to meet the training needs of individuals, as distinct from those of employers and industry which were the concern of the boards. It included the continuing and growing work of the government vocational-training scheme, but it greatly expanded the scale and nature of training opportunities to include all levels of occupation, from semiskilled to managerial and professional. A great variety of vocational further education courses lasting up to a year was made available for adults. The government undertook to meet the cost of training and supporting trainees. The aim was to train several thousand people a year by 1975, reaching an annual target of 100,000 as soon as possible thereafter. Extensive use was to be made of facilities in colleges of further education.

The growth of advanced further education: the Council for National Academic Awards
A fourth stage of development, involving advanced further education, stemmed from the Robbins Report of 1963. The Robbins Committee

had regarded advanced work provided in the technical colleges as coming within their terms of reference, and their report contained one recommendation affecting this sector which was to prove of very great importance.

This was their proposal that the National Council for Technological Awards should be replaced by a council, to be called the Council for National Academic Awards (CNAA), established under royal charter, with power to award both degrees and higher degrees to students in maintained colleges outside the university sector.

This recommendation was accepted by the government and quickly implemented. The CNAA received its charter in September 1964. By 1965 it had set up boards of studies for each of the main subject fields, and by 1965-6 there were eighty-four CNAA degree courses in progress, with some 4,000 students. CNAA degree courses have come to provide an alternative to the University of London external degree system, which, being entirely external, was open to the criticism that it afforded the colleges little or no influence on syllabuses or examinations. The CNAA and its boards have from the outset aimed for close working relations with the colleges. Colleges devise their own courses and syllabuses, generally in consultation with the relevant industry or professional body; and once the CNAA is satisfied that courses are of appropriate standard and that college facilities are adequate, the college is free to conduct courses and examinations, subject to moderation by the CNAA. Teacher representatives on the CNAA have a voice in determining its general policy. A notable feature of CNAA courses is the admissibility of course work in the final assessment of students.

In the early stages the CNAA was mainly concerned with technological subjects, and one of its early decisions was retrospectively to validate the awards of the National Council for Technological Awards as degree awards. Courses are now approved in a much wider range of subjects, for example, business studies, sociology and librarianship. The CNAA has also instituted higher degrees, both masters' and doctors'.

A high proportion of the courses approved are of the full-time or sandwich type, but the CNAA is also prepared to approve part-time courses, and these are increasing in number.

In the matter of standards the CNAA has from the beginning set itself the aim proposed by the Robbins Committee of ensuring that its degrees should be in fact as well as in name equivalent to those of universities. It is widely agreed that this aim has been achieved. It is also widely accepted that the CNAA system is one particularly suited for courses closely geared to industry and commerce, and one which encourages experiment and innovation.

The comparable body for degree-level courses in art and design is the National Council for Diplomas in Art and Design (NCDAD). This body was created as a result of the First Report of the National Advisory Council on Art Education (NACAE), and its courses were first introduced in 1963. Its awards at degree level were referred to as the Diploma in Art and Design (DipAD) and at postgraduate stage as the Higher Diploma in Art and the Higher Diploma in Design. Recommendations for a broadening of the structure of DipAD courses and changes in arrangements for entry and preparation were made by a joint committee of the NACAE and the NCDAD which reported in 1971.

Early in 1973 the CNAA and the NCDAD announced jointly that they had decided in principle that they wished to amalgamate. This decision was given effect on 1 September 1974.

The polytechnics
In the later 1960s the numbers on advanced courses in the technical colleges built up rapidly for a number of reasons: the establishment of the CNAA, the increased output from the secondary schools, improved student grants resulting from the Education Act 1962, and growing awareness in industry that students educated in this type of course were particularly well suited to its needs. It also came to be seen that, from the point of view of national policy for higher education, there were advantages in encouraging the development of a variety of institutions. These views, which had been implicit in the policy of developing advanced education within the maintained sector pursued by governments of both parties, were made explicit in speeches by ministers during the 1960s. At this time the policy of developing higher education in both the university and the maintained sector was commonly referred to as the 'binary' policy.

In pursuance of this line of thought, the government in May 1966 published a White Paper, *A Plan for Polytechnics and Other Colleges*.[15] This proposed that there should be a limited number of major centres in the maintained sector, mainly for students aged 18 and over, concentrating on degree and other advanced-level work in a wide range of subjects. These centres were to be designated as 'polytechnics'. They would aim at a student population of some 2,000 students doing advanced full-time or sandwich courses, together with advanced part-time students drawn from their areas. They were to be primarily teaching institutions, and to develop further the close links that the constituent colleges already had with industry and commerce. Their governing bodies were to be given considerable autonomy on lines foreshadowing the Education (No. 2) Act 1968. (See Chapter 7.)

The White Paper did not specify the exact number of colleges to be designated as polytechnics. But it included a provisional list of colleges and groups of colleges (some fifty institutions in all) which *prima facie* appeared to be suitable to constitute some twenty-eight polytechnics. In 1967 the Secretary of State informed Parliament that, having completed his review of this provisional list in the light of views expressed by regional advisory councils for further education and other bodies, he proposed to make one further addition to the list and also accepted the need for a second addition later. By November 1974 thirty polytechnics had been designated, and these contained some 159,000 students.

One of the characteristics of the polytechnics, as their name implies, is the wide range of subjects covered (with the consequent possibility of interdisciplinary studies). Another is the variety of levels at which subjects may be studied. The polytechnics offer not only courses leading to degrees and higher degrees but also advanced courses below degree level. Thus a student who finds a degree course too exacting may be able to transfer to another at a lower level, or vice versa.

A substantial proportion of polytechnic students are on courses of the sandwich type, or on part-time courses designed to cater for the needs of local industry. Polytechnics usually also offer a wide range of 'degree-equivalent' courses, part-time as well as full-time and sandwich, leading to the qualifications of professional bodies or (where they have incorporated colleges of art) to awards in art and design. A number of polytechnics have developed education departments.

Since their creation the polytechnics have established for themselves a distinctive role in the system of higher education. In the 1972 White Paper, *Education: A Framework for Expansion*, the government of that time put on record that they had been 'impressed by the speed and vigour' with which the polytechnics had 'assumed and pursued their innovative task', and announced their intention to allot to them a major share in the expansion of higher education during the remainder of the decade. (See Chapter 10.)

The Technician and Business Education Councils
Parallel with these developments in advanced further education, a fifth stage of development may be noted at what may be broadly described as technician level, that is, the very wide range of courses between degree work at one end and craft work at the other. Towards the end of the 1960s the NACEIC turned its attention to this area of the colleges' work and set up a committee under the chairmanship of Dr H. L. Haslegrave to consider its needs. The Haslegrave Report,

published in December 1969, recommended the establishment of a Technician Education Council and a Business Education Council, each with responsibility in its sector for planning and developing a new unified pattern of courses for technician and equivalent students (the term 'technician' has no equivalent in the business world). These new courses are intended eventually to replace the courses for National Certificates and Diplomas and those for the technician-level qualifications of the City and Guilds of London Institute.

The Technician Education Council was established by the Secretary of State in March 1973, and the Business Education Council in May 1974.

Adult education

Most of the provision for the education of adults is made by LEAs as part of their further education arrangements, in the form of courses in a wide range of vocational, cultural and recreational subjects, in evening institutes or centres. In some instances these may have their own premises. More often they are housed in school premises. In some areas colleges of further education provide courses for adults as well as for the younger age-groups. Several LEAs also maintain residential colleges, or centres, often housed in country mansions, offering short-term courses for adults ranging from a weekend to a week or more. LEAs make grants, to which the Department may also contribute, towards the cost of erecting village halls and community centres, where local funds are also forthcoming.

Courses in liberal adult education are also provided by university extramural departments and by certain voluntary bodies, notably branches of the Workers' Educational Association (WEA). These are directly grant aided by the Department as 'responsible bodies' under the further education regulations, and they may also receive help from LEAs. The Department also directly aids six 'long-term' residential colleges, such as Ruskin College in Oxford and Coleg Harlech in Wales, which offer courses for adult students lasting for one year or more.

Provision for all forms of adult education was the subject of an inquiry by a committee appointed by the Secretary of State in February 1969 under the chairmanship of Sir Lionel Russell. This committee reported in 1973.[16] This was not an area in which development could be expected to command a high priority in a period of economic constraint.

The youth service

The youth service is operated as a partnership between the public authorities and voluntary youth organisations. LEAs maintain their own youth clubs and centres as part of their further education provision. In most cases they also give assistance to branches of voluntary bodies towards both current expenses and the capital cost of building projects. The Department may also make contributions towards the capital cost of such projects. And it makes grants towards the headquarters administrative costs of a number of national youth organisations, for example, the Young Men's Christian Association (YMCA) and Young Women's Christian Association (YWCA), the National Associations of Youth Clubs and Boys' Clubs, the Boys' Brigade, the Scouts and Girl Guides.

COLLEGES, COURSES AND STUDENT NUMBERS: GROWTH SINCE 1947

There are about 620 major establishments of further education in England and Wales, ranging from the polytechnics concentrating on advanced work to local colleges offering mainly part-time courses for those in the 16–18 age range, although many also offer full-time courses for students aiming at GCE and similar qualifications. Table 8.1. gives some idea of the growth of numbers in this sector from 1947 to 1975.

Table 8.1 *Students in major establishments of further education*

		1947[1]	1975
All students	about	700,000	1,943,000
Full-time	less than	50,000	351,000[2]
Sandwich		—	47,000
Part-time day	less than	200,000	744,000
Evening		450,000	802,000
Students released by their employers		159,000	541,000
Students on advanced courses		40,000[3]	250,900
Students on degree courses	about	10,000[3]	70,000

[1] The figures given for 1947 are not strictly comparable with those for 1975, as during this period the coverage of the statistics has been extended and many definitions have been changed. Nevertheless it is possible with some adjustments to give figures for the two dates which are broadly comparable and indicate the main trends.
[2] Including about 12,000 students on initial teacher-training courses.
[3] Excluding a certain number on evening courses.

There are some 7,300 LEA-maintained evening institutes or centres providing courses of adult education, mainly in vocational and recreational subjects.

There are forty-four responsible bodies, mainly extramural

departments of universities and districts of the WEA, providing courses of liberal adult education. Growth over the period from 1947–8 to 1975 is shown in Table 8.2.

Table 8.2 *Adult education (figures to the nearest thousand).*

	1947	1975
Provision by LEAs (mainly in evening institutes)	0·75 m.	1·982 m.
Provision by responsible bodies	140,000	275,000

NOTES AND REFERENCES

1 LEAs were also required to submit plans for county colleges. This provision has never been implemented on the lines envisaged in the Act. But it has been the aim of successive administrations to encourage day release on a voluntary basis.

2 Certain of the older-established institutions are 'assisted', not maintained.

3 A few specialist colleges are directly grant aided by the Department. There are also a number of independent specialist establishments which are recognised as efficient by the Department.

4 An advanced course in this context is, broadly, any course (lasting more than one month full-time or forty hours part-time) having a minimum entry age of 18 and being of a standard above ONC or GCE 'A' level.

5 Except that the regulations require the Department's approval for individual items of teaching or research equipment costing £1,000 or more.

6 White Paper, *Technical Education*, Cmnd 9703 (London, HMSO, 1956).

7 Circular 305 of 21 June 1956.

8 From 350,000 to 700,000.

9 White Paper, *Better Opportunities in Technical Education*, Cmnd 1254 (London, HMSO, 1961) See also Circular 1/61.

10 DES, *Day Release*, report of a committee set up by the Minister of Education in 1962 (Chairman: Mr C. Henniker-Heaton) to inquire into day release recommended that there should be a target of at least an additional 250,000 boys and girls obtaining day release by 1969–70 (the Henniker-Heaton Report, London, HMSO, 1964).

11 White Paper, *Industrial Training: Government Proposals*, Cmnd 1892 (London, HMSO, December 1962).

12 Administrative Memoranda 2/69 and 12/70.

13 Administrative Memorandum 25/67.

14 White Paper, *Employment and Training: Government Proposals*, Cmnd 5250 (London, HMSO, March 1973).

15 White Paper, *A Plan for Polytechnics and Other Colleges*, Cmnd 3006 (London, HMSO, 1966).

16 *Adult Education: A Plan for Development: Report of the Committee on Adult Education* (the Russell Report) (London, HMSO, 1973).

PART THREE

The Department and the Universities

CHAPTER 9

The University Grants Committee;
the Robbins Report; Student Grants

HISTORICAL BACKGROUND AND FRAMEWORK

In no part of the educational scene in Britain[1] has the transformation been greater than in the university sector. When the Forster Act reached the statute book in 1870 there were only four universities in England – Oxford and Cambridge, which were then still Anglican preserves, and London and Durham – and four in Scotland. When the Board of Education came into being in 1900, charters had been granted to only two more universities in England (Manchester and Birmingham; the latter received its charter in 1900) and to the federal University of Wales, although others existed in embryo as university colleges. The total student population at this time was about 20,000. Even in 1939 there were only twelve universities and five university colleges in England and Wales; and these, with the Scottish universities, had a total student population of about 50,000. By 1975–6 there were forty-three universities in Great Britain, with a student population of over 261,000.

There have also been far-reaching changes in the arrangements for financing the universities and the students attending them. Before 1900 most universities were self-supporting. Only a few of the newer civic foundations were aided on a small scale from Exchequer funds. Even after the First World War, when the universities were suffering from the after effects of four years of war, government grants to universities in Great Britain and Ireland (excluding Oxford and Cambridge, whose needs were at that time being examined by a royal commission) totalled about £1 million. In 1976–7 recurrent grants to universities in Great Britain (excluding the Open University) totalled over £600 million. Exchequer assistance accounted for not far short of three-quarters of the universities' recurrent costs and a still higher proportion of their capital costs.

In 1900 the number of students receiving assistance from public funds was insignificant. As late as 1938 probably less than a sixth of all students were in receipt of awards from the Board or from local education authorities (LEAs). By the 1970s the proportion was over 90 per cent.

The Department's concern with the universities

It is a much-prized characteristic of British universities, modern as well as ancient, that they are self-governing institutions, usually operating under the provisions of royal charters, with virtually complete academic autonomy and a large measure of administrative autonomy, which they have for the most part retained despite their growing dependence on public funds. The Department is, however, directly concerned with the universities in several ways.

Its most important responsibility, although in point of time its most recently acquired one, is that of grant-aiding them as institutions. Since 1964 grants to universities and university colleges have been carried on the Department's vote. They are distributed on the advice of the University Grants Committee (UGC), which also advises the government on the financial needs of the university sector as a whole. (See p. 158.)

Secondly, the Department is concerned with the salary scales of academic staff in universities. There is a special negotiating machinery, involving the university authorities, university teachers and the Department. The scales apply nationally, and the government normally meets the cost of salary awards by supplementing the universities' recurrent grants.

Thirdly, the Department is concerned with grants to university students (in England and Wales). Most home-based students receive grants from public funds towards their fees and maintenance. Payments to individual students (other than postgraduate students) are made not by the Department but by LEAs. But the Department frames the regulations determining the amounts and conditions of awards, is responsible for general policy on student grants and pays 90 per cent grant on LEAs' expenditure on them.

Fourthly, because of the Secretary of State's responsibility for the supply and training of teachers, the Department is closely concerned with the work of the university departments of education (UDEs) and, during their lifetime, with that of the university-based area training organisations. It also has a more general concern with the output of university graduates in so far as they are potential recruits for teaching in the schools.

Fifthly, the Department is concerned with the universities' work in adult education, making direct grants to university extramural departments providing courses of liberal adult education.

Less directly, the Department is involved with the universities in its capacity as the department responsible for civil science, because a substantial proportion of the science budget for which the Secretary of State is responsible is applied by the research councils to the support of scientific research, and training in research, in universities. (See Chapter 13.)

The Department is also interested in the universities' activities in the field of secondary school examinations and in such matters as the entrance requirements and admissions policies of universities, because of the effects that these have on the schools. And it has a close interest in the work of universities in educational research.

This chapter deals mainly with the Department's responsibilities under the first and third of these heads: namely, the financing of the universities as institutions, and student grants.

Government grants to universities: Origins of the University Grants Committee

To the outside observer it may seem a characteristic oddity of the British educational system that during a crucial period of expansion of the universities in the two decades after the Second World War the responsibility for grant aiding them lay not with the Department but with the Treasury. This is not, as is sometimes supposed, an arrangement of great antiquity; it is of quite recent origin.

Government assistance to individual universities had started on a small scale in the 1880s. When the Board of Education came into being in 1900 it took over the payment of most of these grants, although in some cases the moneys continued to be paid directly by the Treasury, and in 1910 a Universities Branch of the Board was established. At about the same time an Advisory Committee was appointed to advise the Board on their distribution.

Immediately after the First World War, at a time when the civic universities urgently needed increased aid and Oxford and Cambridge were also asking for help, the arrangements were changed. It was decided that all grants to the universities as institutions should be paid directly by the Treasury and not through the Board. Under a Treasury Minute of July 1919 the Advisory Committee was re-constituted as a committee advisory to the Treasury, to be called the University Grants Committee (UGC). There was a technical reason for this decision, namely, that grants to Scottish and Irish universities as well as to those in England and Wales were involved, and the Board's jurisdiction did not extend to Scotland and Ireland. The then President of the Board, H. A. L. Fisher, would have liked to maintain the close relationship that had existed up to that time between the Advisory Committee and the Board, but other views prevailed.[2]

This arrangement by which the Treasury, on the advice of the UGC, made grants directly to the universities was not without its advantages for the universities. But from the point of view of the educational system it had considerable disadvantages. One of these was pointed out by the late Lord Bridges:[3] it left the Chancellor of the Exchequer 'in a sense doubling the roles of a Departmental and a Treasury Minister'. Another was that the planning of developments in the university sector was in effect divorced from that in the schools and in the maintained sector as a whole.

These disadvantages became increasingly apparent as, during the 1950s, the expansion of secondary education stemming from the 1944 Act got under way; and the number of candidates for universities was further swollen as a result of the growth in school population, the trend towards staying on to 18, and the inducement to attempt university entry offered by generous student grants. By the later 1950s the number of qualified applicants for university places had increased to an extent that almost no one had foreseen.

CRISIS OVER UNIVERSITY PLACES:
THE ROBBINS REPORT

During the 1950s the universities were expanding, but on a very modest scale. Undergraduate numbers increased from about 68,500 in 1953–4 to a little under 90,000 in 1960–1. By then it was becoming clear that the expansion was nothing like enough to keep pace with the escalating demand for places. It was estimated that between 1958 and 1965 the number of school leavers qualified to enter university would double while university places would increase by only 50 per cent.[4]

There was thus widespread public disquiet, and a growing concern that, when the larger age groups of the 'bulge' reached higher education, the situation would become critical. The basic problem was that of the availability of all forms of higher education. But at this point of time it was the increasing competitiveness of university entry that attracted most attention and had the most serious impact on the schools. The Crowther Report put its finger on the danger: 'If a fully qualified sixth former's chance of securing a [university] place is going to shrink, we fear a disastrous reaction on the willingness to stay on at school into the sixth form, and a consequent loss to the nation of some of its potential supply of trained brain power.'[5]

From 1958 onwards the government, on the advice of the UGC, embarked on a considered policy of development, creating new universities as well as expanding existing ones. Between 1959 and 1965 seven new universities were established in England and Wales.[6] But it is in the nature of new foundations that in the initial stages numbers build up slowly. The expansion proved insufficient to ease the pressure on university places, and public criticism continued to grow.

In 1961 the government appointed a committee under the chairmanship of Lord Robbins to review the whole pattern of full-time higher education in Great Britain. Amongst other things the committee were asked to advise on 'whether modifications should be made in the existing arrangements for planning and co-ordinating the development of the various types of institution'. They reported in October 1963.[7]

This was the first time, as the committee observed, that any such body had been given such a remit. There had been royal commissions or committees on particular universities, and on various aspects of technical education and teacher training. There had never before been a comprehensive survey of higher education as a whole.

For the purposes of their report the Robbins Committee took higher education to include degree and higher degree courses provided at universities, full-time courses for the education and training of teachers, and systematic courses of further education beyond General Certificate of Education (GCE) 'A' level or its equivalent for technology, commerce and art. This is the definition of higher education now generally in use.

The committee's recommendations, and the actions that have flowed from them, have had major consequences for all sectors of higher education: for the teacher-training colleges and the leading technical colleges as well as for the universities, and also for the machinery for central control. This chapter is mainly concerned with two groups of the committee's recommendations that have been of particular importance for the Department's work: those on the machinery of central control of higher education, and those on the expansion of the universities.

The Robbins proposals on the machinery of control, and government action

On machinery the Robbins Committee had two main proposals. First, they wanted to see a single grants commission which would advise the government on the needs of all institutions of higher education in England, Wales and Scotland, including the teacher-training colleges and advanced technological institutions as well as the universities. This was to be modelled on the UGC, but with a larger staff. Secondly, they proposed that ministerial responsibility for the higher education sector should rest not with the Minister of Education, but with a new minister called the Minister of Arts and Science, who would combine the functions of what would in effect be a minister of higher education (although they rejected this designation) with those exercised by the Minister for Science and those of a minister for the arts.[8]

The government, although they agreed with the Robbins Committee on the need for changes in machinery, reached conclusions about the changes needed that differed from those of the majority of the committee. Their solution was a single Department of Education and Science, with responsibility for all sectors of education (except in Scotland, where education other than in universities would remain with the Secretary of State for Scotland) and also for those aspects of civil science that were at that time the responsibility of the Minister for Science. The enlarged ministry became a department of state, its ministerial head designated Secretary of State for Education and Science.[9] At the outset the Department consisted of two distinct administrative units, each with its own permanent head: one concerned with schools and other non-university education (in England and Wales), and the other concerned with universities (in England, Wales and Scotland) and also with civil science. Two ministers of state were appointed. Grants to the universities were transferred from the Treasury vote to that of the new Department and were to be made as before on the advice of the UGC. This body's terms of reference continued to be limited to the universities and were not extended to cover other sectors of higher education as the Robbins Committee had proposed.

Subsequently the two administrative units established in 1964 were merged into a single unit under one permanent secretary. This is, in its main essentials, the shape of the machinery as it exists today.

THE WORK OF THE UNIVERSITY GRANTS COMMITTEE

The reorganisation of 1964 did not result in any fundamental change in the role of the UGC, which is to act as an intermediary between the government and the universities,[10] channelling public funds to the universities in a way that reconciles the interest of the state as paymaster and guardian of national policies with the autonomy of the universities. Its main functions are to ascertain the financial needs of the universities, both individually and collectively, to advise the government on the application of grants made by Parliament to meet them, and in consultation with the universities to assist in the preparation and implementation of national plans for the development of the sector.[11]

In performing these functions the UGC may be said to have an executive as well as an advisory role. But it is not a statutory body, and there is no legislation governing its work. Its members are appointed by the Secretary of State for Education and Science in consultation with the Secretaries of State for Scotland and Wales. There are at present twenty-one members including the chairman, who serves full-time. Of these, some two-thirds are university people, usually chosen for their expertise in a particular field, but also for their general experience of university affairs, and there are members from other sectors of education and from industry. No university vice-chancellor may be a member. A member of the UGC who becomes a vice-chancellor during his term of office is required to resign. All members serve in an individual capacity and not as representatives of any university or organisation.

The UGC is served by a permanent secretariat, who are civil servants and are for establishment purposes members of the staff of the Department, but during their period of service with the UGC they are responsible to the UGC alone. The secretariat numbers somewhat over 100.

Some of the UGC's work is done through advisory subcommittees covering the main subject fields. These are chaired by UGC members but include members drawn from the universities and elsewhere who are not members of the main UGC. The UGC's advice to the Secretary of State is confidential.[12]

The UGC keep in touch with the universities in a variety of ways. It has formal meetings from time to time with the Committee of Vice-Chancellors and Principals and with the Association of University Teachers. At least once in each quinquennium it pays visits to individual universities, which are occasions for wide-ranging discussions with staff and students. Apart from these more formal occasions, there is constant coming and going of vice-chancellors and university staffs to the UGC's headquarters and of members of the UGC and secretariat to individual universities.

The grant system: quinquennial recurrent grants

Since the UGC came into existence it has been the practice for the recurrent grants to universities, that is, grants to cover their running expenses, to be fixed for a quinquennium. In recent years it has been the UGC's practice, in preparing the ground for discussion with universities, to frame a 'planning hypothesis' for the university sector as a whole, in the light of expectations about the objectives that the government wants to see achieved in terms of student numbers and mix, and the resources that can be made available. The UGC then invite each institution to submit detailed estimates of its needs for the quinquennium, indicating the developments it would like to attempt. In doing so they give indications, based on the planning hypothesis, of the objectives that they think each institution might set itself, of the building priorities required to achieve them, and so forth.

The universities' proposals and cost estimates are then aggregated; and in the light of a review of the global effect of university proposals and their own assessment of the way in which total university expenditure should change, the UGC make their recommendations to the government on the total sums needed in each year of the quinquennium and on the objectives to be achieved. It is the established convention that the UGC's submission to the Department is made in global terms. It may deal in detail with particular fields of study, student numbers, academic priorities, unit costs, and so forth, but it does not make recommendations about individual institutions.

It is the government – that is, education ministers in consultation with their colleagues in Cabinet – who decide, after discussion with the UGC, on the main policy issues as regards student numbers and mix and the total sums that can be made available in each year of the quinquennium to achieve their objectives. When the government's decisions are known, the UGC make the allocations to individual universities, with advice from their subject subcommittees. Their aim is to make allocations that ensure the optimum use of resources, are seen to be fair, and are so far as possible in line with the wishes of individual institutions while serving national policies. When notifying universities of their allocations, the UGC give guidance about the student numbers and mix to be aimed at and about the developments for which provision has (or has not) been made. A reserve is retained by the UGC, partly for contingencies and partly to enable them to initiate developments not fully provided for in the universities' proposals.

The grants are block grants covering the full five-year period, which universities are by and large free to spend as they think fit. They are free to carry over unused balances from year to year within the quinquennium, and there is a minimum of 'earmarking' of grants for specific purposes. These provisions accord with the principle, basic to the work of the UGC and subscribed to by successive governments, that universities should be allowed maximum freedom in determining their own priorities, subject to broad guidance on national policies and the financial constraints that the receipt of public funds involves. But in practice the use of allocations by any given university usually bears a fairly close relation to its broad objectives arrived at in discussion with the UGC.

It has sometimes been suggested[13] that in a period of inflation a fixed quinquennium inhibits long-term planning and that some form of rolling quinquennium would be more satisfactory. But on the whole the system of fixed quinquennial grants, with provision for supplementation to meet salary increases and rising costs, has been valued by the universities as affording the maximum of freedom and flexibility compatible with subvention from public funds. The government have taken the view that, provided the long-term strategy for the development of higher education is clearly stated (as in the White Paper of December 1972), planning can proceed effectively within the framework of existing financial arrangements.[14]

The grants are normally supplemented for one of two reasons: salary increases for academic and related staff agreed in negotiation with the government, and increases in cost. Increased commitments due to agreed salary increases have normally been met in full by additions to grants. As salaries are the largest single item in the universities' expenditure, this is an important provision from their point of view. Supplementation to meet other increases in costs has become increasingly needed as a result of inflation, and this has posed formidable problems. In recent years the government has usually been willing to negotiate supplementary grants from time to time to help meet cost increases, on the basis of an agreed formula. The effect of the formula is to ensure that at least half of the extra costs arising from price increases are met from public funds, and in some cases more, although in some circumstances (for example, the economic crisis in the winter of 1973–4) some supplementary grants have had to be withdrawn.

Non-recurrent grants
There are non-recurrent grants for three specific purposes: buildings, sites and professional fees. The most substantial are for buildings, and these largely determine the requirements under the other two heads. The amounts are fairly closely regulated from year to year, by means of an annual building programme procedure not unlike that operated in other sectors of education, except that in this instance the cost of building is met from Exchequer funds. There are also 100 per cent grants to cover the purchase of sites and professional fees.

The total amount of the programme is determined by the Department in the light of the resources available, the UGC's advice about national requirements, the objectives of the universities themselves (in terms of student numbers and mix), their existing capacity and the need to replace obsolescent accommodation. Once the total of starts for a particular year has been agreed, the Department accepts liability to provide in successive annual estimates for the grants necessary to complete the buildings. As in the case of recurrent grants, there may in times of economic stringency be reductions in or even temporary suspension of building and equipment allocations.

The UGC have to ensure that the amounts are fairly distributed amongst universities according to need. The bulk of the allocations are for named projects, which will usually have been proposed by the universities themselves. There is also provision for universities to undertake small jobs or 'minor works'. Since 1972 this has taken the form of an unindicated addition to university recurrent grants, with authority to use up to $2\frac{1}{2}$ per cent of recurrent grant for capital expenditure.

Since 1968 it has been the practice for each university to receive an annual grant for equipment, related to the planned number and mix of students; and since 1972 there have been grants specifically for the purchase or repair of furniture.

The provision and running costs of central computers at universities are the responsibility of an autonomous Computer Board for Universities and Research Councils, set up in 1966, which within its own sphere operates in much the same way as the UGC.

Special problems have arisen over residential accommodation to enable universities to house a reasonable proportion of their student population. In the early postwar years residence for students was usually provided in the form of halls of residence, with catering and communal facilities. But this is a costly form of provision; and students themselves tend to prefer student houses or flats. Since 1970 the UGC have ceased to provide 100 per cent grant aid for halls of residence; they now offer up to 25 per cent subsidy (sometimes more) for loan-financed student-housing projects sponsored by universities. This has made possible a large increase in the provision of student accommodation.

Universities' accountability

In 1967 the then Secretary of State accepted a recommendation by the Public Accounts Committee that the Comptroller and Auditor-General should be given access to the books of the UGC and of individual universities. The government emphasised at the time that the Comptroller and Auditor-General's function would be to comment and advise on the propriety, regularity and efficiency with which moneys voted by Parliament were administered, not to question policy or academic decisions. The new arrangements were accepted by the UGC and also by the universities – though with some initial misgivings because of their possible implications for academic freedom. Anxieties arose, not so much from the fact that the Comptroller and Auditor-General would have access to the universities' books, as from the possibility that his reports to Parliament might lead to pressures that would result in their autonomy being eroded.

In the event 'the world did not come to an end'.[15] It is probably true to say that, by and large, British universities continue to enjoy 'a position of freedom in relation to their own Government which has no parallel in Europe, East or West'.[16]

The Robbins Report and university expansion

The Robbins Committee, as earlier remarked, surveyed higher education as a whole, and their recommendations for further university expansion were made in that context. Their thinking started from the 'axiom' that 'courses of higher education should be available for all those who are qualified by ability and attainment to pursue them and who wish to do so'. This is sometimes referred to as the principle of 'constant opportunity', and it has influenced all subsequent thinking and government action on higher education.

With this end in view the Robbins Committee attempted forecasts of demand for higher education up to 1980, and of the expansion in the various sectors needed to meet it. As regards demand, they arrived at what at that time seemed the startling conclusion that the number of places in higher education would need to be increased by 80 per cent (from 216,000 in 1962–3 to over 390,000) by 1973–4, and by 160 per cent (to 558,000) by 1980–1.[17]

It was within this framework that they looked at the need for expansion of the universities. Like the Crowther Council and Secondary School Examinations Council (SSEC), they found evidence of sharply increasing competition for university entry. They noted that this had forced up standards in sixth forms of schools[18] and that it was having other and less desirable effects on the schools, such as excessive and premature specialisation. They foresaw that with the arrival of the 'bulge' at university age the competition would intensify. They concluded that, to limit the damaging effects on the schools, measures must be taken to ensure that the competitiveness of entry should not become more intense. They thought it desirable that eventually it should become less so.

To this end they proposed a further massive expansion of the universities. They recommended that, of the 390,000 or so places that they reckoned would be needed in higher education by 1973–4, 218,000 should be in universities (an increase of 100,000); and that, of the 558,000 places needed in 1980–1, 346,000 should be in universities (an increase of 228,000).

To achieve these targets they proposed: first, that existing universities should be expanded; secondly, that university status should be conferred on the ten colleges of advanced technology and on the comparable Scottish institutions; and thirdly, that six new universities should be established (one of them in Scotland). They further thought that the government should give university status, either singly or in combination, to some ten regional colleges, central institutions (in Scotland) and colleges of education. They asked for a 'crash programme' for the period up to 1967–8 when the larger age groups of the 'bulge' would be passing through higher education.

This is not the place to discuss the Robbins Committee forecasts and proposals in detail.[19] There are, however, four points about their proposals that call for comment. First, their estimates of the expansion required were made in terms of what has been called the 'private demand' approach, that is, student demand for places. The committee did not overlook the importance of other approaches – for example, the 'manpower' approach, which tries to measure the need for expansion in the light of national requirements for particular categories of highly qualified manpower – but they took the view that, except in a few sectors such as teachers for the schools, there was an insufficient theoretical and statistical base from which to obtain reasonably precise forecasts for a period of years ahead.

Secondly, their forecasts were made in terms of demand by those qualified for higher education by ability and attainment, as measured by examination results.[20] The significance of this method of forecasting demand is that it implies a standard, and therefore has a bearing on university standards generally.

A third point to note is that the committee's approach was largely university oriented. It contained an implicit assumption that the most effective means of meeting student demand was through the expansion of university-type courses and institutions (except in so far as there was a need to expand the colleges of education to meet the needs of the schools for teachers). Their over-riding concern was to limit the competitiveness of university entry. Hence, for example, their proposal that the universities' share of higher education places should increase from 55 per cent in 1962–3 to 62 per cent by 1980–1. Hence also their recommendation that the colleges of advanced technology and certain other institutions should be incorporated into the university sector. Their proposals for the teacher-training system also in effect envisaged the integration of the colleges of education into the university system. By contrast they treated advanced education provided in the further education sector as a residual balancing item, and assumed a fall in its share of entrants to higher education.[21]

Fourthly, it is to be noted that the Robbins forecasts, startling as they seemed at the time, quickly proved to have underestimated student demand. By 1968 the Robbins forecasts of school leavers with two GCE 'A' level qualifications in England and Wales had already been exceeded by nearly 17,000, and it was estimated that by 1976 they would be exceeded by over 46,000.[22]

Government action on the Robbins proposals for university expansion
Within twenty-four hours of the publication of the Robbins Report, the government published a White Paper[23] announcing their acceptance of the report's axiom that higher education courses should be available for all those who are qualified by ability and attainment to pursue them and who wish to do so.

They also accepted the Robbins estimates of the number of places needed, both in higher education as a whole and in universities, and adopted the committee's target figures for 1967–8 and 1973–4 as their objectives for those years. As regards the universities, they recognised the urgency of the need to provide more places for the years when the bulge reached university age; they specifically accepted the Robbins targets for institutions of university status (197,000 places by 1967–8, and 218,000 by 1973–4); and they announced their intention of adjusting university grants accordingly. They did not commit themselves to the suggested targets for 1980–1, although they made it clear that their programme took account of the need for further big expansion after 1973–4.

They accepted some but not all of the Robbins recommendations for achieving the targets in the university sector. They accepted the proposal that the colleges of advanced technology, and certain Scottish institutions, should have university status. They postponed consideration of the proposal that further new universities should be established in England and Wales and that other existing institutions should be associated with the university system. (In 1965 it was decided that, except in Scotland, no new universities should be created.) Further developments in this and other sectors of higher education are discussed in Chapter 10.

GRANTS TO STUDENTS

The arrangements evolved since 1944 for assisting university and other students from public funds are a feature of higher education in Britain, which is in many ways unique.[24] They have played a major role in the expansion of higher education, and it might well be argued that they have of themselves constituted something of a social revolution in ensuring a career open to talent within the educational system.

Private benefactions to support needy students at universities have a history almost as long as the universities themselves, but before the present century virtually no grants were available from public funds.[25] Early in the twentieth century the newly established LEAs began to offer grants on a modest scale to enable the abler children coming up through grant-aided schools in their areas to attend university.

In 1911 the Board of Education instituted a scheme of grants to enable students who undertook to become teachers to pursue a university course followed by a year of professional training. From 1920 the Board offered state scholarships unencumbered with a commitment to teaching, but the numbers were small. In 1920 it offered 200; by 1936 the number was 360.

These state and local scholarships, together with the open scholarships offered by universities, enabled a small proportion of the ablest boys and girls coming up through the publicly provided schools to get to university. But a student's chance of getting an award varied from one area to another, and the value of the awards bore little relation to his costs at university. A student from a poor home had to collect two or three awards, or beg or borrow from other sources. As late as 1938 the number entering universities from grant-aided schools in England and Wales with help from public funds was probably less than a sixth of all entrants.

Awards provisions of the Education Act 1944
The 1943 White Paper had noted the inadequate number of scholarships available, and the 1944 Act contained important provisions designed to increase it and thus to achieve greater equality of opportunity for higher education. It required the Minister to make regulations empowering LEAs to grant scholarships and other awards 'for the purpose of enabling pupils to take advantage without hardship to themselves or their parents' of any educational facilities available to them; and it empowered the Minister himself to make provision in similar terms (Sections 81 and 100(1)(c)).

The Ministry implemented these requirements in two ways: it substantially increased the number of state scholarships, and it also undertook to 'supplement' university open scholarships, to bring them up in value to state scholarships. Two new categories, namely, 'technical' and 'mature' scholarships, were added. (These were not numerically significant.) At the same time the Ministers required LEAs to submit schemes of 'scholarships and other benefits',[26] and this procedure was used to encourage LEAs greatly to increase the number of awards they offered. In the early 1950s the great majority of students obtaining places at universities could thus count on obtaining state or local awards.

There was also an important innovation as regards the value of awards. To give effect to the principle of avoidance of hardship, the Ministry adopted, and recommended to LEAs, a proposal originally put forward in the Norwood Report of 1943: that, subject to a contribution from parents according to an income scale, state scholars should receive the full cost of their fees and maintenance at university. The Ministry itself undertook to work out 'standard figures of maintenance', in consultation with the local authority associations and in the light of information provided by the universities.

The Anderson Committee and the Education Act 1962

With the growth during the 1950s of the number of school leavers entering university, the system of student awards deriving from the 1944 Act proved unsatisfactory. The LEAs found that the number of local awards, and thus their share of the financial burden, was growing faster than had been anticipated. Some authorities became reluctant to continue increasing the number of their awards, and not all of them accepted the Ministry's recommendations on levels of grant. Thus a candidate's chances of getting a grant, and its amount if he got one, varied from one area to another. The Ministry's powers were insufficient to ensure uniformity, and the consequent variations led to growing public criticism.

In 1958 a committee under the chairmanship of Sir Colin Anderson was appointed to consider the system of awards from public funds to students attending first-degree courses at universities and comparable courses at other institutions. This committee in its report of 1960[27] proposed that there should be a uniform system of grants for England and Wales (and also for Scotland). Their main recommendation was that a duty should be placed on LEAs to make awards available to all students accepted for university first-degree or comparable courses and having appropriate qualifications. It followed that state scholarships would be discontinued.

The government accepted the Anderson Committee's main recommendations. New legislation, which received the Royal Assent as the Education Act 1962, imposed a duty on LEAs to make awards to all students from their areas who had the requisite qualifications and obtained places on undergraduate courses at universities or comparable courses in other institutions. These came to be known as mandatory or 'duty' awards. The regulations made under this Act specify the residential and educational qualifications that a student needed to obtain a duty award (the educational qualification is defined as two passes at GCE 'A' level or equivalent), the rates of grant payable, the conditions of grant and the scale of parental contribution. A schedule lists courses at non-university institutions designated as 'comparable'. (This list has been extended from time to time.)

The 'mandatory' provisions of the 1962 Act apply only to first-degree or undergraduate courses. Section 2 of the Act continues the LEAs' power to make awards at their discretion for courses not attracting 'duty' awards. A subsequent section deals with awards to students at colleges of education. Guidance on discretionary awards has been given in successive circulars.

In the terms of the Act, grants for postgraduate students fell within the field of 'discretionary' awards. With the passage of time and the mounting cost of mandatory awards, LEAs became increasingly reluctant to finance postgraduate students. Eventually agreement was reached between the Department and the local authority associations that as from 1968–70 all postgraduate awards, with the exception of certain limited categories, should be financed by central government (mainly the Department itself and the research councils). This was given statutory authority by regulations (now made under the Education Act 1973).

In 1962 a standing advisory committee was constituted, on lines recommended in the Anderson Report, to advise on the level of grants, but this machinery did not enjoy the confidence of the local authority associations. In 1967 the then Secretary of State dispensed with this committee and appointed a small expert advisory panel to give technical advice on adjustments to grants needed to meet cost-of-living increases. This arrangement also proved unsatisfactory. The present arrangement is that the Department invites the National Union of Students (NUS) and the corresponding Scottish body to confer with officials of the education departments in a preliminary factual investigation of the changes in the amounts of awards needed to maintain their real value. The government then decides, in consultation with the local authority associations, the university authorities and the students' associations, on how the available resources should be spent.

It is important to note the timing of the 1962 Act. It was on the statute book in time to provide an improved framework of student support for the great expansion of higher education that was launched following the Robbins Report. The extent of the increase can be seen from Table 9.1, which shows the growth in the number of awards to students over the period 1950–75.

By the early 1970s the local authorities were becoming seriously concerned about the financial burden imposed by their commitments under the provisions of the 1962 Act, since this was expenditure over whose growth they had no control.

In 1973 the then Secretary of State announced that as from 1 April 1974 arrangements would be made for grant at a special rate of 90 per cent to be paid on local authority expenditure on students' awards, although the local authorities would continue to administer the grants as before. Provisions to this effect were incorporated in the Education Act 1973.

Table 9.1 Awards to students taken up and current¹ 1950–1 to 1975–6

	1950–1	1960–1	1970–1	1975–6
Awarded by the Department				
State scholarships (including mature and adult education bursaries)²	2,006 (5,495)	3,549 (12,041)	21 (75)	252 (448)
State studentships and bursaries	—	262 (540)	1,560 (2,551)	1,764 (2,882)
Awards to students in UDEs	—	—	5,184 (5,184)	—
Awarded by research councils	—	—	6,823 (12,355)	6,642 (13,285)
Awarded by LEAs³				
Full value awards	10,538 (24,278)	28,903 (74,057)	95,079 (245,142)	112,360 (273,144)
Lesser value awards	6,408 (12,113)	7,840 (12,278)	19,454 (25,898)	28,791 (38,458)

¹ Figures in brackets show awards current.
² State scholarships (other than mature scholarships) were discontinued following the Education Act 1962. The adult education bursary scheme has operated from 1975.
³ Not including teacher-training awards.

NOTES AND REFERENCES

1 The Department's general responsibilities in the university sector cover Great Britain. Its responsibilities for grants to students extend only to England and Wales.
2 See Fisher's papers relating to this period, especially a letter from Fisher to the then Secretary of State for Scotland of 27 January 1919 (unpublished papers now in the Public Records Office, Ed 24/1968).
3 Lord Bridges, *The Treasury*, New Whitehall Series (London, Allen & Unwin, 1964), pp. 58–9.
4 *The General Certificate of Education and Sixth Form Studies: Third Report of the Secondary School Examinations Council* (London, HMSO, 1960), App. C, p. 24.
5 *Fifteen to Eighteen: Report of the Central Advisory Council for Education (England)* (the Crowther Report), Vol. I (London, HMSO, 1959), para. 439.
6 Sussex, Essex, Kent, East Anglia, Warwick, York and Lancaster.
7 Committee on Higher Education (Chairman: Lord Robbins), *Higher Education*, Cmnd 2154 (London, HMSO, 1963).
8 In their recommendations on ministerial control, the committee were not unanimous. A note of reservation by one member (the late Sir Harold Shearman) urged the case for a single minister responsible for both school and higher education.
9 Secretary of State for Education and Science Order 1964 (SI 1964 No. 490).
10 In England, Wales and Scotland. It also advises the Northern Ireland authorities.
11 For an authoritative account of the work of the UGC see: HC Expenditure Committee (Session 1970–1), *2nd Report*, HC 545 (London, HMSO, 1971), p. 194; memorandum submitted by the secretary of the UGC; Paper No. 1 by the secretary of the UGC; *and* HC Expenditure Committee (Session 1972–3), *Report, Appendices and Index, Further and Higher Education*, Vol. III, Evidence, Appendices and Index, HC 48–III (London, HMSO, 1972), p. 522; memorandum submitted by the UGC; Paper No. 2 by the secretary of the UGC.
12 But it publishes its Quinquennial Reports, Annual Surveys, Annual Statistics and Returns, and other papers.
13 See, for example, HC Expenditure Committee (Session 1972–73), *Report: Further and Higher Education*, Vol. I, HC 48–I (London, HMSO, 1972), paras 40*ff*.
14 White Paper, *Government Observation on Report on Further and Higher Education*, Cmnd 5368 (London, HMSO, 1973).
15 Sir Richard Clarke, *New Trends in Government*, Civil Service College Studies (London, HMSO, 1971), p. 87.
16 Letter to *The Times* from Sir John Hackett, then Principal of King's College, London (4 July 1973).
17 Figures for Great Britain.
18 Robbins Report, op. cit., ch. VII, paras 195 and following.
19 For a more detailed analysis see DES, *Student Numbers in Higher Education in England and Wales*, Education Planning Paper No. 2 (London, HMSO, 1970), especially para. 2.4.
20 This concept is not entirely straightforward, as different forms of higher education require different entry qualifications. The Robbins calculations allowed for this. Subsequent estimates have tended to work on the simplified assumption that the attainment of two GCE 'A' levels or their equivalent qualifies for higher education (other than at colleges of education).

21 See *Student Numbers in Higher Education*, op. cit., paras 2.8 and 5.11. In the event the advanced further education grew more than twice as fast as the university sector between 1960–1 and 1970–1.

22 ibid., para. 3.3.

23 White Paper, *Higher Education: Government Statement on the Report of the Committee under the Chairmanship of Lord Robbins, 1961–63*, Cmnd 2165 (London, HMSO, 1963).

24 The Robbins Committee, which made a detailed study of higher education in nine other countries, found that none of them, except the USSR, made provision from public funds for assisting as high a proportion of students as Britain, and that many countries did not pay grants of comparable value (Robbins Report, op. cit., para. 116 and app. V).

25 Some local authorities used their powers under the Technical Instruction Act 1889 to assist students in their areas.

26 Scholarships and Other Benefits Regulations. See also Circular 26 of 13 March 1945.

27 *Grants to Students: Report of the Committee Appointed by the Minister of Education and the Secretary of State for Scotland in June 1958* (the Anderson Report), Cmnd 1051 (London, HMSO, 1960).

PART FOUR

The Growth of Higher Education

CHAPTER 10

Higher Education: A Decade of Rapid Growth, and Some Problems

This chapter aims to bring together the threads of the discussion in the preceding three chapters, to give a conspectus of the development of the higher education sector as a whole up to the mid-1970s, and of some of the major problems that have arisen.

The 1960s were a period of growth in higher education that was remarkable by any standards. Between 1961–2 and 1971–2 the number of full-time and sandwich students in higher education in Great Britain more than doubled, from 192,000 to 464,000 – an average annual growth rate of 9 per cent. The number of advanced part-time students increased by two-thirds. The proportion of each age-group entering higher education increased from 7 per cent to 14 per cent.

The major factor accounting for this explosion was the upsurge of demand resulting from the continuing increase in the output of qualified school leavers. During the early and mid-1960s the larger age-groups of the bulge were reaching higher education. Superimposed on this was the continuing increase in the proportion of each age-group qualifying for higher education, as a result of the continuing trend towards staying on at school and of improved examination performance by those staying on. The proportion of the age-group obtaining two or more General Certificate of Education (GCE) 'A' levels (or three or more Scottish Higher levels) rose from 6·6 per cent in 1961 to 11·4 per cent in 1967.

In consequence the Robbins[1] forecasts of demand were far exceeded, as may be seen from a comparison made by the Department in 1970 (Table 10.1).[2]

Table 10.1   *School leavers with two or more 'A' levels (thousands).*

	1968	1976
Robbins forecast	57·7	78·2
DES (1970)	74·4 (actual)	124·6

At the beginning of the 1970s the indications were that the number of qualified leavers would continue to increase with little or no abatement throughout the decade. The Department's projections published by the Department in 1970[3] indicated that between 1971 and 1981 the number would again almost double; and although by the early 1970s there was a falling off in the trend of staying on after 16, and of the proportion of qualified young people opting for higher education, it was at that time considered too early to draw firm conclusions from this change.

Welcome as the growth in higher education was, it posed formidable problems for national policy. As noted in Chapter 9, the then government had in 1963 endorsed the Robbins 'axiom' that courses of higher education should be available for all who were qualified by ability and attainment to pursue them, and who wished to do so. Subsequent governments adhered to this principle. Thus, despite economic constraints and competing claims, it was government policy to ensure that higher education institutions should grow so as to keep pace broadly with rising student demand. Problems of two kinds, however, had to be faced.

The most obvious was cost. Superimposed on the increase in numbers there had been a continuing increase in the cost of provision. Higher education is the most costly form of education, and costs in this sector tend to rise more rapidly than in other sectors. Given that the total amount of resources that can be made available to education, under any government, is necessarily limited, there was a growing danger that the escalating demands of higher education would pre-empt resources to an extent that would virtually preclude advance in other sectors.

Problems of a different kind emerged as a result of the difficulty, in a society in which higher education is rapidly expanding and there is continuing technological change, of 'matching' the outputs of higher education with the needs of the labour market. These problems only began to attract wide public attention in the early 1970s, largely as a result of the difficulties experienced by university graduates in obtaining first employment.[4] Indeed until late in the 1960s successive governments were more concerned with continuing shortages of highly qualified manpower, notably in science and technology and teachers for the schools.

Nevertheless there was from the outset an inherent likelihood that, in a society hitherto geared to absorbing only some 6–8 per cent of each age-group into employment for which graduate or comparable qualifications were required, problems of adjustment would arise when 15 per cent or more of larger age-groups were obtaining such qualifications. The Robbins Committee proposals for the expansion of higher education, as noted in Chapter 9, were based entirely (except as regards teachers for the schools) on forecasts of student demand, the committee having taken the view that, except in certain limited fields, it was impracticable to use the manpower approach. But the resulting problems of matching outputs to opportunities have become increasingly evident.

The changing requirements of industry and of society generally due to technological change and demographic factors have accentuated these problems. One instance is the falling off in demand for certain categories of scientists and technologists. Another, already touched on in Chapter 7, is the impact of the fall in birth rate on the longer-term requirement for teachers.

Such difficulties are liable to be complicated by what may be described as the job expectations of those with higher education qualifications. These are inevitably coloured by the experiences of a previous generation which may no longer be relevant. Thus there can be little doubt that the intensification of demand for university places in the 1950s was in part generated by a widespread assumption, amongst parents, teachers and students, that a university degree, whatever the subject or grade, constituted a safe conduct to the better paid posts and careers. A decade or so later, this was to be the cause of not a little disenchantment.

THE 1972 WHITE PAPER AND HIGHER EDUCATION

The government which came into office in 1970 was committed to an expansion of education over a broad front, with greater emphasis on primary and preschool education, on improved staffing standards in schools and the development of teacher training, and also on a continued expansion of higher education. Its objectives were set out in the White Paper of December 1972, *Education: A Framework for Expansion*,[5] which was intended to indicate 'the general direction of a ten-year strategy for the education service'. The aim was, within the resouces available, to secure a balanced programme of advance on all fronts over a ten-year period.

The White Paper paid special attention to the higher education sector, where the greatest need exists for long-term planning to match growing demands and limited resources in relation to other priorities.

The government foresaw that the trend to increased staying-on to 18 might continue after the raising of the school leaving age, and that the proportion of young people achieving GCE 'A'-level qualifications (or their equivalent) might continue to increase. The planning of higher education, they thought, must make allowance for these factors as well as for the increasing size of the age-groups.

They pointed out that it was harder to foresee likely trends in the attitudes and intentions of young people towards higher education, and their requirements within it. In this connection they drew attention to some of the manpower problems mentioned above. The expansion of higher education, it was suggested, had already reached the point at which employers' requirements for highly qualified people in the forms of employment that were traditionally available were, in the aggregate, largely being met. Although patterns of employment were changing and would continue to do so as employers enlarged the areas of work in which highly qualified recruits could be made good use of, it seemed likely that the continuing expansion of output from higher education would more than match the expansion of graduate employment opportunities as understood at that time.

In this context the White Paper drew attention to the plurality of objectives served by the higher education system. The availability of opportunities for higher education should not, it argued, be determined primarily by reference to estimates of the country's future need for highly qualified people. Higher education was valuable for its contribution to the personal development of those who pursued it. Moreover its continued expansion must be seen as an investment in the nation's human talent in a time of rapid social change and technological development.

On a balanced judgement, and allowing for these and other difficulties in forecasting needs for almost a decade ahead, the government estimated that by 1981 provision should be made for a modest development, allowing for some 200,000 entrants to higher education annually (from within Great Britain. This allowed for some reduction in postgraduate numbers.) This would be about 22 per cent of the age-group aged 18, compared with 7 per cent in 1961 and 14 per cent in 1971. It was estimated that this requirement could be met by the provision of 750,000 full-time and sandwich places in higher education by 1981. This figure was adopted as the basis for the government's longer-term planning for the higher education sector up to 1981.

The White Paper gave indications of the government's thinking about the rate of development to be provided for in the different sectors, to achieve these targets with maximum flexibility and cost effectiveness. Provision would be made for the universities to continue their expansion. But, allowing for the additional capacity already created, and the growing opportunities for qualified leavers to take degree courses outside universities, it was thought desirable that the universities should maintain 'a reasonably smooth rate of increase' over the period up to 1981. The aim would be a full-time university student population of the order of 375,000 (including sandwich students) by 1981, or an increase of nearly 60 per cent over the 1971–2 figure. This, it may be noted, was somewhat higher than the target envisaged by the Robbins Committee for the universities for 1981 (namely, 350,000) on the basis of lower forecasts of the number of qualified leavers. But the universities' contribution to the total number of higher education places would be proportionately smaller than that envisaged by the committee.

The polytechnics and other colleges in the non-university sector offering advanced further education were to provide for some 335,000 full-time and sandwich students (England and Wales) in 1981, a net expansion of some 130,000.

The major contribution was to be made by the polytechnics, which were singled out for specially rapid expansion. The government, as remarked earlier, had been impressed by the speed and vigour with which the polytechnics had gone about their task. Moreover expansion of the polytechnics could provide important economies of size. The polytechnics' own development plans suggested that they were capable of reaching a target of 180,000 places by 1981. This would provide well over half the total number of places to be contributed by the advanced further-education sector.

The task of expanding to provide for the remaining 155,000 students was allocated to the other colleges in the non-university sector, including the colleges of education. Here the anticipated changes and developments in the teacher-training sector (see Chapter 7) had to be taken into account. In some cases places in the colleges of education would cease to be available for higher education. Others might diversify their role, in closer association with the non-university sector of higher education as a whole. Thus, while there would be a reduced output of teachers, the colleges would be able to make a substantial contribution, with other further education colleges, to meeting the overall demand for higher education.

Another important objective that the government had in mind at this time in proposing reorganisation in the maintained sector was a better geographical distribution of facilities for higher education over the country as a whole. Previously there had been a tendency for such facilities to be concentrated in the larger conurbations, on a scale liable to give rise to serious problems of transport and student residence. The government were anxious to secure a distribution that, amongst other things, would facilitate home-based study and extend the social and cultural benefits of higher education to areas not so far provided for. It was the intention that in the long run every major conurbation or other catchment area with a population of more than perhaps 250,000 should have an institution offering higher education, including teacher training.[6]

THE DIPLOMA OF HIGHER EDUCATION, AND OTHER PROPOSALS

The government believed that the existing structure of courses in higher education was unduly restricted. Those wanting to continue their education beyond school had the choice either of entering employment and studying part-time or, in the main, of committing themselves to courses lasting three years or more. Only a limited range of two-year courses existed at that time, all in specific vocational areas. The government believed that here was a gap that ought to be filled.

The James Report had already proposed a Diploma in Higher Education (DipHE), obtainable at the end of a two-year course in a college of education. The government believed that courses on these lines, designed to serve a wider purpose, could meet an important need not hitherto met and would be valuable in achieving greater flexibility in higher education. There should, in their view, be a range of two-year courses – no less intellectually demanding than the first two years of a degree course, and normally with an entry qualification similar to that for a degree or comparable course. There should be both general and specialised courses, and these should be on offer in each of the main sectors of higher education: universities, poly-technics and other colleges. They would provide both a terminal qualification (for example, for entry to appropriate forms of employ-ment), and a foundation for further study, as staging posts towards degrees or requirements of professional bodies. This, the government thought, might be best achieved if the courses were developed on a unit basis.

The courses would be validated by existing degree-awarding bodies. The Council for National Academic Awards (CNAA) had already expressed a willingness to undertake this work. There was reason to think that a number of universities were ready to offer DipHE them-selves, and would be prepared to validate courses where colleges did not seek validation from the CNAA.

The White Paper announced the government's intention of en-suring that DipHE students should qualify for mandatory awards.

The government proposed to give the new courses a fair wind as employers and to encourage other employers to do likewise.

They envisaged that the introduction of the proposed DipHE would enable many students to complete their higher education in two years instead of three or more.

The government had also looked for other ways of achieving the objectives of their programme more effectively and economically. Thus they hoped that with increasing numbers there would be scope for economies of scale in the larger institutions.

They thought that it would now be reasonable for staffing policies in both the university and non-university sectors to be modified, to give an average staff–student ratio of about 1:10 by the end of the decade, and that this could be done without lowering standards.

They hoped for a more widespread adoption of a break between a student's leaving school and entering higher education. This too would ease the financial burden as well as enabling students to gain more from their higher education.

They also shared the frequently expressed view that it was unnecessary for such a high proportion of students to reside and study at a distance if equally acceptable courses were available to them within daily travelling distance of their homes. In universities, for example, only 16 per cent of students at that time were home based. The government's intention was that greater geographical dispersion would make it possible for more students to attend higher education within reach of their homes, and thus reduce the high cost of residential accommodation.

The government wanted to see better arrangements for co-ordinating provision in the non-university sector, to ensure that expansion was planned to the best advantage. This has been facilitated by the formation by the local authority associations of a higher education committee formed by the local authority associations in 1972, to discuss matters of common interest to local education authorities (LEAs) in the higher education sector. There were those at this time who would have liked to see a more radical revision of arrangements for the co-ordination of higher education development. For example, the House of Commons Expenditure Committee[7] favoured a 'higher education commission', somewhat on the lines of that proposed in the Robbins Report, which would advise the Secretary of State on the administration and finance of the whole higher education sector. The government, in a White Paper of July 1973,[8] rejected this proposal on the grounds that such a body (unless purely advisory) would be 'an undesirably centralised bureaucracy with very extensive powers', and that the long-term effect would be 'to diminish the scope of education ministers' accountability to Parliament and to weaken control by locally elected representatives and by governing bodies of the institutions themselves'. They believed that existing arrangements had been shown to be capable of establishing a clear policy for the distribution and use of resources for higher education.

DEVELOPMENTS IN HIGHER EDUCATION FOLLOWING THE 1972 WHITE PAPER

In the course of 1973 important progress was made in implementing the policies for higher education outlined in the 1972 White Paper. The quinquennial settlement for the universities provided for an increase in undergraduate numbers to 254,000 and in postgraduate numbers to 52,000, giving a total of 306,000 full-time students by 1976–7. Substantial building programmes were provided for at polytechnics and other further education colleges, continuing the expansion already under way. A circular issued in March 1973[9] set an administrative framework and a timetable for the preparation and submission of plans by LEAs for the development of higher education in their areas.

The ensuing economic crisis and the consequent reduction in the resources that the government could make available for higher education resulted in what was undoubtedly a serious setback in plans for its expansion. At the same time there were indications of a falling off in demand for higher education. At the beginning of 1974 the view of ministers was that the effective demand for places could be met despite the cutbacks, even if there were no further falling off in numbers applying, and that the requirement for places in 1981 was likely to be substantially less than the 750,000 assumed for that year in the White Paper. The government's 1976 White Paper on *Educational Expenditure to 1979–90*[10] announced revised plans for the expansion of student numbers in higher education (full-time and sandwich) to 600,000 by 1981. It pointed out that, while this figure implied some increase in competitiveness of entry in some subjects and economies in operating standards, it allowed for a further rise in the proportion of the postschool age-group entering higher education, to 15 per cent.

NOTES AND REFERENCES

1 Committee on Higher Education (Chairman: Lord Robbins), *Higher Education*, Cmnd 2154 (London, HMSO, 1963).
2 DES, *Student Numbers in Higher Education in England and Wales*, Education Planning Paper No. 2 (London, HMSO, 1970), p. 12, table 2.
3 ibid., p. 11, table 1.

4 See, for example, HC Expenditure Committee (Session 1972–73), *Report: Further and Higher Education*, Vol. I, HC 48-I (London, HMSO, 1972), para. 22.

5 White Paper, *Education: A Framework for Expansion*, Cmnd 5174 (London, HMSO, December 1972).

6 Circular 7/73 of 23 March 1973.

7 *Further and Higher Education*, op. cit.

8 White Paper, *Government Observations on Report on Further and Higher Education*, Cmnd 5368 (London, HMSO, 1973).

9 Circular 7/73 of 23 March 1973.

10 White Paper, *Educational Expenditure to 1979–90*, Cmnd 6393 (London, HMSO, 1976).

PART FIVE

The Department's Responsibilities in Other Fields

CHAPTER 11

The Department and the Library Services

HISTORICAL BACKGROUND

The postwar period has been one of unprecedented expansion of public library services, both national and local.[1] Some of the main factors at work have been the continual rise in the general level of education, the increase in leisure time and the sheer growth in knowledge – which is still primarily embodied in the printed word.

Some idea of the rate of growth in the printed word is given by the following figures for books published in the United Kingdom in selected years from 1929 to 1975.

1929	14,904
1951	18,066
1961	24,893
1969	32,393
1975	35,608

At the same time major technological developments are transforming the way in which library services operate.

Up to 1965 the Department's concern in this field was strictly limited. It had direct responsibility for two national collections (the Victoria and Albert Museum, and the Science Museum Libraries); it had certain limited powers in relation to public library authorities; and it had a general concern with library provision made by local education authorities (LEAs) in their schools and colleges. Responsibility for maintaining or aiding other major national libraries was dispersed amongst other departments.

THE LOCAL LIBRARY SERVICE

A local-authority-provided public library service had existed for more than fifty years before the LEAs were created. William Ewart's Act of 1850 allowed any borough with a population of over 10,000 to establish a free library on the rates. Later legislation empowered other local authorities, including parishes, to establish libraries, and by 1900 almost all the county boroughs and a number of non-county boroughs and urban districts had adopted the Acts. But development was haphazard, and much of the population, mainly but not only in rural areas, was not provided for.

After the First World War the idea of a nationwide public library service forming part of the education service was mooted by the Adult Education Committee of the Ministry of Reconstruction,[2] which proposed that counties and county boroughs (which were the education authorities for higher education) should exercise library (and museum) powers, with grant aid from central funds. But these proposals proved controversial, and little was done to implement them.

The pattern of library authorities remained haphazard. Some hundreds of smaller authorities, many of them serving very small populations, continued to exist alongside the county and county borough councils. Authorities had no duty to provide; expenditure on libraries continued to be borne entirely on the rates; and the central department had no effective powers to co-ordinate and develop the service.

THE NATIONAL CENTRAL LIBRARY

There was one development in the interwar period that prepared the way for a co-ordinated national service. One of the proposals made by the Adult Education Committee was that the Central Library for Students, founded by Albert Mansbridge in 1916 to meet the needs of university extramural and Workers' Education Association (WEA) students, should be developed into a national lending library. This proposal was developed by a departmental committee (the Kenyon Committee)[3] which recommended that the Central Library should be established as a national institution, grant-aided by the government, to serve as the nucleus of a national system of interlibrary co-operation. In 1931 the Central Library received a royal charter as the National Central Library, and its first grant-in-aid from the Exchequer, and in the following years a system of regional library networks linked with the National Central Library was developed to cover the whole of England and Wales.

THE ROBERTS
REPORT AND THE PUBLIC LIBRARIES
AND MUSEUMS ACT 1964

When local government in England and Wales was reviewed in the 1950s it was recognised that the public library and museum service needed separate consideration. In 1957 the then Minister of Education set up a committee under the chairmanship of Dr (later Sir) Sydney Roberts to look at the public library service. They reported in 1959.[4]

The Roberts Committee considered public libraries to be 'of vital importance to the whole community as an instrument in the education of the modern citizen'. They thought that it should be a statutory duty of a local authority, not merely a power, to provide an efficient public-library service. They recommended that a minister of the Crown should have a general responsibility for the oversight of the service and the power to enforce the proper exercise by local authorities of their library duties.

They proposed that the existing voluntary regional committees for interlibrary co-operation should be given statutory recognition, and should be required, under schemes to be approved by the Minister, to provide an effective system of library co-operation within their regions and to work in conjunction with the National Central Library in providing a national system.[5]

To assist the Minister in the exercise of his new duties the committee proposed that two advisory bodies should be appointed: one for England and one for Wales.

THE PUBLIC
LIBRARIES AND MUSEUMS ACT 1964

In 1964 a Bill, based largely on the Roberts Committee's recommendations, reached the statute book as the Public Libraries and Museums Act, and this came into operation in April 1965. Its principal provisions concerned libraries, but it also made certain changes in the law governing museums. In main essentials this is still in operation, although some of its provisions were modified by the Local Government Act 1972.

As proposed by the committee, the Act converted the library authorities' powers to provide a service into a duty to provide a comprehensive and efficient service. The Secretary of State was given the duty to superintend and promote the improvement of the service, and to secure the proper discharge by library authorities of their functions.[6] He was given power to obtain information from library authorities, to arrange inspections and to hold inquiries. He was also given powers of last resort in the event of a library authority failing to carry out its duties.

The criteria of a comprehensive and efficient library service were stated in broad terms in the Act. Library authorities were required to have regard to the desirability of securing adequate stocks for borrowing and for reference, both by keeping stocks themselves and by arrangements with other library authorities.[7]

The Secretary of State was given responsibility for designating library regions for interlibrary co-operation, and for making schemes for each region. There was provision for the appointment of a Library Advisory Council for England and one for Wales.

DEVELOPMENTS SINCE 1965

The period following the coming into effect of the 1964 Act was one of major expansion in the library service, with extensive programmes of public library building.

However, the continuing increase in demand for library services, more particularly specialist services, and developments in library technology led to growing doubts about the then existing pattern of authorities, many of them too small to provide an effective service.

The setting up of the Royal Commission on Local Government in England (the Redcliffe–Maud Commission) gave an opportunity for fuller study of the question of the local authority area best suited to exercise public library powers. The Department, in evidence submitted to the commission in 1967,[8] argued that, from the point of view of efficiency, convenience and economy, the best pattern would be a library service linked with the education service under large authorities. They thought that the minimum size for an efficient service was an area with a population of about 100,000.

The commission concluded that the library service ought to be the responsibility of the all-purpose unitary authorities that they proposed,[9] or, in the metropolitan areas, of the metropolitan district councils.[10] Thus library functions in England would in all cases be in the hands of authorities that were also education authorities, as the Department had recommended.

In its provisions for England the Local Government Act 1972 followed the commission's recommendations. Outside Greater London only the counties and, in metropolitan areas, the metropolitan district councils have library powers.[11]

The effect of these provisions has been to reduce the number of library authorities in England and Wales from 385 to 121 (including the City of London and the Isles of Scilly).

THE PUBLIC LIBRARY SERVICE TODAY,
AND THE DEPARTMENT'S ROLE

The locally-provided public-library service in England and Wales may be said to have two main aims, complementing the work of the education service: to satisfy the needs of individuals for their personal development, and to meet the needs of society for specialised knowledge and accurate information. Within these aims its main task is the provision of books and information on request. This requires an increasingly sophisticated system of interlending, to ensure access to stocks of national and specialised libraries, including foreign libraries.

Public libraries also have to meet a growing demand for 'non-book' material – microtexts, photocopies, tapes, film-slides, prints, gramophone records – and more attention needs to be given to specialist needs – for example, information services to industry and commerce, or material for those interested in local history, or the needs of particular groups such as inmates of old people's homes. Another major function of the service is to provide bibliographical services and advice. Table 11.1 gives some details of the growth in public libraries in England and Wales since 1965–6.

The Local Government Act 1972, by its provision that (with the possibility of exceptions in Wales) the library function shall be operated over the same areas as the education function, has made possible closer co-operation between the public library service and the libraries of institutions in the maintained sector – that is, of polytechnics and other colleges of higher and further education, schools and teacher centres.

Table 11.1 *Growth of public libraries in England and Wales from 1965–6 to 1975–6.*

Totals	1965–6	1969–70	1975–6
Total expenditure (£'000)	33,217	49,185	148,884
Expenditure on books (£'000)	8,355	11,171	25,435
Bookstock (volumes) ('000)	81,514	97,673	113,073
Staff:			
professional	5,090	6,346	7,529[1]
non-professional	11,976	12,605	13,955[2]
Lending issues ('000)	511,452	594,342	571,600
Books on loan			
(on a particular day) ('000)	17,502	21,767	31,741
Total expenditure per 1,000 of			
population (£)	698	1,006	3,029

[1] Total staff occupying professional posts (change of definition since 1969–70).
[2] Includes staff undergoing training.

Sources:
(a) For lending issues, *The Municipal Yearbook*.
(b) For other statistics, *Public Library Statistics*, issued by the Institute of Municipal Treasurers and Accountants (as from 1 April 1974 The Chartered Institute of Public Finance and Accountancy) and The Society of County Treasurers.

THE DEPARTMENT'S ROLE

By virtue of the Public Libraries and Museums Act 1964 the Department has come to have a role in relation to the public library service that is not unlike its role in relation to the local-authority-provided education service. Its main task is to assist local authorities to identify the changing needs of society for library-based services and to provide such services efficiently. It issues policy circulars and published reports (some based on research findings) to indicate the main lines of development.

The Secretary of State also has the duty to superintend standards. This is done mainly by the collection of statistical information, and also by studies and inspections carried out by the professional library advisers. These operate in much the same way as HM Inspectors, issuing reports and offering advice to library authorities. They are also concerned with general library policy, including library provision in colleges and schools, and they act as technical assessors to the library advisory councils.

The Department also sponsors library research from departmental funds; and it is involved, along with the local authority associations and other government departments, in the negotiations on rate support grant for which local authorities' expenditure on libraries is reckonable.

The Department is not only concerned with local-authority-provided services and with libraries in schools and colleges. It is also closely involved in the development of national libraries and in national library policy. The resources of the British Library (see p. 193) have assumed increasing importance as a central resource backing the facilities provided by local libraries.

THE LIBRARY ADVISORY COUNCILS
FOR ENGLAND AND WALES

In all its work in connection with libraries, local and national, the Department is advised by the Library Advisory Council for England and that for Wales. These councils are appointed by the Secretary of State, and must include persons who have had experience of the service provided by local authorities and persons with experience of libraries managed by other bodies. These are standing councils. They may offer advice to ministers on any matters relevant to library provision, whether under the 1964 Act or otherwise, as well as on matters specifically referred to them by ministers. Their secretariat is provided by the Department, which also appoints assessors.

Policy on national libraries: origins of the British Library
In the three decades since the Second World War the need to bring together all the public library resources of the country, both national and local, into a single inter-related system has become increasingly apparent. As mentioned earlier, the first step in this direction had already been taken in 1931 with the establishment of the National Central Library as the clearing house for a national system of interlending.

But this was only a first step. This country possesses a number of major national libraries and services between whose activities there was until recently little co-ordination. Of these the most important, apart from the National Central Library, are the British Museum Library (including what was the National Reference Library of Science and Invention, NRLSI), the National Lending Library of Science and Technology (NLLST), the Science Museum Library and the British National Bibliography (a private non-profit company). Scotland and Wales also have their national libraries, housing collections of special interest to these countries; and in Scotland the Scottish Central Library (now part of the National Library of Scotland) combines the functions of a regional library headquarters with some of the wider responsibilities of a national central library.

Up to the end of the 1960s all these, except the NLLST and the Science Museum Library, were autonomous bodies pursuing largely independent policies.

In 1967 a committee under the chairmanship of Dr F. S. (later Sir Frederick) Dainton, FRS, were appointed by the Secretary of State to examine the organisation and working of these institutions, and to consider whether in the interests of economy and efficiency they should be brought into a unified framework. Their report was published in June 1969.[12]

Their main recommendation was that a new statutory and independent authority should be established which would assume responsibility for the administration of four of the major national bodies: the British Museum Library (including the NRLSI), the National Central Library, the NLLST and the British National Bibliography. The new authority would also assume many of the functions of the Office of Scientific and Technical Information (OSTI) and of the Association of Special Libraries and Information

Bureaux (ASLIB). They proposed that the loan stocks of the National Central Library should be moved to Boston Spa (Yorkshire), already the headquarters of the NLLST, and that this should also be the headquarters of an interlibrary loan location service and a national reports centre.

They proposed that the British Museum Library, renamed the National Reference Library (NRL), should be located in central London, preferably immediately adjacent to the British Museum. They proposed that the National Reference Library of Science and Invention, renamed the Central Science and Patents Collection (CSPC), which they thought should aim to provide a comprehensive collection of Biritish and foreign patents and relevant technical literature, should also be housed in central London.

They further proposed the establishment of a national bibliographical service to combine and develop the bibliographical activities of the British National Bibliography, the British Museum Library, the NRLSI and the NLLST.

The Dainton Committee's recommendations were accepted in principle by the government in April 1970. In January 1971 the Paymaster-General (at that time the minister concerned with the arts and libraries) presented a White Paper, *The British Library*,[13] giving the government's detailed ideas for implementing them.

The White Paper set out proposals for 'the creation of a national library system without rival', which would also 'provide in the centre of London the most significant complex of museums and library resources in Europe'. It went on to propose – as had the Dainton Committee – that the British Museum Library (including the NRLSI), the NLLST, the National Central Library and the British National Bibliography should be brought together in a unified system under a new national authority to be called the British Library. This would be an independent body corporate, with maximum freedom to conduct its own affairs consistent with the broad objectives of government policy, and would receive grant aid from the department. The legal obligation on publishers to deposit one copy of each item they publish at the British Museum would be amended so as to become an obligation to deposit with the British Library.

The British Museum Library and the NRLSI, which were 'bursting at the seams', would be rehoused. The integration of the NLLST and the National Central Library into a single national lending service would necessitate expansion at Boston Spa so that it could accommodate all the lending facilities of the British Library. A bibliographic services division would be established by combining the British National Bibliography with the bibliographic functions and the copyright receipt office of the British Museum Library. The operation as a whole would thus be concentrated on two complexes: one in London for reference and bibliographical services, and the other in Boston Spa for lending services.

Other major national libraries such as those for Scotland and Wales were to remain independent. The British Library would develop close working relations with them.

A study into the feasibility of applying automatic data-processing to the operations and services of the British Library was commissioned; and its report[14] was considered by an organising committee under the Paymaster-General's chairmanship, to prepare the way for the establishment of the British Library. The results of these five years' preparatory work came to fruition with the passing in July 1972 of the British Library Act.

The Act sets out the duty of the British Library Board as 'to manage the Library as a national centre for reference, study and bibliographical and other information services, in relation both to scientific and technological matters and to the humanities'. It is given power to sponsor research both in achieving the objects of the Act and for contributing to the efficient management of other libraries and information services.

The board is also empowered to contribute to the expenses of public libraries and other libraries. Subject to reasonable safeguards it is empowered to lend any item. The board consists of a chairman appointed by the Secretary of State and not less than eight, nor more than thirteen, members (of whom at least one, who may be the chairman, shall be whole-time), preference being given to those with knowledge and experience of library or university affairs, finance, industry and administration. Provision is also made for advisory councils, for the registration of the British Library as a charity, and for the payment of a grant-in-aid by the Secretary of State.

The British Library Board was established in April 1973. By the end of July 1973 the stock from the National Central Library had been moved to Boston Spa and the Lending Division of the British Library was fully operational. The work of the board concentrated initially on the reorganisation of the Reference and Bibliographical Services Divisions of the British Library and on the provision and planning of accommodation for these services. Responsibility for the OSTI, which up to that time had been part of the Department. was transferred to the British Library in April 1974.

NOTES AND REFERENCES

1 The Department's responsibilities in respect of public libraries extend only to England. Public libraries in Wales are the responsibility of the Welsh Office.

2 Ministry of Reconstruction, *Third Interim Report of the Adult Education Committee*, Cd. 9237 (London, HMSO, 1919); and *Final Report of the Adult Education Committee*, Cmd 321 (London, HMSO, 1919).
3 Board of Education, *Public Libraries in England and Wales*, report of the Public Libraries Committee, Cmnd 2868 (London, HMSO, 1927).
4 Ministry of Education, *The Structure of the Public Library Service in England and Wales*, report of the committee appointed by the Minister of Education in September 1957 (the Roberts Report), Cmnd 660 (London, HMSO, 1958).
5 The implications of the committee's main recommendations were examined by two technical working parties; one on the standards of library service, the other on interlibrary co-operation. That on standards (London, HMSO, 1962) suggested yardsticks by which library authorities could measure the efficiency of their service. That on interlibrary co-operation (London, HMSO, 1962) proposed the reorganisation of the eight English regions into four or five, and drafted a model scheme for regional co-operation.
6 Since 1966 local authorities' expenditure on public libraries has been reckonable for rate support grant.
7 In an appendix to Circular 4/65 of 29 March 1965 the Department set out the criteria in greater detail, drawing largely on the report of the Working Party on Standards of Public Library Service, op. cit.
8 Royal Commission on Local Government in England, *Written Evidence of the Department of Education and Science* (London, HMSO, 1967); see especially app. VI.
9 *Royal Commission on Local Government in England 1966–69* (Chairman: Lord Redcliffe-Maud), Cmnd 4040 (London, HMSO, 1969), para. 384. (This applied only to England; Wales was not within the Royal Commission's terms of reference.)
10 ibid., para. 338.
11 Circular 5/73. In the case of Wales the Act includes a provision allowing district councils to seek the approval of the Secretary of State to exercise library powers in certain circumstances.
12 *Report of the National Libraries Committee*, Cmnd 4028 (London, HMSO, June 1969).
13 White Paper, *The British Library*, Cmnd 4572 (London, HMSO, January 1971).
14 DES, *Scope for Automatic Processing in the British Library: Report of a Study into the Feasibility of Applying ADP to the Operations and Services of the British Library* (by M. B. Line) (London, HMSO, 1972).

CHAPTER 12

The Department's Concern with the Arts and Museums

Before 1965 the Department (Ministry) had no responsibility for patronage and preservation of the arts.[1] This came mainly from two sources: the Arts Council of Great Britain, and the local authorities.

The Arts Council was established by royal charter in 1946 as an autonomous body, to carry on in peace time the work that had been done with outstanding success during the Second World War by the Council for the Encouragement of Music and the Arts (CEMA). The moving spirit in the creation of the Arts Council was the late Lord Keynes, who had served as chairman of the CEMA. Lord Keynes died before the council received its royal charter. The council's task was, in the words of its charter, the development of 'a greater knowledge, understanding and practice of the fine arts . . . and in particular to increase the accessibility of the fine arts to the public' and 'to improve the standard of execution . . . of the fine arts'. It was required to advise and co-operate with government departments, local authorities and other bodies on any matters concerned directly or indirectly with these objects.

The Arts Council became the main instrument for public patronage of the arts throughout Great Britain, and the channel for grants from Exchequer funds for a number of major national enterprises such as Covent Garden, the Royal Ballet, Sadlers Wells and, later, the Royal Shakespeare Company and the National Theatre. From the outset it has also had as one of its main aims the encouragement of the arts outside London, in the English provinces and (through its Scottish and Welsh Committees) in Scotland and Wales – for example, by supporting leading orchestras, repertory theatres and arts festivals, and by assistance to regional and local arts associations.

From its creation in 1946 up to 1965 the Arts Council received its grant directly from the Treasury. The then Ministry of Education was concerned only to the extent that the council's charter required education ministers to be consulted on the appointment of its chairman and members, and officials of the education departments served as assessors on the council.

As regards preservation of the arts, the Department's responsibility was until 1965 confined to administering two national museums: the Victoria and Albert Museum (with its dependencies in and around London: Apsley House, the Bethnal Green Museum, Ham House and Osterley Park), and the Science Museum. For both of these, responsibility had rested with the central department since their establishment in 1857.[3] It had no responsibility for the major trustee museums and galleries in London, or those in Scotland and Wales. These received grant aid either from the Treasury, or from the Scottish or (more recently) the Welsh Office.

Local authorities had powers to maintain or grant-aid local museums and galleries, and these were clarified and extended by the Public Libraries and Museums Act 1964, which also gave the central department certain limited powers in relation to local museums. By 1965 there were some 900 provincial museums and galleries supported or administered by local authorities. Purchases by local museums and galleries were assisted through a modest fund administered by the Victoria and Albert Museum.

During the 1960s the first steps were taken, on the advice of the Standing Commission on Museums and Galleries, towards the development of an area museum service, to co-ordinate improvements and extensions of the work of provincial museums and galleries, through a network of area museum councils, with assistance from Exchequer funds. Under the Local Government Act 1972, county and district authorities, the Greater London Council and London boroughs and the Isles of Scilly only were designated as museum authorities for the purposes of the Public Libraries and Museums Act 1964.

The 1965 White Paper A Policy for the Arts
A White Paper of February 1965, *A Policy for the Arts*,[4] announced that responsibility for grant aiding the arts would be transferred from the Treasury to the Secretary of State for Education and Science, who would delegate it to a minister in his department. There were to be appropriate arrangements to meet the special interests of Scotland and Wales. The Arts Council's charter was amended accordingly.

The arrangement by which the greater part of Exchequer aid for the arts was channelled through the Arts Council was to be maintained, and it was made clear that, within the broader context set by the government's policy, the council would retain its autonomy and its freedom in allocating grants.

Amongst the policy objectives that the government at that time singled out as having a special claim on the increased funds to be made available were: more financial help to living artists, greater encouragement for the arts outside London, and a programme to overcome the dearth of suitable buildings for housing the arts – theatres, arts centres, and so forth. Subsequent ministers concerned with the arts have continued to support these objectives.

An increasing amount of the Arts Council's grant has been devoted to the sponsoring of the arts in the regions, particularly through grants to regional arts associations. These started in 1965 and grew up independently of the Council. By 1974 most of the country was covered by associations and their income had begun to grow rapidly.

The Arts Council decides, within the total grant available, the resources to be made available to the Arts Councils of Scotland and Wales, which are constitutionally committees of the Arts Council of Great Britain.[5] The branch of the Department that is responsible for advising on grants to the Arts Council, and to certain other bodies such as the British Film Institute and the National Film School, has a general concern with the administrative efficiency of the bodies receiving aid, to ensure that the grants effectively promote agreed policy objectives. This branch is also responsible for advising, with the assistance of an advisory committee, on government policy on the export of works of art.

Increasing help has also been given to the crafts, as a result of a government pledge in 1970 that there would be a better deal for the artist craftsman. Responsibility for this field was transferred to the Department of Education and Science from the Department of Trade and Industry, and a new advisory committee structure was established. The Crafts Advisory Committee has aimed to bring fuller understanding by the public of the importance of the work of the artist craftsman, to strengthen and rationalise the craft associations and to improve the quantity and quality of the product. The committee is also examining the crafts of conservation alongside those of new production.

MUSEUMS AND GALLERIES

The Administration that took office in the summer of 1970 extended the responsibilities of the minister concerned with the arts and libraries to include oversight of policy and development for the major trustee museums and art galleries in London,[6] and also a general concern with provincial museums and galleries.

A White Paper of 1971[7] announced an expanded programme of building for the national museums and galleries, resources for which were to be augmented by a scheme of admission charges which were introduced in January 1974. The Minister also announced the government's intention to review the needs of provincial museums and galleries and their links with the national institutions. Members of the committee appointed for this purpose were drawn from the Standing Commission on Museums and Galleries, the Museums Association, the local authorities associations, and Scotland and Wales.

This committee reported in June 1973. It made recommendations on standards of accommodation, staff and training, communication, education, aid from the national museums, resources and organisation, and the special problems confronting university and private museums and museums in Scotland and Wales. One of its principal recommendations was a new fund to give capital assistance from central government for building projects for local museums. This was not accepted by the government because they considered that the essential responsibility for housing their museums must rest with the local authorities concerned; but they undertook to consider with the local authorities what could be done within the resources available to assist cases of museums of 'more than local significance', remitting to the Standing Commission on Museums and Galleries the task of looking at possible cases.

NOTES AND REFERENCES

1 The Department's responsibilities for the arts (but not museums and galleries) cover Great Britain as a whole.

2 The power of local authorities to contribute to the arts prior to 1974 derived mainly from the Local Government Act 1948, which permitted municipal authorities in England and Wales to spend the product of a sixpenny rate (together with proceeds from charges) on entertainment of all kinds. By the provisions of the Local Government Act 1972 all county and district authorities are expressly permitted to support the arts by providing or encouraging performances or exhibitions, by assisting arts assoc .tions and centres and in other ways (Circular 9/73, para. 11).

3 For a brief account of the history of these two museums up to 1950 see Education 1900–1950, report of the Ministry of Education and Statistics of Public Education for England and Wales, Cmd 8244 (London, HMSO, 1951). pp. 126ff. Accounts of subsequent developments may be found in the publications of these two establishments.

4 White Paper, A Policy for the Arts, Cmnd 2601 (London, HMSO, 1965).

5 Full accounts of the activities of the Arts Council of Great Britain, and of those of Scotland and Wales, are contained in their annual reports, published together in a single volume.

6 The most important are the British Museum, the Imperial War Museum, the London Museum, the Transport Museum, the National Maritime Museum, the National Gallery, the National Portrait Gallery, the Tate Gallery and the Wallace Collection. (For the British Museum (Natural History) see Chapter 13). The National Museums of Scotland and of Wales are the responsibility of the Secretaries of State for Scotland and Wales respectively.

7 White Paper, *Future Policy for Museums and Galleries*, Cmnd 4676 (London, HMSO, 1971).

CHAPTER 13

The Department and Civil Science

BEGINNINGS OF GOVERNMENT SUPPORT FOR CIVIL SCIENCE: THE DEPARTMENT OF SCIENTIFIC AND INDUSTRIAL RESEARCH

The history of government support for civil science goes back to the First World War.[1] The country had been profoundly shaken by the experience of fighting a war against a power with highly developed scientific and technological resources, and one of the conclusions drawn by the wartime Administration was that a more effective deployment of the country's resources in these fields would be needed to meet the industrial problems of the postwar period, and that the state must play its part. The chosen instrument was to be a Department of Scientific and Industrial Research (DSIR).[2]

The original function of the DSIR was to develop knowledge required for the application of science to industry. One of the means that it employed was the grant-aiding of research in universities and the making of awards for postgraduate training in research. It also undertook research in its own establishments and aided autonomous bodies.

This is not the place for a detailed account of the DSIR.[3] There are, however, two features of its work that are relevant here. The first concerns its organisation. The DSIR's Advisory (subsequently Executive) Council consisted mainly of scientists of repute, who enjoyed a large measure of autonomy in deciding on research to be encouraged and on the allocation of resources. It thus commanded the confidence of both scientists and leading industrialists. This was an arrangement to which great importance was attached by those who created the organisation, and it was one that largely influenced the pattern of organisation of the more specialised research councils established later.

The philosophy underlying this arrangement has commonly been referred to as the 'Haldane principle' after Lord Haldane, former War Minister and a senior member of the wartime Administration, who had a major influence in the creation of the DSIR. The Report of the Committee on the Machinery of Government,[4] of which he was chairman, held up the Advisory Council as a model for future public research bodies in the field of civil science.

Secondly, because much of the work of the DSIR was concerned with universities, it had from the outset close links with the higher education system and with the body that became the University Grants Committee (UGC).[5]

THE RESEARCH COUNCILS

In the following years further research councils concerned with particular aspects of science were established. These represented a. new concept, following in some ways, but not in all, the DSIR pattern. The Medical Research Council (originally established in 1913) received its first royal charter in 1920. The Agricultural Research Council followed in 1931, and the Nature Conservancy in 1949.

The main functions of these bodies were to support scientific research, to provide a fundamental research capability and to advance the standards of scientific excellence in their fields, as well as meeting the needs of departments for applied research. They might operate either through their own establishments, or through independent agencies (including international agencies) or by aiding research and research training in universities, and they were responsible for giving expert advice to the government. Unlike the DSIR none of these bodies at any time became a government department. While the arrangements for their direction and financing varied,[6] from the outset they have had certain features in common. Their membership has in most cases (although not all) consisted of independent individuals, both scientists and laymen. Their permanent staff are not civil servants, but are on terms of service similar to those of the civil service (or in some cases of university staffs). Although they have at all times been formally subject to ministerial direction and are mainly dependent on grant aid from the Exchequer, they have considerable independence in determining their own programmes within the resources made available to them by the government.

THE ADVISORY COUNCIL ON SCIENTIFIC POLICY

In 1947 an Advisory Council on Scientific Policy was established, with terms of reference covering the whole field of government involvement in scientific and industrial research.[7] This had an independent scientist as chairman; and its members included independent scientists and scientific industrialists, together with the senior officers of the research councils, the chairman of the UGC, and a representative of the Treasury.

A MINISTER FOR SCIENCE

During the 1950s there was growing pressure on the government to appoint a minister responsible for government science in name as well as in fact – up to that time it had been the responsibility of the Lord President. In 1959 a minister in the Cabinet was for the first time designated Minister for Science, combining this title with that of Lord President, and having responsibility for 'broad questions of scientific policy'. He was given oversight of the DSIR and the research councils, and assumed chairmanship of the Privy Council committees to which they then reported. He also exercised ministerial functions under the atomic energy Acts and in relation to the programme of space research.

He was at that time advised by the Advisory Council on Scientific Policy; and he was also given a small office of civil servants, designated the Office of the Minister for Science.

THE TREND REPORT
AND CONSEQUENT REORGANISATION

These arrangements did not work satisfactorily. In March 1962 a small committee of senior civil servants and scientists were appointed, under the chairmanship of the then Secretary of the Cabinet, Sir Burke Trend, to review the arrangements for government-sponsored civil science. They reported in October 1963.[8]

The Trend Committee identified two main defects in the arrangements: they did not 'in the aggregate constitute a coherent and articulated pattern of organisation'; and there was insufficient clarity and precision about the arrangements for co-ordinating the government's scientific effort and for apportioning resources between the different agencies.

One of the committee's main criticisms concerned the pattern of research councils. They found that, except in medicine and agriculture, this was not such as to provide a comprehensive and coherent coverage of civil science as a whole. They also took the view that the attempt to combine in one agency – namely, the DSIR – the function of supporting basic scientific research and that of promoting technological development, had had the result of producing an unwieldy organisation.

Among their main recommendations was one that the DSIR should be dissolved. They proposed that its responsibilities for industrial research and development should be assigned to a new agency created for the purpose. To discharge its functions in supporting scientific research and training (other than in agriculture, medicine and the environment) they proposed a new body, to be called the Science Research Council. This would be concerned with research in both 'pure' and 'applied' science. It would amongst other things be responsible for the National Institute for Research in Nuclear Science (NIRNS), for the scientific aspects of the United Kingdom's relations with the European Organisation for Nuclear Research (CERN), for the UK programme of space research and relations with the European Space Research Organisation (ESRO), and for the royal observatories.

They also proposed the establishment of a new research council concerned with natural resources, which would take over the work of the Nature Conservancy, including its responsibility for national nature reserves, its research activities and other related functions – notably research into hydrology, fisheries and related aspects of aquatic biology; the Geological and Soil Surveys; long-term forestry research; and (jointly with the Admiralty) research into oceanography.

The Trend Committee in general endorsed the Haldane principle as they understood it – that is, the principle that responsibility for scientific research should be in the hands of a minister who is 'immune from any suspicion of being biased by administrative considerations against the application of the results of research', and the allied concept that public funds for civil scientific research should be administered by autonomous research councils.

They also endorsed the principle of dual support of university science, that is, the arrangements by which scientific research in universities is supported both by the research councils and by the UGC.

They thought that the scope for initiative of the Minister for Science was too circumscribed.[9] While accepting it as axiomatic that he should not interfere with the scientific judgement of the research councils, they thought that he should be enabled to take a more positive role in promoting research and development, and that he should be responsible for assessing the resources needed by each agency and deciding on priorities.

They also thought that he should be responsible for keeping the whole field of civil scientific research under review, and where necessary adjusting the distribution of functions, creating new agencies and eliminating any that had outlived their usefulness.

They proposed that the Privy Council committees supervising the research councils should be dissolved, and that the Minister should assume the power to appoint the governing bodies of the agencies and to issue formal directions. He should also be responsible for the government's relations with the Royal Society and other learned bodies, and for the government's international relations in scientific matters.

They proposed that the Minister should have the advice of a Council for Scientific Policy (CSP), which should supersede the existing Advisory Council for Scientific Policy and consist entirely of independent members, half of whom should be scientists. The CSP would advise the Minister on all his scientific functions, including the broad allocation of resources, and on national scientific needs as a whole, including scientific manpower, administrative machinery and international scientific policy.

They proposed that the Office of the Minister for Science should be strengthened so that it could provide an effective secretariat for the CSP and assume responsibility for co-ordinating the research agencies.

GOVERNMENT ACTION ON THE TREND REPORT: ARRANGEMENTS FROM 1964

The government accepted the main recommendations of the Trend Report. In April 1964 the functions of the Minister of Education and those of the Minister for Science were transferred to the newly created Secretary of State for Education and Science.

In July 1964 the new Secretary of State announced his intention to dissolve the DSIR and to establish a Science Research Council and a Natural Environment Research Council, with substantially the range of functions proposed in the Trend Report, and also to establish an Industrial Research and Development Authority, which would take over most of the functions of the DSIR in industrial research.

These changes required legislation; and this, although on a somewhat modified pattern, was carried through by the Labour Administration that came into office in October 1964, reaching the statute book as the Science and Technology Act 1965. This made new and uniform provision for the financing and direction of civil science by the Secretary of State. It established the two new research councils, and also provided for the creation of others; and it dissolved the DSIR, providing for the transfer of its functions either to the research councils or to appropriate government departments. (In its provisions for industrial research the Act embodied policies differing from those envisaged by the previous Administration.)

The Advisory Council for Scientific Policy was replaced by a Council for Scientific Policy (CSP), with terms of reference limited to science and excluding technology. One of its main tasks was to be to advise on the distribution of resources to the research councils.

In December 1965 the government, on the recommendation of the Heyworth Committee on Social Studies, established a Social Science Research Council to cover a range of subjects including economics, political science, social anthropology, sociology, psychology, management studies and education. At first the vote for this council was determined directly by the Department of Education and Science (DES) and it had no links with the CSP; but in 1971 its allocation of funds came within the purview of the CSP. Consequently the scope of the CSP was widened to include the social as well as the natural and life sciences; but neither the CSP nor its successor body, the Advisory Board for the Research Councils (see below), has embraced the humanities. Thus the range of science policy is narrower than that comprehended by the German term *Wissenschaft*, and the activities of the CSP and its successor body have been more restricted than those of similar bodies in, say, Germany or Switzerland.

THE DES SCIENCE BRANCH AND THE SCIENCE BUDGET

The Office of the Minister for Science in 1965 became the Science Branch of the DES.[10] The functions of this branch include responsibility for advising the Secretary of State on general policy for civil science (including support for postgraduate students), and on matters requiring specific approval referred by the research councils and the Natural History Museum. It advises on appointments to the research councils and to the Advisory Board for the Research Councils, and it services the Advisory Board.

With the assistance of the Advisory Board for the Research Councils it deals with what is known as the science budget. This consists mainly of grants in aid to the rescarch councils under the Science and Technology Act 1965. There are two other votes: that for the British Museum (Natural History); and that for 'science: grants and services', which covers grants to the Royal Society and other bodies.[11]

The Science Branch is also responsible for handling important aspects of the international relations of science. Thus it co-ordinates briefing for research council commitments towards international scientific organisations, and is responsible for scientific matters in the field of international agencies such as the North Atlantic Treaty Organisation (NATO), the Council of Europe, the European Economic Community (EEC), the Commonwealth Scientific Committee and the Organisation for Economic Co-operation and Development (OECD).

RESEARCH COUNCIL SUPPORT FOR SCIENTIFIC RESEARCH IN UNIVERSITIES

As earlier noted, much of the work of the research councils is carried out in their own establishments or associated institutes. This has particularly been the case with the Agricultural, Medical and Natural Environment Research Councils. But from the early days the research councils have also pursued their objectives by supporting scientific research in universities, and postgraduate training in research.

Research council grants to universities are not intended to assist with their general upkeep – this is the responsibility of the UGC. They are earmarked for scientific research, or for postgraduate training, in subjects related to the research councils' activities. Their purposes are to help to maintain the universities as the foundation of the country's scientific activity; to promote high scientific standards in all universities – and the highest international standards in some; to help individual scientific enterprise to flourish, and to make use of the quality and breadth of knowledge within universities in developing new areas of research or in tackling specific problems of national importance.

Their support of university research takes various forms. They may make direct grants to individuals or groups for work judged to be of timeliness and promise. They may give assistance for ancillary services, such as libraries, computers or supporting staff. Some – the Science Research Council in particular – provide for the joint use by groups of universities of expensive facilities that would be beyond the means of any one university, for example, the Rutherford and Daresbury nuclear physics laboratories. In some cases university scientists may benefit from facilities provided through research council contributions to international establishments, such as CERN.

The provision of shared facilities, and the concentration of costly facilities at a limited number of centres, has assumed increasing importance as costs, particularly for what is called 'big science', have continued to rise and there has been a falling off in the rate of growth of the resources available to the research councils.

Research council awards for postgraduate training in science are broadly of three kinds: research studentships for training in methods of research; advanced course studentships for postgraduate courses in specialised fields; and research fellowships (strictly limited in number) for those who show promise of capacity for original research. Research councils also make grants to university departments in which holders of postgraduate awards work, to be used at the departments' discretion for research-training purposes.

HIGHLY QUALIFIED MANPOWER FOR SCIENCE AND TECHNOLOGY

One of the functions of the Advisory Council for Scientific Policy, which was inherited by the CSP, was to advise on scientific manpower. Between 1965 and 1970 two influential reports were produced by groups working in this field in collaboration with the Committee on Manpower Resources for Science and Technology.[12]

In 1968 a group under the chairmanship of Dr F. S. (later Sir Frederick) Dainton produced a Report on the Flow of Candidates in Science and Technology into Higher Education.[13] This drew attention to the phenomenon known as the 'swing from science' in school sixth forms and in universities, and to the potentially harmful consequences of this trend. Amongst their recommendations for counteracting it was a broadening of the sixth-form curriculum and a revision by universities of their entrance requirements to encourage this development. The report of this group had a considerable influence on thinking about the sixth-form curriculum, both in the Schools Council and in the universities.

In the same year a second working group, under the chairmanship of Professor M. M. (later Sir Michael) Swann, studied the flow into employment of qualified scientists, engineers and technologists.[14] They found that there was excessive concentration of scientific talent in fundamental research in universities and government establishments, and that this was depriving both industry and the schools of the qualified manpower that they needed. Amongst the measures that they proposed were the development of undergraduate courses combining science with preparation for teaching, the revision of both undergraduate and postgraduate courses to make them more suitable to the needs of industry, and the development of refresher or post-experience courses for qualified manpower in industry.

NEW THINKING ON THE WORK OF THE RESEARCH COUNCILS: THE 1971 GREEN PAPER AND 1972 WHITE PAPERS

Shortly after the change of government in June 1970, the research council system was the subject of several reviews, which were to have important consequences for their structure and financing.

The first in point of time was one undertaken by a working group under Sir Frederick Dainton, set up by the CSP to advise on effective arrangements for supporting pure and applied scientific research. The immediate occasion for this inquiry was a proposal to transfer the Agricultural Research Council to the Ministry of Agriculture. The CSP also thought that, as nearly six years had elapsed since they were set up, the time had come to consider how the system had evolved. Shortly afterwards the government, as part of a review of departmental functions, commissioned Lord Rothschild, the then head of the Central Policy Review Staff, to report on the whole range of government research and development, including work in relation to defence and industry. The results of these two inquiries were published together in November 1971 as a Green Paper,[15] which also included a memorandum giving a preliminary indication of the government's views.

In 1971–2 the House of Commons Select Committee on Science and Technology made a review of government research and development (R and D) as a whole and the part played in it by the research councils, publishing their conclusions in their First and Fourth Reports for that session.[16] The government's considered conclusions in the light of these inquiries were published in White Papers of July 1972[17] and December 1972.[18]

LORD ROTHSCHILD'S REPORT

Lord Rothschild's report was essentially concerned with the method of funding government R and D – that is, R and D with a practical application as its objective. One of its main theses was that this should be on a consumer–contractor basis; that is, the government department concerned should decide what programmes of R and D it needed, for what objectives and at what cost, and should foot the bill.

His views had important implications for some of the research councils. He found that much of the work of the Agricultural, Medical and Natural Environment Research Councils fell into the category of applied research, and should therefore be financed on the customer–contractor principle.[19] The customers would be the departments concerned, namely, the Ministry of Agriculture, the Department of Health and Social Security and the Department of the Environment (and Welsh and Scottish Offices); and he proposed that, as soon as these departments were organised to undertake the work, a substantial proportion of the science budget should be transferred to them.

Consequential changes would be needed in the functions and composition of the three research councils affected and in the arrangements for the appointment of their officers. Thus Lord Rothschild thought that it would be appropriate for the Secretary of State, when appointing their chief executives, and also their part-time chairmen, to consult the departmental ministers concerned, and for the chief scientists of the customer departments to be full members of the research councils with which their departments were mainly concerned.

He thought that the CSP should continue to advise on the distribution between the research councils of funds remaining on the DES vote, but that they should not be responsible for the funds provided by the customer departments for research commissioned from the research councils.

VIEWS OF THE DAINTON GROUP

The Dainton group were concerned only with the work of the research councils and not with government R and D as a whole, although they were well aware of the variety of national objectives to which science is relevant. They thought it more useful to think in terms of three categories of scientific work: 'tactical' science, needed by government and industry to further their immediate objectives; 'strategic' science, that is, the broad spread of more general scientific effort needed to maintain the vigour of the relevant disciplines; and 'basic' science, that is, research and training having no specific application but needed to ensure the advance of knowledge and the maintenance of a corps of able scientists.

They believed that the organisation required to manage basic and strategic research must be one that unifies rather than fragments scientific activity, in which the determination of programmes is in the hands of scientists who recognise the benefits of the interactions between disciplines and is not dispersed to executive departments, and one that retains a close association with the education and training of future scientists. This amounted in their view to a reaffirmation of what they saw as the research council principle, although they recognised that the machinery must be such as to ensure closer links between the research councils.

At the same time they acknowledged that it was important, if 'ivory-towerism' was to be avoided, that those making judgements on the allocation of resources should be continually aware of national needs and objectives, and that there should be closer contacts between the research councils and the departments concerned. For this reason they endorsed Lord Rothschild's view that the Secretary of State, when appointing chairmen of individual research councils, should consult the ministerial colleagues concerned.

They also saw a need for changes in the machinery for supervising the research councils' work. They proposed that the CSP should be replaced by a board which – in addition to the scientific heads of the research councils, the President of the Royal Society, a UGC representative and independent members – would include members from relevant departments and a representative of the chief scientific adviser (Cabinet Office).

Their proposed board, like its predecessor, would be responsible to the Secretary of State for Education and Science, but it would be constituted under a charter designed to protect the independence of government-supported basic and strategic science. Amongst its responsibilities would be that of ensuring that the requirements of the executive departments for scientific support from the research councils were properly met. They also thought that this board should be consulted by the Secretary of State when appointing the chairmen and members of individual research councils.

VIEWS OF THE HOUSE OF COMMONS SELECT COMMITTEE ON SCIENCE AND TECHNOLOGY

As already indicated, the House of Commons Select Committee were mainly concerned, in their First Report, with government R and D as a whole; and on this their recommendation was that there should be a cabinet minister for R and D, concerned with the whole range of government science, both defence and civil, and advised by a statutory Council for Science and Technology with similarly comprehensive terms of reference. They did, however, have a view about the research council system, which was that it should be retained because (and here they quoted words used by Sir Frederick Dainton in his oral evidence) it provided 'a mechanism by which the overall programme can best be devised, best monitored and where all the elements of the customer and the contractor and the man doing the work on the bench can be brought together'. They also attached great importance to a continuing close relationship between the research councils and the universities. And they were clear that the link between the research councils and the DES should be retained.

But they thought that the government should define more clearly what the role of the research councils should be within the whole field of government R and D. They also thought that individual research councils needed to keep in closer touch with government departments and industry, and to this end they proposed that their membership should be reconstituted to ensure wider representation.

While they accepted Lord Rothschild's views about the importance of the customer–contractor principle, they thought that its application required further consideration, and proposed that any reallocation of responsibilities between the research councils and departments should await a joint review of current programmes and needs.

They further recommended that their proposed Council for Science and Technology should set up a committee for the research councils – with membership based on the Rothschild and Dainton proposals, but with the addition of independent representatives from industry, the trade unions and other outside interests – to take the place of the CSP, advising the Secretary of State on the allocation of the science budget and on policies affecting the research councils as a whole.

In their Fourth Report the Select Committee reverted to their theme of the inadequacy of the existing machinery of government R and D, and the need for a minister for R and D advised by a statutory council.

THE GOVERNMENT'S CONCLUSIONS: THE 1972 WHITE PAPERS

In their preface to the Green Paper of November 1971 the government had already given a preliminary indication of their views on three points. They had agreed that applied R and D commissioned by the government should be organised on a customer–contractor basis. Subject to this, they had made clear their view that the research councils should be preserved under the sponsorship of the DES. Thirdly, they believed that authoritative advice should continue to be available to the Secretary of State on the allocation of the science budget.

In a White Paper of July 1972 the government developed these conclusions in the light of the views expressed by Lord Rothschild, by the Dainton group, in subsequent consultations, and in the First Report of the House of Commons Select Committee. Many of their conclusions concerned R and D in government departments generally and are not directly relevant here.

But an important section of the White Paper dealt with the work of the research councils. This pointed out that the purpose of the research supported through the five research councils and the UGC was: to develop the sciences as such, to maintain a fundamental capacity for research and to support higher education. Much of it was in subjects for which government departments did not have the necessary facilities. For these and other reasons they reaffirmed their intention of retaining the system of research councils responsible to the Secretary of State for Education and Science.

However, they accepted that in future the departments most directly concerned should be more closely associated in framing the research councils' programmes, and should be provided with funds to commission applied research in some areas covered by the research councils. The research councils would be asked to seek amendments to their charters so as to include as full members representatives of departments with a substantial interest in their work, and the Secretary of State would in future agree such appointments with the ministerial colleagues principally concerned. Subject to the establishment of chief scientist organisations in the main customer departments, part of the DES science budget would be transferred over a three-year period to those departments, to meet their needs for commissioned research. The departments would have final responsibility for defining the objectives of commissioned research, although it would be open to the research councils to refuse work on reasonable grounds.

In place of the CSP the government stated its intention to establish an Advisory Board for the Research Councils, whose membership would include the chairmen or secretaries of the five research councils, the Chairman of the UGC, senior scientists from departments with a major interest in the work of the research councils, a representative of the chief scientific adviser, and independent members drawn from the universities, industry and the Royal Society.

At the same time they announced their intention of making changes in the responsibilities of the National Environment Research Council. Its activities in managing national nature reserves, its advisory, educational and protective work on wildlife conservation, and its applied research connected with these activities, would in their view be more appropriately funded through an environmental programme budget. Accordingly funds for these activities would from 1973–4 onwards be transferred from the DES science budget to the Department of the Environment.

In September 1972 the Secretary of State announced the setting up and terms of reference of the new Advisory Board for the Research Councils. The government's White Paper of December 1972,[20] published following the Fourth Report of the House of Commons Select Committee, was mainly concerned with rehearsing the arguments against the Select Committee's proposal for a minister for R and D. But it again made clear, in a passage dealing with the research councils and the DES, that the composition of the Advisory Board, which was to replace the CSP, would be such as to ensure that customer departments, as well as the chief scientific adviser, would be represented as full members. It also confirmed that the Secretary of State would consult the ministerial colleagues principally concerned when appointing chairmen and ministerial nominees of research councils. These arrangements should, in the government's view, do much to promote co-operation between all the partners, and to ensure that the work of the Advisory Board was closely related to the total scientific effort of government.

They also made it clear that, like the Select Committee, they attached great importance to the support that the research councils gave to the universities, and that this would continue.

Civil science, along with all other aspects of the work of the DES, has had to accept the retrenchment resulting from the country's economic situation. The cutback has fallen particularly heavily on 'big science', which, on the advice of the Advisory Board, has been held back in order to make it possible to sustain the work of other sciences (including applied science) supported by the Science Research Council, and to enable the Agricultural, Medical, Natural Environment and Social Science Research Councils to continue to develop programmes based on social need as well as scientific opportunity.

NOTES AND REFERENCES

1 The responsibilities of the DES for civil science extend to Great Britain as a whole.
2 White Paper, *A Scheme for the Organisation and Development of Scientific and Industrial Research*, Cd 8005 (London, HMSO, July 1915).
3 This may be found in Sir Harry Melville, *The Department of Scientific and Industrial Research*, New Whitehall Series (London, Allen & Unwin, 1962).
4 Ministry of Reconstruction, *Report of the Committee on the Machinery of Government* (Chairman: Viscount Haldane of Cloane), Cd 9230 (London, HMSO, 1918).
5 The White Paper of 1915 was presented by the then President of the Board of Education, which was at that time directly concerned with the universities. (See Chapter 9.) The president was a member of the Privy Council committee responsible for overseeing the DSIR. Up to 1929 there was a further link because the administrative chairmanship of the DSIR and that of the UGC were held by the same person (Sir William McCormick).
6 For details of the research councils' constitutions and functions see the DES annual report for 1967, pp. 88–90.
7 Initially the Advisory Council on Scientific Policy advised on defence as well as on civil science. With the replacement of Sir Harry Tizard by Lord Todd as its chairman, its terms of reference were limited to civil science.
8 *Report of the Committee of Enquiry into the Organisation of Civil Science* (the Trend Report), Cmnd 2171 (London, HMSO, 1963).
9 The Robbins Committee, which reported at about the same time, also had views on the control of government science (Committee on Higher Education, *Higher Education*, Cmnd 2154, London, HMSO, 1963, para. 784). In

discussing the machinery for central control of higher education they proposed a Minister for Arts and Science, who would in effect combine the functions of a Minister for Science with those of a Minister for Higher Education and a Minister for the Arts.

10 Initially there were two science branches, but these were merged in 1969. (See p. 158.)

11 For an authoritative account of the science budget see HC Expenditure Committee (Session 1970–71), *2nd Report*, HC 545 (London, HMSO, 1971); memorandum by the Department of Education and Science, p. 183.

12 In 1970 the Department of Employment took over from DES responsibility for co-ordination of government policy in relation to highly qualified manpower.

13 *Report of the Enquiry into the Flow of Candidates in Science and Technology into Higher Education*, Cmnd 3541 (London, HMSO, 1968).

14 CSP, *The Flow into Employment of Scientists, Engineers and Technologists*, Cmnd 3760 (London, HMSO, 1968).

15 Green Paper, *A Framework for Government Research and Development* (Lord Rothschild's report), Cmnd 4814 (London, HMSO, November 1971).

16 HC Select Committee on Science and Technology (Session 1971–72), *First Report: Research and Development*, HC 237 (London, HMSO, 1972); *Fourth Report: Research and Development*, HC 308 (London, HMSO, 1972).

17 White Paper, *Framework for Government Research and Development*, Cmnd 5046 (London, HMSO, 1972).

18 White Paper, *House of Commons Select Committee on Science and Technology, Session 1971–72: Government Observations on First and Fourth Reports*, Cmnd 5177 (London, HMSO, December 1972).

19 Lord Rothschild found that the Science Research Council was unaffected, as it was largely concerned with pure and, to a lesser extent, applied science, which he did not regard as synonymous with applied research. He did not include the Social Science Research Council in his review because its work was in its infancy.

20 *Government Observations on First and Fourth Reports*, op. cit.

PART SIX

Organisation and Personnel; and some Conclusions

CHAPTER 14

Organisation and Personnel

THE HEADS OF THE OFFICE

The ministerial head of the Department[1] is the Secretary of State, who is responsible to Parliament for all that is done – or left undone – by the Department, to whom all major issues of policy are referred, and who decides which of them need to be discussed with colleagues in Cabinet.

There are normally three or more ministers of state or parliamentary under-secretaries of state attached to the Department, and it is usual for the Secretary of State to ask ministerial colleagues to concern themselves with particular functions or areas of policy. Thus policy for the arts has, from the time at which the Department became responsible for this sector, been the concern of a particular minister.

The permanent or civil service head of the Department is the permanent secretary – traditionally referred to simply as 'the secretary'. He is the Secretary of State's chief adviser on policy, but as in all departments he also has other major functions. He has managerial functions in relation to the organisation and staffing of the Department. Thus he decides (with the advice of the director of establishments and, for certain levels of appointment – after consultation with the deputy secretaries, the Civil Service Department and the Secretary of State) on the selection of personnel for senior posts, and he is ultimately responsible for all matters to do with the running of the Department. He is the Department's accounting officer, responsible for appearing before the Public Accounts Committee, and he may be required to appear, or to arrange for his senior colleagues to appear, before other parliamentary committees. He has to deal, in consultation with the legal adviser and the director of establishments, with complaints of mal-administration made about his Department to the Parliamentary Commissioner (Ombudsman). He also has diplomatic or representational functions which, because of the decentralised nature of the educational system, are of special importance – dealings on major policy issues with the local authority associations, with university vice-chancellors, with representatives of the teachers' associations, and so forth.

The permanent secretary is assisted by four deputy secretaries, along with the chief legal adviser, and the senior chief inspector. Each of the deputy secretaries has responsibilities for a group of branches or functions. The deputy secretaries also act as chairmen of policy groups within the departmental planning organisation; and they, along with the senior chief inspector, the director of establishments and the accountant-general, serve on the policy-steering group which is chaired by the permanent secretary.

THE HEADQUARTERS ORGANISATION

The Department's headquarters staff in London is organised in seventeen branches, each usually headed by an under-secretary, together with a Welsh Education Office, the directorates of the Victoria and Albert Science Museums, and the headquarters group of HM Inspectorate.

A distinction is commonly made between what are loosely called 'policy' branches – that is, those dealing with particular sectors of policy such as schools, further and higher education, the arts and libraries or science – and the 'general' or 'service' branches such as those dealing with finance, establishments, legal matters, architects and building, and statistics. It would be misleading to make too much of this distinction, as the general branches are often as much involved in policy issues as policy branches. But it is convenient to make the distinction here.

The oldest of the policy branches are those dealing with the Department's policy responsibilities in relation to schools. Schools Branch I deals with the supply and organisation of schools in the maintained sector (including school building programmes and the establishment and closure of schools), nursery provision, and such matters as the management and government of schools, choice of school, school transport, school attendance and the employment of school children. This branch also deals with grants and loans to voluntary schools and with independent schools. A senior official of the branch acts as registrar of independent schools.

A feature of Schools Branch I is that it has traditionally been organised on a territorial as well as a functional basis. The territorial teams, each headed by a principal, have general responsibility, subject to the policy of the branch, for each of the ten geographical areas into which the country is divided for this purpose. This territorial form of organisation is regarded by the local authority world as a helpful feature of the Department's organisation. Members and officers of individual local education authorities (LEAs) know that there is a group of officials in the branch who, with the help of advice fed in by HM Inspectors for their area, are well informed about their educational needs and problems.

A second schools branch (Schools Branch II) was created in 1972 with special responsibility for policy on deprived children and immigrant children; on school meals, milk and other welfare benefits; on problems related to violence, indiscipline and truancy; and on the identification of handicapped children and the provision of special schools. It is in close touch with the Department of Health and Social Security on matters concerning the school health service, which is now part of the national health service. Matters concerning the school curriculum and examinations, including liaison with the Schools Council, and other related matters such as educational and careers guidance and educational technology, formerly part of Schools Branch II, are now the responsibility of the new Schools Branch III.

In 1962 a separate Teachers Branch was created to deal with the teacher shortage, which was one of the Department's main preoccupations at that time. This branch now deals with all questions concerning the qualifications, supply, salaries and conditions of service of teachers in the maintained system. It represents the Department in Burnham negotiations, and also in negotiations on the salaries of university teachers; and it deals with issues arising under the teachers' misconduct regulations.

Pensions Branch deals with the administration of the superannuation Acts relating to teachers and certain other staffs employed by LEAs and other bodies. It is supervised by the under-secretary in charge of Teachers Branch.

As a result of reorganisation following the White Paper of December 1972 four branches were created dealing with higher and further education (HFE); these were subsequently reduced to three. One branch, then designated as HFE Branch I, dealt with teacher training, the development of higher education in the non-university sector, co-ordination of investment programmes, and policy in relation to the Diploma of Higher Education.

From 1 January 1978 HFE Branch I was split, responsibility for initial and in-service training of teachers being transferred to Teachers Branch, and responsibility for the finance and government of colleges of education being allocated to the branch dealing with polytechnics, now renamed HFE Branch 1. This branch also deals with particular matters in the field of advanced further education, including liaison with the Council for National Academic Awards, with further education building programmes and finance for further education, and with adult education and education within the further education system for agriculture, art and design.

A second branch, HFE Branch 2 (formerly HFE III) is concerned with industrial training, day release, technician and business education and the councils that supervise them. It also has general responsibility for educational provision for 16–19-year-olds not in school, and also for the youth service.

A third, HFE Branch 3 (formerly HFE IV) has the responsibility for advising on the broad lines of government policy and finance for the university sector which the Department assumed in 1964, and is the main point of contact with the University Grants Committee (UGC). It is further responsible for general policy on student grants, administers centrally awarded postgraduate awards in the humanities and services the Computer Board. It also is concerned with grants to the Open University and to two other university-level institutions: the Royal College of Art and the Cranfield Institute of Technology.

Arts and Libraries Branch deals with national and local libraries, including relations with the British Library; with arts policy generally, including relations with the Arts Council; with policy matters relating to museums and galleries, both national and local; and with such questions as the export of works of art.

After the merger of the Ministry of Education and the Office of the Minister for Science in 1964, two Science Branches came into being. These were merged in 1969 when responsibility for the Office of Scientific and Technical Information (OSTI) was transferred to the then newly created Libraries Division. (In 1974 responsibility for OSTI was transferred to the newly established British Library.) The unified Science Branch thus formed advises on the Secretary of State's responsibilities for civil science, and deals with the science budget, with advice from the Advisory Board for the Research Councils. It services the Advisory Board, and is the main link between the Department and the research councils, as well as with the Royal Society, and it is responsible for grant aid to the British Museum (Natural History). It is responsible for UK policy for, and participation in, a number of international scientific organisations, such as the European Organisation for Nuclear Research (CERN) and the European Space Research Organisation, and it co-ordinates

UK policy on the scientific activities of the Organisation for Economic Co-operation and Development (OECD), the North Atlantic Treaty Organisation (NATO), the United Nations Educational, Scientific and Cultural Organisation (UNESCO) and the Council of Europe.

In September 1977 Science Branch was renamed Science and International Relations Branch when the division responsible for international relations was moved to the branch for Schools Branch II. This division is responsible for handling the extensive contacts that the Department has with international organisations concerned with education, in co-operation with the Foreign and Commonwealth Office. It is the Department's link with the Council of Europe, UNESCO and other specialised agencies of the United Nations; it provides the secretariat serving the Conference of European Ministers of Education; and it organises British participation in the educational programme of the OECD. The division also represents the Department's interests in the negotiation of bilateral and multilateral agreements on educational and cultural matters with foreign countries. It deals with arrangements for the interchange of teachers and modern language assistants with other countries, and with educational visits and exchanges generally. It is responsible for liaising with the institutions of the European Economic Community (EEC) on matters concerning education.

There are seven general or service branches, or units, several of which, because of the Department's role as a national policy and planning agency for services operated by local government or by autonomous bodies, have functions not only for the Department's work but also for the educational system as a whole.

The work of the Department's Finance Branch is of special importance for the system as a whole, for several reasons. (See Chapter 5.) Besides performing the normal functions of a departmental Finance Branch – looking after the Department's financial and accounting arrangements, processing departmental estimates, acting as the Department's liaison with the Treasury, doing internal audit, and so forth – it has major responsibilities in relation to the educational system as a whole. Thus it works with the local authority associations in the preparation of forecasts for local authority expenditure on education and libraries for the purpose of the rate support grant, and takes part with other departments of central government and the local authority associations in the negotiations on rate support grant orders and increase orders. The accountant-general, who is its head, chairs the committee dealing with pooling and extradistrict payments. With the development of the public expenditure surveys, and more recently of Programme Analysis and

Review (PAR), it has also come to have a key role in longer-term forward estimating for the education service as a whole (including the university sector), and in the costing of policies, as well as in providing economic advice on educational policies. The accountant-general and his senior officials (who include professional economists and cost accountants) thus have an important role in the departmental planning organisation.

Legal Branch advises ministers, branches of the Department and the research councils on any legal matters with which they are concerned. It undertakes preparatory work for educational legislation, and is responsible for drafting subordinate legislation (regulations, rules, orders, etc.) and certain other instruments. In a decentralised system, in which the powers and duties of the Department and its relationship with the local authorities are largely determined by statute, these functions are of unusual importance.

Until 1974 Legal Branch also exercised the Secretary of State's jurisdiction over educational and quasi-educational charities. This function was then transferred to the charity commissioners.

Establishments and Organisation Branch performs the usual functions of such a branch in a government department, and is the liaison with the Civil Service Department. One division of the branch is responsible for recruitment, promotion, transfer and retirement of staff, career management, conditions of service and staff training. A second division deals with grading, complementing and management services, and has a broad overall concern with establishment arrangements of a number of autonomous bodies in receipt of grant from the Department, such as the research councils, the national museums and galleries and certain other art institutions. The third is responsible for common services.

The director of establishments is also responsible for the Information Division which looks after the Department's relations with the press, radio and television, providing information about the Department's activities and about the education service generally through all the media: press and broadcasting (including press conferences, interviews, press material and briefing of correspondents), publications, publicity and advertising campaigns and films.

Also within Establishments and Organisation Branch is the Department's library – an educational library of considerable importance containing nearly 200,000 books and publications, a substantial collection of official reports and documents and a wide range of educational journals. The library's main function is to service ministers, officials of the Department and HM Inspectorate. It also prepares small *ad hoc* collections for teachers' short courses organised by HM Inspectors, and provides a service for those engaged in educational research.

Architects and Building Branch was brought into being in its present form in the immediate postwar period, to provide the professional and technical advice needed to deal with the formidable educational building problems that arose at that time. It has responsibility for co-ordinating and processing educational building programmes for all sectors, in consultation with policy branches concerned with the compilation of programmes. It advises generally on cost, techniques and performance of educational buildings, on procedures and on periodic revision of cost limits. Working with HM Inspectorate, LEAs and the UGC, it investigates the architectural and technical implications of new educational trends, and provides a service of information and guidance on developments in design, technique and supply of materials and components, through the publication of Building Bulletins and in other ways. The head of the branch is a professional architect, having the title of chief architect to the Department. Its senior personnel includes a number of professional staff, mainly architects but also engineers and quantity surveyors. Professional staff, administrators and HM Inspectors work in very close association in all the branch's work.

Statistics Branch also has responsibilities in relation to the education service as a whole. It is responsible for the Department's statistical and automatic data-processing services, providing statistical information relating to the educational system (including universities) and to civil science. It gives an extensive service of information, forecasts and advice to branches of the Department and in particular to the departmental planning organisation, as well as to the UGC. It also publishes annual statistics of education, the range of which has steadily grown in recent years. Six volumes are now published annually, and also special *ad hoc* series.

The Planning and Programmes Unit services the departmental planning organisation which was brought into being in 1970. It is responsible for servicing all component parts of the organisation, and for co-ordinating their activities, although it does not itself initiate policies. The head of the unit, who is an under-secretary, also acts as the Department's liaison with the Central Policy Review Staff.

The Department's headquarters staff includes the directorates of the two museums that are the direct responsibility of the Department: namely, the Victoria and Albert Museum and the Science Museum.

The headquarters group of HM Inspectors in England, consisting of the senior chief inspector, six chief inspectors and many of the staff inspectors, are also accommodated alongside the headquarters staff of the Department in London. (The headquarters of HM Inspectorate in Wales is in Cardiff.)

SOME CHARACTERISTICS OF THE DEPARTMENT'S STAFF

One fact about the Department's staff that is perhaps worth mentioning, although it is now of purely historical interest, is that the Department, in its earlier incarnation as the Board of Education, was the last of all the major Whitehall departments to fall in with orthodox civil-service recruitment procedures. Up to the end of the First World War it continued to appoint its own officers by nomination. Although a source of embarrassment to successive governments, this practice was not without its advantages. As the Ministry's Annual Report for 1950 engagingly remarks, it 'enriched the work of administration with a leaven of scholarship and humanity which was in the best tradition of public life'.[2] Thus the Board in the early days of the century counted amongst its senior officials men of distinction in literature, history, philosophy and educational studies, such as E. K. Chambers, Sir Amherst Selby-Bigge, Michael Sadler and G. M. Young.

After the First World War the Board came into line with the rest of the civil service in its recruitment arrangements, including those for HM Inspectorate – although the arrangements for recruiting HM Inspectors differ in that they require candidates to have had previous experience, either in teaching or in industry and commerce.

If there is one characteristic of the Department as it is today that must strike the informed observer, it is its modest size. Of all the nine or ten major departments of central government (other than the central departments) it is by far the smallest. Its total staff (including HM Inspectorate but excluding curatorial and other museum staffs) numbers less than 3,000. (With museum staff, the total is about 4,000. Corresponding 1975 figures for the Ministry of Defence (non-industrial staff) were 130,321, and for the Department of Health and Social Security 89,465.) The Department has a higher ratio of senior officers (principal and upwards) to junior than is usual in Whitehall departments.

This is largely a consequence of the decentralised character of the system, and the resulting fact that the Department is largely a policy and planning department with few executive functions. This small size has advantages, not the least of which is that it is possible for all the senior staff to know each other fairly well, and to work together in what has been described as a 'collegiate' atmosphere.

There is another characteristic of the Department that is also largely a consequence of its small size. The working relationships between administrators and the professionals (including HM Inspectors) are exceptionally close. This is perhaps most noticeable in the Department's Architects and Building Branch, where administrators and professionals work continuously together in teams, particularly but not only in the development groups. But it may also be seen in other branches, for example, in Arts and Libraries Branch and Science and International Relations Branch.

It may also be said that, for reasons given in earlier chapters, civil servants in the Department are well accustomed to the practice of 'open government'. It is not only that everything they do in the name of ministers is almost always in the public eye and subject to the scrutiny of unusually well-informed journalists, broadcasters and researchers, as well as Members of Parliament. But because education is largely a locally administered service, they also must be constantly aware of the views and reactions of local councillors and officers, of the bodies that represent them, of the teachers who are the third main element in the partnership operating the service, and, not least, of parents.

It is perhaps legitimate to venture one further comment. It is often said that the staff of the Department (including HM Inspectors and other professional groups) are 'dedicated' to their work to an extent that is not usually found in other government departments. To make too much of this would be to do an injustice to a large body of civil servants in many other departments who go about their work with dedication. What can be said without casting any reflection on civil servants in other departments is that, because so much of the Department's work is concerned with policy making and because education has, for most of the time since 1944, been a growing service which can be seen to have a vital role in the country's future, the Department offers exceptional opportunities for creative work. This is perhaps one of the reasons why it has in recent years tended to be specially attractive to new entrants who join as executive officers or administrative trainees.

NOTES AND REFERENCES

1 This chapter describes the organisation of the Department as it was at 1 January 1978.
2 *Education 1900–1950*, report of the Ministry for Education and Statistics of Public Education for England and Wales, Cmd 8244 (London, HMSO, 1951), ch. 1, para. 4.

CHAPTER 15

Some Conclusions

Conclusions are the stock in trade of civil servants. They are, as one who must have been a civil servant wrote in 1553, 'the clerkly gathering of all the matter that has gone before'. What conclusions can a bureaucrat draw from the preceding chapters of this book?

The history of a department of state like the Department of Education and Science (DES) cannot help but be largely a history of a developing education system and service. Looking back now over the thirty or so postwar years, the main determinants of educational development might be thought to have been successive ministers bringing with them into office explicit political commitments (and occasionally educational convictions), or the permanent officials who advise ministers during their terms of office from a base of professional skills, accumulated knowledge and a concern for the continuity of things. Yet in the final analysis this is not perhaps the right first conclusion. Certainly ministers, and occasionally officials, by personal characteristics like clarity of mind, strength of character or instinctive tactical skills, have made distinctive contributions to the shaping of events. But in the matter of objectives, and often of the means to those ends, they have themselves been shaped by more deep-seated forces. The obscure tides of moral, social and economic change which have run with singular strength in the postwar years have in this sense been the main determining factors.

In the 1920s and 1930s recovery from one world war was separated mainly by economic crisis and slump from the threat and then the outbreak of another war. The social and economic condition of the country and within it of the education system can best be described as static. None but a small minority received full-time education beyond the age of 14. Higher education was the preserve of the rich and the very ablest. Night classes and teacher training, however, provided a measure of social mobility; the determined man – and, less often, woman – could move from clerical to submanagerial or subprofessional employment, assuming that there was employment to be had at all. The number of pupils, students and teachers remained relatively constant. There were few new institutions and the social composition, curricula and output of existing institutions changed hardly at all. In 1938–9 defence accounted for some 20 per cent of tax and rate-borne public expenditure; housing was the biggest social service (13 per cent); then came education (nearly 8 per cent), health (5 per cent), unemployment benefits (the 'dole', 4 per cent) and pensions (2–3 per cent).

One of the biggest changes following the Second World War was the assumption that change itself was an essential objective of social policy. There was not merely an expectation of radical change but also a radical change in expectations. The drab world of the 1930s was to be reconstructed into the welfare state of full employment, a widening range of social services, and new homes, factories and towns. Prosperity, opportunity and equality were to be the key notes of the succeeding years – the confident expectations of rising personal and public affluence; the widening of opportunities to cross the traditional boundaries of class and occupation and to challenge the conventions of received morality and authority; the pursuit of greater equality between the worlds of privilege and disadvantage. These have been the tidal forces that have affected virtually every aspect of our national life. They have, in consequence, largely shaped the personalities, policies and programmes of the educational world and the environment in which the Department has had to do its work.

The consequences may be judged from the following figures. In 1974–5 defence accounted for some 9 per cent of public expenditure. The principal social services, which in 1938–9 represented about one-third of the total, accounted for nearly one-half in 1974–5, made up as follows: pensions and social security 17 per cent, education 12 per cent, health and personal social services 10 per cent, housing 9 per cent and unemployment services (but very largely unemployment benefits) less than 1 per cent.

The consequences for the education system have been little less than astonishing, although this is perhaps less recognised precisely because the changes have been steady and expected. Although the economic growth rate in Britain has long been below that of its main industrial competitors, it has still been sufficient to permit a substantial rise in its internal standard of living, although less than in these other countries. Included in this rising standard of living has been the community's purchase of education, which has exceeded that of private consumption generally.[1] The reader who has followed the preceding chapters will have seen the documentary evidence for this. In this concluding chapter only the briefest summary is called for.

The education service has taken a rising share of the increased internal affluence of the country: in 1975 7 per cent of gross national product and 12 per cent of public expenditure, compared with 3 per cent and 8 per cent respectively in 1938. The school leaving age has been raised twice; the period of compulsory school attendance is now among the longest in the world. Five million more people are currently receiving education than before the war. One in seven young people are enjoying higher education, compared with hardly more than one in 100 in the 1930s. The number of teachers in schools, colleges and universities has doubled in the last twenty years. Pupil–teacher ratios in schools have improved by nearly one-third (21:1 compared with 30·5:1 before the war). About two out of every three pupils are in postwar buildings. Twenty-one new universities and thirty new polytechnics have been established. An essentially evolutionary system has produced its own innovations: middle schools, sixth-form colleges, the Open University, the Council for National Academic Awards, the Schools Council, the Business Education Council, the Technical Education Council, the Certificate of Secondary Education, the Bachelor of Education (BEd) degree and the Diploma of Higher Education (DipHE), not to mention the more controversial trend towards a fully comprehensive system of secondary schools.

A number of qualifications are needed before any conclusive judgements can be made about this striking record.

First, the period of uninterrupted expansion that made these developments possible came to an end in 1973, and subsequent developments up to the time of writing (March 1978) have confirmed that more than just a transient background change has taken place. The dramatic rise in oil prices in 1973 placed massive new strains on the United Kingdom's already weak external trading position, while spiralling domestic inflation continued to erode the appearance of our internal affluence. New keynotes were sounded: restraint, economy, sacrifice. The expectation was now to be of a lowering of real living standards. The education service which had risen with the upswing was now to be carried, along with everything and everybody else, with the downswing. So began a new era. How long it will last no one can tell, but certainly long enough to challenge existing attitudes, practices and priorities. It may even prove to be just the stimulus that any system needs when it has fallen into the habit of seeing progress mainly in terms of growth and taking growth for granted.

The era of expansion, while it had significantly extended the boundaries of the education system and widened access to it, had not done so uniformly over all stages and sectors. There were gaps that had not been filled and areas that had been bypassed either by the flow of resources or by the failure to innovate, and sometimes by both. In short, prosperity had widened opportunities and diminished inequalities for many, but not for all.

In terms of the structure of the system the two sectors that had advanced least were nursery education and non-advanced further education. Nursery education had been held back throughout the 1950s and 1960s for lack of resources; the necessary teachers and buildings were needed to meet the prior claims of the ever-rising school population and the explosive demand (a world, not only a British, phenomenon) for more higher education. The 1972 White Paper *Education: A Framework for Expansion*[2] at last turned to this neglected sector, promising the resources to extend nursery education to 90 per cent of 4-year-olds and 50 per cent of 3-year-olds. But, as already noted, by 1973 the economic tide had begun to change. Nursery education for all who need or want it remains a clear objective; in an era of restraint it will take longer to achieve.

The disappointment about non-advanced further education is of a different kind. A systematic nationwide scheme of part-time attendance at colleges for all those under 18 who are not in school is the only major objective of the 1944 Act that has proved unattainable. Any compulsory system was, and in the new period of restraint is likely to remain, too costly. In any event, the growing maturity of young men and women and their changed attitude to authoritarianism must raise doubts about the acceptability today of any new measure of compulsion. Successive governments have therefore chosen or been forced to rely upon a system of voluntary attendance, through day release and in conjunction with industrial training. The only honest judgement must be that the results remain unsatisfactory. Ways have still to be found of stimulating more 16–19-year-olds to seek postschool further education and training, of making that education more relevant to their needs and aspirations and of integrating vocational training far more closely with the continued personal education of these young people. When 40 per cent of boys and girls leave school with no qualifications and have no further contact with either education or training it is clear that this is an area to which priority must be given, even in an era of restraint.

There is one other aspect of 'gaps and problems'. The pursuit of widening opportunities and diminishing inequalities has given rise over most of the postwar years to widespread debate about the primary objectives of the education system and process. The debate has led to many contradictory conclusions, amongst them: that education can and should have only educational objectives; that education has social as well as educational objectives; that the social objectives can and must include widening opportunities and diminishing inequalities (there are debates within debates about whether these objectives are best described as 'opportunity and equality', 'equality of opportunity' or 'opportunity for equality'); that noble though these social objectives, however expressed, may be, there is no evidence that they can be effectively attained; that other factors such as home influence, peer group attitudes or the mass media of communication, notably television, are now seen as influencing social attitudes, values and choices more powerfully than education. These issues have been debated for centuries. Only a foolish bureaucrat would suppose that by some 'clerkly gathering of all the material that has gone before' he can reach a definitive conclusion.

Two perspectives, however, seem to emerge. On the one hand the majority of children and their parents do not see the issues in these intellectual terms. For them the educational process is in itself a sufficient objective. They participate in it happily and constructively, protected by supportive homes. Their incentives and rewards are standards of performance and self-fulfilment that, it is not too much to claim, are on average higher than those achieved by their predecessors. For them their educational attainments will provide the most satisfying key to all the later opportunities of life.

In contrast, there is a minority – and not a negligible minority – of children for whom this rewarding path to educational attainment is blocked. They start their journey handicapped. The education service has had long experience of dealing with physical and congenital mental handicaps. A marked feature, however, particularly over the later span of the postwar years, has been a pervasive concern with those handicaps that are not inherent in the child but have their roots in environmental social conditions: namely, parental support, ethnic origins, bad housing, urban decay but, above all, poverty. That these disadvantages cruelly impede the educational process is beyond dispute. That attention should be focused as it has been on developing techniques and programmes to mitigate the consequences is right. That progress is not quickly apparent is true. That the attempt to make progress is futile is not a view that will or should prevail. Any civilised state and any compassionate educational system must continue its effort in the belief that the strong must help the weak, and in the faith that they can ultimately do so.

One other qualification is perhaps needed in interpreting the list of achievements earlier recorded; it is not unconnected with the point last made about helping the disadvantaged or with the thoughts with which this last chapter will end. It will be noticed that the record of achievement is couched in terms of money, numbers, percentages, school places, examinations and institutional organisations. These are important indices; for the technocrat they measure the input of effort and resources into the system and even, in a crude intermediate way, the output – so many buildings, teachers, graduates, etc. But they remain, nevertheless, only a description of a *system*, of the outer shell within which the *process* of education takes place. This process is personal to every individual; it is essentially a private process intricately working within the mind and heart of every child, even every adult throughout life. It is fostered in countless ways. It happens as each child learns to work the loom of language, sees the magnitude of things, drives a chisel, leaps a stream, feels the first tremors of sex or Schubert, struggles with pain or grief, makes connections and asks questions and little by little comes to judge the enveloping world around him. This is the inner mystery within the outer shell, and the shell exists only to protect and develop this process.

A fair criticism of the postwar years, or at any rate, of those who claim to have shaped them, is perhaps that they preoccupied themselves too much with the shell of the system and not enough with the inner mystery of the process itself. To acknowledge that structure does not appear to determine function directly or in the ways often predicted or sometimes promised; to admit the primacy of the process over the system; to recognise the tremendous complexity of this inner process and the need for a greater understanding of it; to search for better ways of assessing the quality of the results of this process ('the output of the system'), of defining and measuring standards of achievement and of identifying the factors that block or encourage attainment to the highest level: all these may prove to be amongst the most significant conclusions emerging from the ending of one long phase of educational development and administration and therefore amongst the central preoccupations of the educational world in the remaining quarter of this century.

It will not be forgotten that since 1964–5 the responsibility of the Department has been widened to include science and the arts as well as education. The story of growth and change is the same.

The government funding of scientific research for purposes other than defence, which amounted to less than £10 million in 1945–6, rose to some £45 million by 1955–6, £200 million by 1965–6, and £650 million by 1975–6. Within this expenditure, somewhat under one-half has consistently been devoted not to the applied research undertaken by particular departments in support of their executive functions, but to maintaining the basic scientific capability of the country, represented by the research activities of the universities and other establishments of higher education and work carried out by, or supported by, the research councils and (before 1965) the Department of Scientific and Industrial Research. The Department inherited this role first through its assumption of responsibility for the support of the universities through the University Grants Committee (UGC), and later through the reorganisation and elaboration of the research council system effected by the Science and Technology Act 1965, which made the Department the legatee of the diverse forms of government organisation that had hitherto had responsibility for sustaining the country's scientific capability.

The last ten years have seen many attempts to define the precise nature of this responsibility. Whether called 'pure research', 'basic research' or 'strategic research', it may perhaps best be negatively defined as the support of research that is not policy orientated, although it must be influenced to some extent by socioeconomic needs. This concept finds characteristic expression in a system of 'buffer' bodies: the five research councils themselves, and the advisory machinery through which government support is distributed between them. Total government support in this field amounted to just under £90 million when the Department assumed responsibility in 1965-6, divided almost equally between the funds provided indirectly to university departments through UGC grants (a sum that can only loosely be quantified since university expenditure on research cannot strictly be separated from that on teaching) and the more clearly identifiable sums spent by the research councils from DES grant-in-aid on supporting specific projects in universities and on maintaining their own research establishments. This 'dual system' expanded at a healthy rate in the earlier part of the last decade, and although the last few years have seen a much less buoyant rate of growth, the input into the system has tripled over the past ten years, to reach some £270 million in 1975-6.

The changes in this system effected by the 1972 White Paper *Framework for Government Research and Development* may perhaps now be seen in perspective as little more than a modest adjustment in the boundary between the policy-orientated research effort of particular departments and the non-policy-orientated research support provided through the Department, coupled with an attempt to define more clearly the relationship between these two sectors. A much more significant development has been the sharp decline in the expected future growth of the DES science budget. From an annual growth of 4–5 per cent in the early 1970s, the research councils have moved abruptly into an era of negative or at best zero growth which looks like continuing until the end of the 1970s. This has called for new strategies of resource allocation, the effects of which are not easy to see at the present time.

Until 1965, the funding of the Arts Council, the postwar successor to the wartime Council for the Encouragement of Music and the Arts, and of the national museums and galleries was the direct responsibility of the Treasury. In that year the functions were transferred to the Department and a minister was appointed to the Department with a special responsibility for the arts. This step marked the initiation of a policy of deliberate expansion of interest in and Exchequer resources for the arts, which was checked only with the financial crisis of the mid-1970s. The grant to the Arts Council rose from £2·73 million in 1963–4 to £17·138 million in 1973–4, and expenditure on the national museums and galleries from £6 million to £19·4 million. The appointment of a minister meant that there was a member of the government responsible not only for dealing defensively with questions of the moment but also for propagating politically a view about the importance of the arts and their place in national life. At the same time the system was carefully preserved whereby decisions on matters of aesthetics and artistic choice were insulated from direct political influence by the Arts Council, and in the case of most of the national museums and galleries by the system of trustees. In this period the development of central government support took place both as a matter of deliberate policy and, to some extent, to replace the relative decline in the scale of private patronage of the arts.

The growth in public expenditure on the arts has accompanied, and presumably to a significant extent caused, the remarkable development in public interest in enjoying the arts and indeed public concern for artistic issues. The development of television especially has contributed to this growth, and together with the consequences of educational development it has meant that there is an ever increasing demand for facilities to enjoy the arts and an increase in the expectations of high standards both in performance arts and in displays in museums and galleries.

The main consequence of these developments is that the arts have become noticeably significant claimants for resources in competition with other social expenditure.

This then is the record, blemishes and all. In presenting it the writer has tried to give a picture of the stuff of administrative life within the Department: the issues, the considerations, the horizons and the constraints.

The role of the officers of the Department has been, and is likely to remain, first to listen (for example, through a network of committees representing all the relevant interests, through deputations and visits and through widespread press coverage); then to reflect and relate (for example, through the departmental planning organisation); then to advise ministers and, when ministers have taken their decisions, to promulgate and explain the government's policies and views to the outside world (for example, through circulars, White Papers or speeches); and so finally to administer those policies and the powers underlying them. The domain within which these functions are exercised is very varied, but the issues tend to be ones either of determining policy objectives (for example, whether or not to give priority to nursery provision or how high to rate the development of comprehensive secondary education); or of allocating resources (for example, as between capital or recurrent expenditure); or of operating and sometimes modifying the principal structural statutory controls (for example, Section 13 of the Education Act 1944). Often all these aspects are simultaneously involved in a major issue.

There is, however, one issue that the reader will notice has not been featured prominently amongst the Department's responsibilities: that of the content of the curriculum in general, or of teaching methods or materials in particular. The long tradition of this country has been to leave those matters in the hands nominally of local education authorities (LEAs) or school governors but effectively of individual teachers. Except in relation to religious instruction, the law assigns no powers or responsibilities to the Secretary of State. The immense freedoms that rest in professional rather than political or bureaucratic hands have undoubtedly produced over the years much of the richness and flexibility that are characteristic of the British education process. Moreover, these freedoms have never been unlimited; they have been moderated for better or worse by the school examination system. But it is becoming increasingly clear that this very examination system is now being called in question, and growing doubts are being expressed about what is taught to children and how it is taught. These are legitimate questions to ask of any educational system. Another major preoccupation, therefore, of the years ahead is likely to be not only the content of the curriculum, but also who in the last analysis should control it and be accountable for its results.

Because of its role as the national policy-making and resource-providing agency the Department's contribution to the record of achievement – or of shortcomings for that matter – has been important, at times decisive. In its main field of education the Department has indisputable powers – although perhaps more influence than power – but it has a monopoly of neither. Power and influence are also wielded by local authorities, teachers' unions and pressure groups of all kinds, including the press. The achievements and short-comings of the education service are in a very real sense the results of the interaction of these forces, whether acting, as more often than not, in partnership or, as occasionally, in tension.

The biggest single virtue of the Education Act 1944, it can be argued, was that it determined that no one interest group should have a monopoly of power, and the distribution of power that it enacted has proved over thirty years to have been stable, effective and appropriate. It produced what has earlier and aptly been des-cribed as 'an all-embracing network of dispersed responsibility'. There have been, and remain, critics of such a system. They point to the absence of a clear demarcation of responsibility between the centre and the local authorities or, in the higher education sector, between the Department, the UGC-administered university sector and the local-authority-maintained institutions in the field. There is recurring pressure, some of it from well-informed and responsible quarters, for more central control. In particular, the financing of educational expenditure partly from rates but predominantly from grants raised by central taxation, together with a complicated system of distributing such grants, is said to blur accountability; the government meets some two-thirds of the cost but it is the local authorities who decide on what to spend it, even whether to spend it on education or some other local service. There are those who argue that a decentralised system of this kind, based on partnership, can work only when there is a broad consensus about objectives and policies and that that consensus no longer exists, either educationally or politically, locally or nationally. The search for a consensus, moreoever, has become more difficult because of the sheer multi-plicity of groups and interests to be consulted in the process of policy formulation.

These factors, amongst others, are liable to cause conflicts of purpose, delays and impasses which even the most ingeniously devised machinery for planning and consultation cannot always eliminate. They are particularly liable to give rise to difficulties in times of economic crisis when reductions in the resources available for education become inevitable, or in a period of inflation when escalating costs disrupt forward planning.

But there are weighty arguments on the other side. This complex system of 'dispersed responsibilities' came into existence and has been perpetuated because for the best part of a century successive governments of all parties have been convinced that a healthy local democracy is a vital element in a democratic society. Local government, as the Redcliffe-Maud Commission pointed out, is at present the only representative political institution in the country outside Parliament, and is therefore an essential part of the fabric of democratic government. Since 1902 education has been a major function of local authorities; and there are specially cogent reasons why education, which so intimately affects the lives of the vast majority of families in this country, is a suitable activity to be administered by local bodies. If the operation of the education service by elected local bodies sometimes makes it cumbersome, it also helps to make it responsive to local needs. In an age of giant organisations, both public and private, this is a matter of no small importance; and although it would be absurd to claim that the education service is above reproach, it can be argued with a good deal of evidence that it is more responsive than centralised systems, whether for education or other public services. It is not necessary to look outside this country to find examples of public services that, because they are subject to centralised direction unchecked by local democratic controls, have tended to become inflexible and insensitive to 'consumer' needs.

A detached observer might, of course, admit all these advantages and yet say that the price is too high – in loss of efficiency or fairness or capacity to get things done. Yet even on this score a decentralised system is not without its advantages. The efficiency of a centralised system largely depends on the quality and capacity for innovation of a small group of politicians and administrators at the centre. One of the strengths of a decentralised system such as the British is that it can draw on the experience and innovative capacity of those working in the field – officers of LEAs, heads of schools and colleges, officers of examining bodies, and so forth.

The main testimonial to the present system, however, is simply that it has worked well. Over thirty years it has got those things done that had to be done and could be done. It has performed a logistic feat of exceptional difficulty, meeting severe challenges of both demography and demand with the necessary buildings and teachers. In these matters it has rarely if ever broken down or failed to meet its obligations. The Department, the local authorities, both individually and collectively, and the teachers' organisations have each been free to fight their own corner, and have done so. Yet these relationships have been characterised far more by goodwill and mutual respect than by suspicion or hostility.

A former chief education officer wrote:

In a world-wide perspective English education glows like a beacon. Its administration avoids both the fragmentation and near chaos of the United States on the one hand and the rigid centralisation of some European states or the Communist and less developed countries on the other . . . The English genius for flexibility under pressure, for reforms in the nick of time and for the application of sheer common sense when faced with complex problems, has produced an educational machine which works, is capable of evolution at a reasonable rate and which, viewed from outside, has more merit than its internal critics seem to realise . . .

or, might be added hopefully, its external critics.

This machine today has about $1\frac{1}{2}$ million employees.[4] It serves over 14 million people. Allowing for parental or family interest its operation affects about one-half of the total population. The more thoughtful amongst them will always be asking how, in what ways and to what end? This chapter does not, cannot, offer any final conclusions. Its theme is that of a circle of forces: the tides of moral, social and economic change substantially shape the development of the education system and process, these will shape the rising generation of young men and women who will modify this moral, social and economic cycle in their turn.

This cycle of change is essentially slow acting. The full impact of education, both on the individual and on the community, makes itself felt only over a period of time – some of it over a lifetime. It is therefore to generational, not annual, change that one must look for differences. The postwar developments in education have been striking. Yet almost no one over the age of 45 today has benefited from them. The great majority of men and women over this age received all their schooling in what were in effect elementary schools, leaving at 14 or 15. Only one in ten of them, together with a smaller proportion who attended schools outside the maintained system, received an effective secondary education. A still smaller minority received university or other higher education. Those aged between 40 and 45 were educated partly during the war years, with all the dislocation and make-do that that entailed; while those aged between 35 and 40 had their schooling when the education service was still recovering from the after-effects of war and before the reforms of the 1944 Act had had time to emerge. Thus the older and the younger halves of British society (or, at any rate, a substantial and increasing part of the latter) have had quite different experiences of the opportunities and impact of the education process. It will be only as the younger half comes fully to influence, as it is already beginning to do, in politics, industry, trade unions, the professions (including education itself) and the media of communication that the nature of this silent revolution will be known.

O! that a man might know
The end of this day's business, ere it come;
But it sufficeth that the day will end
And then the end is known.

The dilemma of a department of state, charged with the heavy responsibility for 'the education of the people of England and Wales', is that it can powerfully control means, it can propose objectives but it has no certain hold over 'the end'. The mechanism by which societies transmit success or failure is different, as a distinguished doctor and educationalist has recently written, from the genetic code:

The transmission from generation to generation of the institutions of civilised man is an inheritance not of what happens before birth, but of what happens after birth, namely the influences which are brought to bear on the developing child to form his habits, his knowledge and his attitudes of mind. Of these the most important which society can itself control is that embodied in the educational system.[5]

Education is not the only force at work, and the others may be of increasing influence in shaping the minds, hearts, and bodies of the rising generation. But it is unarguably one of them, and the realisation that it can interact with the genetic inheritance and bias human beings towards success or towards failure is a sobering challenge. If one administrator may speak for his company of officials and for the many ministers that they have tried to serve, it is to say that bureaucracies can have their faiths, even a certain optimism.

NOTES AND REFERENCES

1 Some forms of private consumption, however (for example, of car ownership and electrical goods), have risen more than the 'consumption' of education.
2 White Paper, *Education: A Framework for Expansion*, Cmnd 5174 (London, HMSO, December 1972).
3 White Paper, *Framework for Government Research and Development*, Cmnd 5046 (London, HMSO, 1972).
4 Some 740,000 teachers, 200,000 of them part-time; and some 770,000 non-teachers, 500,000 of them part-time, mainly women. The non-teaching jobs include school meal workers, domestic staff, caretakers, clerks, laboratory assistants and manual workers for over 30,000 institutions. The number of administrators (bureaucrats) is probably less than 10,000, of whom the DES accounts for about 3,000. There are under 500 HM Inspectors.
5 Sir George Pickering (formerly Master of Pembroke College, Oxford, and Regius Professor of Medicine in the University of Oxford), *The Challenge of Education* (London, C. A. Watts, 1967), p. 80.

Ministers of Education and Secretaries of State for Education and Science since 1944

MINISTERS

Rt Hon. R. A. (later Lord) Butler
(President of the Board and subsequently Minister)   1941–1945
Rt Hon. Ellen Wilkinson   26 July 1945 to 9 Feb. 1947
Rt Hon. George Tomlinson   10 Feb. 1947 to 1 Nov. 1951
Rt Hon. Florence Horsbrugh   2 Feb. 1951 to 18 Oct. 1954
Rt Hon. Sir David (later Lord)
Eccles   19 Oct. 1954 to 13 Jan. 1957
Rt Hon. Viscount Hailsham   14 Jan. 1957 to 16 Sep. 1957
Rt Hon. Geoffrey Lloyd   17 Sep. 1957 to 13 Oct. 1959
Rt Hon. Sir David (later Lord)
Eccles   14 Oct. 1959 to 16 July 1962
Rt Hon. Sir Edward (later Lord)
Boyle   17 July 1962 to 31 Mar. 1964

SECRETARIES OF STATE

Rt Hon. Quintin Hogg (later
Lord Hailsham)   1 Apr. 1964 to 16 Oct. 1964
Rt Hon. Michael Stewart   19 Oct. 1964 to 23 Jan. 1965
Rt Hon. Anthony Crosland   24 Jan. 1965 to 30 Aug. 1967
Rt Hon. Patrick (later Lord)
Gordon-Walker   31 Aug. 1967 to 5 Apr. 1968
Rt Hon. Edward Short (later Lord
Glenamara)   8 Apr. 1968 to 19 June 1970
Rt Hon. Margaret Thatcher   20 June 1970 to 4 Mar. 1974
Rt Hon. Reginald Prentice   5 Mar. 1974 to 10 June 1975
Rt Hon. Frederick W. Mulley   11 June 1975 to 10 Sep. 1976
Rt Hon. Shirley Williams   11 Sep. 1976–

INDEX